P9-BYL-031

NON SANZ DROICT.

THE TRAGEDIE OF
Anthonie, and Cleopatra.

Decorative headband and title of the earliest printed version of the play, in the First Folio (1623)

William Shakespeare

The Tragedy of Antony and Cleopatra

With New and Updated
Critical Essays
and a Revised Bibliography

Edited by Barbara Everett

THE SIGNET CLASSIC SHAKESPEARE
General Editor: Sylvan Barnet

A SIGNET CLASSIC

SIGNET CLASSIC
Published by the Penguin Group
Penguin Books USA Inc., 375 Hudson Street, New York, New York 10014, U.S.A.
Penguin Books Ltd, 27 Wrights Lane, London W8 5TZ, England
Penguin Books Australia Ltd, Ringwood, Victoria, Australia
Penguin Books Canada Ltd, 10 Alcorn Avenue, Toronto, Ontario, Canada M4V 3B2
Penguin Books (N.Z.) Ltd, 182–190 Wairau Road, Auckland 10, New Zealand

Penguin Books Ltd, Registered Offices:
Harmondsworth, Middlesex, England

Published by Signet Classic, an imprint of Dutton NAL,
a member of Penguin Putnam Inc.
The Signet Classic edition of *Antony and Cleopatra* was first published in 1964,
and an updated edition was published in 1988.

First Signet Classic Printing (Second Revised Edition), October, 1998
10 9 8 7 6 5 4 3 2 1

Copyright © Barbara Everett, 1964, 1988
Copyright © Sylvan Barnet, 1964, 1988, 1998
All rights reserved

 REGISTERED TRADEMARK—MARCA REGISTRADA

Library of Congress Catalog Card Number: 98-7913

Printed in the United States of America

BOOKS ARE AVAILABLE AT QUANTITY DISCOUNTS WHEN USED TO PROMOTE PROD-
UCTS OR SERVICES. FOR INFORMATION PLEASE WRITE TO PREMIUM MARKETING DIVI-
SION, PENGUIN PUTNAM INC., 375 HUDSON STREET, NEW YORK, NEW YORK 10014.

If you purchased this book without a cover you should be aware that this book is
stolen property. It was reported as "unsold and destroyed" to the publisher and neither the author nor the publisher has received any payment for this "stripped book."

Contents

Shakespeare: An Overview

Biographical Sketch

Between the record of his baptism in Stratford on 26 April 1564 and the record of his burial in Stratford on 25 April 1616, some forty official documents name Shakespeare, and many others name his parents, his children, and his grandchildren. Further, there are at least fifty literary references to him in the works of his contemporaries. More facts are known about William Shakespeare than about any other playwright of the period except Ben Jonson. The facts should, however, be distinguished from the legends. The latter, inevitably more engaging and better known, tell us that the Stratford boy killed a calf in high style, poached deer and rabbits, and was forced to flee to London, where he held horses outside a playhouse. These traditions are only traditions; they may be true, but no evidence supports them, and it is well to stick to the facts.

Mary Arden, the dramatist's mother, was the daughter of a substantial landowner; about 1557 she married John Shakespeare, a tanner, glove-maker, and trader in wool, grain, and other farm commodities. In 1557 John Shakespeare was a member of the council (the governing body of Stratford), in 1558 a constable of the borough, in 1561 one of the two town chamberlains, in 1565 an alderman (entitling him to the appellation of "Mr."), in 1568 high bailiff—the town's highest political office, equivalent to mayor. After 1577, for an unknown reason he drops out of local politics. What *is* known is that he had to mortgage his wife's property, and that he was involved in serious litigation.

The birthday of William Shakespeare, the third child and the eldest son of this locally prominent man, is unrecorded, but the Stratford parish register records that the infant was baptized on 26 April 1564. (It is quite possible that he was born on 23 April, but this date has probably been assigned by tradition because it is the date on which, fifty-two years later, he died, and perhaps because it is the feast day of St. George, patron saint of England.) The attendance records of the Stratford grammar school of the period are not extant, but it is reasonable to assume that the son of a prominent local official attended the free school—it had been established for the purpose of educating males precisely of his class—and received substantial training in Latin. The masters of the school from Shakespeare's seventh to fifteenth years held Oxford degrees; the Elizabethan curriculum excluded mathematics and the natural sciences but taught a good deal of Latin rhetoric, logic, and literature, including plays by Plautus, Terence, and Seneca.

On 27 November 1582 a marriage license was issued for the marriage of Shakespeare and Anne Hathaway, eight years his senior. The couple had a daughter, Susanna, in May 1583. Perhaps the marriage was necessary, but perhaps the couple had earlier engaged, in the presence of witnesses, in a formal "troth plight" which would render their children legitimate even if no further ceremony were performed. In February 1585, Anne Hathaway bore Shakespeare twins, Hamnet and Judith.

That Shakespeare was born is excellent; that he married and had children is pleasant; but that we know nothing about his departure from Stratford to London or about the beginning of his theatrical career is lamentable and must be admitted. We would gladly sacrifice details about his children's baptism for details about his earliest days in the theater. Perhaps the poaching episode is true (but it is first reported almost a century after Shakespeare's death), or perhaps he left Stratford to be a schoolmaster, as another tradition holds; perhaps he was moved (like Petruchio in *The Taming of the Shrew*) by

> Such wind as scatters young men through the world,
> To seek their fortunes farther than at home
> Where small experience grows.   (1.2.49–51)

In 1592, thanks to the cantankerousness of Robert Greene, we have our first reference, a snarling one, to Shakespeare as an actor and playwright. Greene, a graduate of St. John's College, Cambridge, had become a playwright and a pamphleteer in London, and in one of his pamphlets he warns three university-educated playwrights against an actor who has presumed to turn playwright:

> There is an upstart crow, beautified with our feathers, that with his *tiger's heart wrapped in a player's hide* supposes he is as well able to bombast out a blank verse as the best of you, and being an absolute Johannes-factotum [i.e., jack-of-all-trades] is in his own conceit the only Shake-scene in a country.

The reference to the player, as well as the allusion to Aesop's crow (who strutted in borrowed plumage, as an actor struts in fine words not his own), makes it clear that by this date Shakespeare had both acted and written. That Shakespeare is meant is indicated not only by *Shake-scene* but also by the parody of a line from one of Shakespeare's plays, *3 Henry VI*: "O, tiger's heart wrapped in a woman's hide" (1.4.137). If in 1592 Shakespeare was prominent enough to be attacked by an envious dramatist, he probably had served an apprenticeship in the theater for at least a few years.

In any case, although there are no extant references to Shakespeare between the record of the baptism of his twins in 1585 and Greene's hostile comment about "Shake-scene" in 1592, it is evident that during some of these "dark years" or "lost years" Shakespeare had acted and written. There are a number of subsequent references to him as an actor. Documents indicate that in 1598 he is a "principal comedian," in 1603 a "principal tragedian," in 1608 he is one of the "men players." (We do not have, however, any solid information about which roles he may have played; later traditions say he played Adam in *As You Like It* and the ghost in *Hamlet*, but nothing supports the assertions. Probably his role as dramatist came to supersede his role as actor.) The profession of actor was not for a gentleman, and it occasionally drew the scorn of university men like Greene who resented writing speeches for persons less educated than themselves, but it

was respectable enough; players, if prosperous, were in
effect members of the bourgeoisie, and there is nothing to
suggest that Stratford considered William Shakespeare less
than a solid citizen. When, in 1596, the Shakespeares were
granted a coat of arms—i.e., the right to be considered
gentlemen—the grant was made to Shakespeare's father,
but probably William Shakespeare had arranged the matter
on his own behalf. In subsequent transactions he is occasionally styled a gentleman.

Although in 1593 and 1594 Shakespeare published two
narrative poems dedicated to the Earl of Southampton,
Venus and Adonis and *The Rape of Lucrece*, and may well
have written most or all of his sonnets in the middle nineties,
Shakespeare's literary activity seems to have been almost
entirely devoted to the theater. (It may be significant that
the two narrative poems were written in years when the
plague closed the theaters for several months.) In 1594
he was a charter member of a theatrical company called
the Chamberlain's Men, which in 1603 became the royal
company, the King's Men, making Shakespeare the king's
playwright. Until he retired to Stratford (about 1611, apparently), he was with this remarkably stable company. From
1599 the company acted primarily at the Globe theater, in
which Shakespeare held a one-tenth interest. Other Elizabethan dramatists are known to have acted, but no other is
known also to have been entitled to a share of the profits.

Shakespeare's first eight published plays did not have his
name on them, but this is not remarkable; the most popular
play of the period, Thomas Kyd's *The Spanish Tragedy*,
went through many editions without naming Kyd, and
Kyd's authorship is known only because a book on the profession of acting happens to quote (and attribute to Kyd)
some lines on the interest of Roman emperors in the drama.
What is remarkable is that after 1598 Shakespeare's name
commonly appears on printed plays—some of which are not
his. Presumably his name was a drawing card, and pub-
lishers used it to attract potential buyers. Another indication
of his popularity comes from Francis Meres, author of *Pal-
ladis Tamia: Wit's Treasury* (1598). In this anthology of
snippets accompanied by an essay on literature, many playwrights are mentioned, but Shakespeare's name occurs

more often than any other, and Shakespeare is the only play-wright whose plays are listed.

From his acting, his play writing, and his share in a playhouse, Shakespeare seems to have made considerable money. He put it to work, making substantial investments in Stratford real estate. As early as 1597 he bought New Place, the second-largest house in Stratford. His family moved in soon afterward, and the house remained in the family until a granddaughter died in 1670. When Shakespeare made his will in 1616, less than a month before he died, he sought to leave his property intact to his descendants. Of small bequests to relatives and to friends (including three actors, Richard Burbage, John Heminges, and Henry Condell), that to his wife of the second-best bed has provoked the most comment. It has sometimes been taken as a sign of an unhappy marriage (other supposed signs are the apparently hasty marriage, his wife's seniority of eight years, and his residence in London without his family). Perhaps the second-best bed was the bed the couple had slept in, the best bed being reserved for visitors. In any case, had Shakespeare not excepted it, the bed would have gone (with the rest of his household possessions) to his daughter and her husband.

On 25 April 1616 Shakespeare was buried within the chancel of the church at Stratford. An unattractive monument to his memory, placed on a wall near the grave, says that he died on 23 April. Over the grave itself are the lines, perhaps by Shakespeare, that (more than his literary fame) have kept his bones undisturbed in the crowded burial ground where old bones were often dislodged to make way for new:

> Good friend, for Jesus' sake forbear
> To dig the dust enclosed here.
> Blessed be the man that spares these stones
> And cursed be he that moves my bones.

A Note on the Anti-Stratfordians, Especially Baconians and Oxfordians

Not until 1769—more than a hundred and fifty years after Shakespeare's death—is there any record of anyone expressing doubt about Shakespeare's authorship of the plays and poems. In 1769, however, Herbert Lawrence nominated Francis Bacon (1561–1626) in *The Life and Adventures of Common Sense*. Since then, at least two dozen other nominees have been offered, including Christopher Marlowe, Sir Walter Raleigh, Queen Elizabeth I, and Edward de Vere, 17th earl of Oxford. The impulse behind all anti-Stratfordian movements is the scarcely concealed snobbish opinion that "the man from Stratford" simply could not have written the plays because he was a country fellow without a university education and without access to high society. Anyone, the argument goes, who used so many legal terms, medical terms, nautical terms, and so forth, and who showed some familiarity with classical writing, must have attended a university, and anyone who knew so much about courtly elegance and courtly deceit must himself have moved among courtiers. The plays do indeed reveal an author whose interests were exceptionally broad, but specialists in any given field—law, medicine, arms and armor, and so on—soon find that the plays do not reveal deep knowledge in specialized matters; indeed, the playwright often gets technical details wrong.

The claim on behalf of Bacon, forgotten almost as soon as it was put forth in 1769, was independently reasserted by Joseph C. Hart in 1848. In 1856 it was reaffirmed by W. H. Smith in a book, and also by Delia Bacon in an article; in 1857 Delia Bacon published a book, arguing that Francis Bacon had directed a group of intellectuals who wrote the plays.

Francis Bacon's claim has largely faded, perhaps because it was advanced with such evident craziness by Ignatius Donnelly, who in *The Great Cryptogram* (1888) claimed to break a code in the plays that proved Bacon had written not only the plays attributed to Shakespeare but also other Renaissance works, for instance the plays of Christopher Marlowe and the essays of Montaigne.

Consider the last two lines of the Epilogue in *The Tempest*:

> As you from crimes would pardoned be,
> Let your indulgence set me free.

What was Shakespeare—sorry, Francis Bacon, Baron Verulam—*really* saying in these two lines? According to Baconians, the lines are an anagram reading, "Tempest of Francis Bacon, Lord Verulam; do ye ne'er divulge me, ye words." Ingenious, and it is a pity that in the quotation the letter *a* appears only twice in the cryptogram, whereas in the deciphered message it appears three times. Oh, no problem; just alter "Verulam" to "Verul'm" and it works out very nicely.

Most people understand that with sufficient ingenuity one can torture any text and find in it what one wishes. For instance: Did Shakespeare have a hand in the King James Version of the Bible? It was nearing completion in 1610, when Shakespeare was forty-six years old. If you look at the 46th Psalm and count forward for forty-six words, you will find the word *shake*. Now if you go to the end of the psalm and count backward forty-six words, you will find the word *spear*. Clear evidence, according to some, that Shakespeare slyly left his mark in the book.

Bacon's candidacy has largely been replaced in the twentieth century by the candidacy of Edward de Vere (1550–1604), 17th earl of Oxford. The basic ideas behind the Oxford theory, advanced at greatest length by Dorothy and Charlton Ogburn in *This Star of England* (1952, rev. 1955), a book of 1297 pages, and by Charlton Ogburn in *The Mysterious William Shakespeare* (1984), a book of 892 pages, are these: (1) The man from Stratford could not possibly have had the mental equipment and the experience to have written the plays—only a courtier could have written them; (2) Oxford had the requisite background (social position, education, years at Queen Elizabeth's court); (3) Oxford did not wish his authorship to be known for two basic reasons: writing for the public theater was a vulgar pursuit, and the plays show so much courtly and royal disreputable behavior that they would have compromised Oxford's position at court. Oxfordians offer countless details to support the claim. For example, Hamlet's phrase "that ever I was born to set it right" (1.5.89) barely conceals "E. Ver, I was born to set it right," an unambiguous announcement of de Vere's authorship, according to *This Star of England* (p. 654). A second example: Consider Ben

Jonson's poem entitled "To the Memory of My Beloved Master William Shakespeare," prefixed to the first collected edition of Shakespeare's plays in 1623. According to Oxfordians, when Jonson in this poem speaks of the author of the plays as the "swan of Avon," he is alluding not to William Shakespeare, who was born and died in Stratford-on-Avon and who throughout his adult life owned property there; rather, he is alluding to Oxford, who, the Ogburns say, used "William Shakespeare" as his pen name, and whose manor at Bilton was on the Avon River. Oxfordians do not offer any evidence that Oxford took a pen name, and they do not mention that Oxford had sold the manor in 1581, forty-two years before Jonson wrote his poem. Surely a reference to the Shakespeare who was born in Stratford, who had returned to Stratford, and who had died there only seven years before Jonson wrote the poem is more plausible. And exactly why Jonson, who elsewhere also spoke of Shakespeare as a playwright, and why Heminges and Condell, who had acted with Shakespeare for about twenty years, should speak of Shakespeare as the author in their dedication in the 1623 volume of collected plays is never adequately explained by Oxfordians. Either Jonson, Heminges and Condell, and numerous others were in on the conspiracy, or they were all duped—equally unlikely alternatives. Another difficulty in the Oxford theory is that Oxford died in 1604, and some of the plays are clearly indebted to works and events later than 1604. Among the Oxfordian responses are: At his death Oxford left some plays, and in later years these were touched up by hacks, who added the material that points to later dates. *The Tempest*, almost universally regarded as one of Shakespeare's greatest plays and pretty clearly dated to 1611, does indeed date from a period after the death of Oxford, but it is a crude piece of work that should not be included in the canon of works by Oxford.

The anti-Stratfordians, in addition to assuming that the author must have been a man of rank and a university man, usually assume two conspiracies: (1) a conspiracy in Elizabethan and Jacobean times, in which a surprisingly large number of persons connected with the theater knew that the actor Shakespeare did not write the plays attributed to him but for some reason or other pretended that he did; (2) a conspiracy of today's Stratfordians, the professors who teach Shakespeare in the colleges and universities, who are said to have a vested interest in preserving Shakespeare as the author of the plays they teach. In fact, (1) it is inconceivable that the secret of Shakespeare's non-authorship could have been preserved by all of the people who supposedly were in on the conspiracy, and (2) academic fame awaits any scholar today who can disprove Shakespeare's authorship.

The Stratfordian case is convincing not only because hundreds or even thousands of anti-Stratford arguments—of the sort that say "ever I was born" has the secret double meaning "E. Ver, I was born"—add up to nothing at all but also because irrefutable evidence connects the man from Stratford with the London theater and with the authorship of particular plays. The anti-Stratfordians do not seem to understand that it is not enough to dismiss the Stratford case by saying that a fellow from the provinces simply couldn't have written the plays. Nor do they understand that it is not enough to dismiss all of the evidence connecting Shakespeare with the plays by asserting that it is perjured.

The Shakespeare Canon

We return to William Shakespeare. Thirty-seven plays as well as some nondramatic poems are generally held to constitute the Shakespeare canon, the body of authentic works. The exact dates of composition of most of the works are highly uncertain, but evidence of a starting point and/or of a final limiting point often provides a framework for informed guessing. For example, *Richard II* cannot be earlier than 1595, the publication date of some material to which it is indebted; *The Merchant of Venice* cannot be later than 1598, the year Francis Meres mentioned it. Sometimes arguments for a date hang on an alleged topical allusion, such as the lines about the unseasonable weather in *A Midsummer Night's Dream*, 2.1.81–117, but such an allusion, if indeed it is an allusion to an event in the real world, can be variously interpreted, and in any case there is always the possibility that a topical allusion was inserted years later, to bring the play up to date. (The issue of alterations in a text between time that Shakespeare drafted it and the time that it was printed—alterations due to censorship or playhouse practice or Shakespeare's own second thoughts—will be discussed in "The Play Text as a Collaboration" later in this overview.) Dates are often attributed on the basis of style, and although conjectures about style usually rest on other conjectures (such as Shakespeare's development as a playwright, or the appropriateness of lines to character), sooner or later one must rely on one's literary sense. There is no documentary proof, for example, that *Othello* is not as early as *Romeo and Juliet*, but one feels that *Othello* is a later, more mature work, and because the first record of its performance is 1604, one is glad enough to set its composition at that date and not push it back into Shakespeare's early years. (*Romeo and Juliet* was first published in 1597, but evidence suggests that it was written a little earlier.) The following chronology, then, is indebted not only to facts but also to informed guesswork and sensitivity. The dates, necessarily imprecise for some works, indicate something like a scholarly consensus concerning the time of original composition. Some plays show evidence of later revision.

Plays. The first collected edition of Shakespeare, published in 1623, included thirty-six plays. These are all accepted as Shakespeare's, though for one of them, *Henry VIII*, he is thought to have had a collaborator. A thirty-seventh play, *Pericles*, published in 1609 and attributed to Shakespeare on the title page, is also widely accepted as being partly by Shakespeare even though it is not included in the 1623 volume. Still another play not in the 1623 volume, *The Two Noble Kinsmen*, was first published in 1634, with a title page attributing it to John Fletcher and Shakespeare. Probably most students of the subject now believe that Shakespeare did indeed have a hand in it. Of the remaining plays attributed at one time or another to Shakespeare, only one, *Edward III*, anonymously published in 1596, is now regarded by some scholars as a serious candidate. The prevailing opinion, however, is that this rather simple-minded play is not Shakespeare's; at most he may have revised some passages, chiefly scenes with the Countess of

Salisbury. We include *The Two Noble Kinsmen* but do not include *Edward III* in the following list.

1588–94	*The Comedy of Errors*
1588–94	*Love's Labor's Lost*
1589–91	*2 Henry VI*
1590–91	*3 Henry VI*
1589–92	*1 Henry VI*
1592–93	*Richard III*
1589–94	*Titus Andronicus*
1593–94	*The Taming of the Shrew*
1592–94	*The Two Gentlemen of Verona*
1594–96	*Romeo and Juliet*
1595	*Richard II*
1595–96	*A Midsummer Night's Dream*
1596–97	*King John*
1594–96	*The Merchant of Venice*
1596–97	*1 Henry IV*
1597	*The Merry Wives of Windsor*
1597–98	*2 Henry IV*
1598–99	*Much Ado About Nothing*
1598–99	*Henry V*
1599	*Julius Caesar*
1599–1600	*As You Like It*
1599–1600	*Twelfth Night*
1600–1601	*Hamlet*
1601–1602	*Troilus and Cressida*
1602–1604	*All's Well That Ends Well*
1603–1604	*Othello*
1604	*Measure for Measure*
1605–1606	*King Lear*
1605–1606	*Macbeth*
1606–1607	*Antony and Cleopatra*
1605–1608	*Timon of Athens*
1607–1608	*Coriolanus*
1607–1608	*Pericles*
1609–10	*Cymbeline*
1610–11	*The Winter's Tale*
1611	*The Tempest*

| 1612–13 | *Henry VIII* |
| 1613 | *The Two Noble Kinsmen* |

Poems. In 1989 Donald W. Foster published a book in which he argued that "A Funeral Elegy for Master William Peter," published in 1612, ascribed only to the initials W.S., *may* be by Shakespeare. Foster later published an article in a scholarly journal, *PMLA* 111 (1996), in which he asserted the claim more positively. The evidence begins with the initials, and includes the fact that the publisher and the printer of the elegy had published Shakespeare's *Sonnets* in 1609. But such facts add up to rather little, especially because no one has found any connection between Shakespeare and William Peter (an Oxford graduate about whom little is known, who was murdered at the age of twenty-nine). The argument is based chiefly on statistical examinations of word patterns, which are said to correlate with Shakespeare's known work. Despite such correlations, however, many readers feel that the poem does not sound like Shakespeare. True, Shakespeare has a great range of styles, but his work is consistently imaginative and interesting. Many readers find neither of these qualities in "A Funeral Elegy."

1592–93	*Venus and Adonis*
1593–94	*The Rape of Lucrece*
1593–1600	*Sonnets*
1600–1601	*The Phoenix and the Turtle*

Shakespeare's English

1. Spelling and Pronunciation. From the philologist's point of view, Shakespeare's English is modern English. It requires footnotes, but the inexperienced reader can comprehend substantial passages with very little help, whereas for the same reader Chaucer's Middle English is a foreign language. By the beginning of the fifteenth century the chief grammatical changes in English had taken place, and the final unaccented *-e* of Middle English had been lost (though

it survives even today in spelling, as in *name*); during the fifteenth century the dialect of London, the commercial and
political center, gradually displaced the provincial dialects,
at least in writing; by the end of the century, printing had
helped to regularize and stabilize the language, especially
spelling. Elizabethan spelling may seem erratic to us (there
were dozens of spellings of *Shakespeare*, and a simple word
like *been* was also spelled *beene* and *bin*), but it had much in
common with our spelling. Elizabethan spelling was conser-
vative in that for the most part it reflected an older pronunciation (Middle English) rather than the sound of the
language as it was then spoken, just as our spelling continues
to reflect medieval pronunciation—most obviously in the
now silent but formerly pronounced letters in a word such as
knight. Elizabethan pronunciation, though not identical with
ours, was much closer to ours than to that of the Middle
Ages. Incidentally, though no one can be certain about what
Elizabethan English sounded like, specialists tend to believe
it was rather like the speech of a modern stage Irishman
(*time* apparently was pronounced *toime*, *old* pronounced
awld, *day* pronounced *die*, and *join* pronounced *jine*) and not
at all like the Oxford speech that most of us think it was.

An awareness of the difference between our pronunciation and Shakespeare's is crucial in three areas—in accent,
or number of syllables (many metrically regular lines may
look irregular to us); in rhymes (which may not look like
rhymes); and in puns (which may not look like puns).
Examples will be useful. Some words that were at least on
occasion stressed differently from today are *aspèct*, *còm-
plete*, *fòrlorn*, *revènue*, and *sepùlcher*. Words that sometimes had an additional syllable are *emp[e]ress*, *Hen[e]ry*,
mon[e]th, and *villain* (three syllables, *vil-lay-in*). An additional syllable is often found in possessives, like *moon*'s
(pronounced *moones*) and in words ending in *-tion* or *-sion*.
Words that had one less syllable than they now have are
needle (pronounced *neel*) and *violet* (pronounced *vilet*).
Among rhymes now lost are *one* with *loan*, *love* with *prove*,
beast with *jest*, *eat* with *great*. (In reading, trust your sense
of metrics and your ear, more than your eye.) An example of
a pun that has become obliterated by a change in pronunciation is Falstaff's reply to Prince Hal's "Come, tell us your

reason" in *1 Henry IV*: "Give you a reason on compulsion? If reasons were as plentiful as blackberries, I would give no man a reason upon compulsion, I" (2.4.237–40). The *ea* in *reason* was pronounced rather like a long *a*, like the *ai* in *raisin*, hence the comparison with blackberries.

Puns are not merely attempts to be funny; like metaphors they often involve bringing into a meaningful relationship areas of experience normally seen as remote. In *2 Henry IV,* when Feeble is conscripted, he stoically says, "I care not. A man can die but once. We owe God a death" (3.2.242–43), punning on *debt,* which was the way *death* was pronounced. Here an enormously significant fact of life is put into simple commercial imagery, suggesting its commonplace quality. Shakespeare used the same pun earlier in *1 Henry IV,* when Prince Hal says to Falstaff, "Why, thou owest God a death," and Falstaff replies, " 'Tis not due yet: I would be loath to pay him before his day. What need I be so forward with him that calls not on me?" (5.1.126–29).

Sometimes the puns reveal a delightful playfulness; sometimes they reveal aggressiveness, as when, replying to Claudius's "But now, my cousin Hamlet, and my son," Hamlet says, "A little more than kin, and less than kind!" (1.2.64–65). These are Hamlet's first words in the play, and we already hear him warring verbally against Claudius. Hamlet's "less than kind" probably means (1) Hamlet is not of Claudius's family or nature, *kind* having the sense it still has in our word *mankind*; (2) Hamlet is not kindly (affectionately) disposed toward Claudius; (3) Claudius is not naturally (but rather unnaturally, in a legal sense incestuously) Hamlet's father. The puns evidently were not put in as sops to the groundlings; they are an important way of communicating a complex meaning.

2. Vocabulary. A conspicuous difficulty in reading Shakespeare is rooted in the fact that some of his words are no longer in common use—for example, words concerned with armor, astrology, clothing, coinage, hawking, horsemanship, law, medicine, sailing, and war. Shakespeare had a large vocabulary—something near thirty thousand words—but it was not so much a vocabulary of big words as a vocabulary drawn from a wide range of life, and it is partly his ability to call upon a great body of concrete language that gives his plays the sense of being in close contact with life. When the right word did not already exist, he made it up. Among words thought to be his coinages are *accommodation, all-knowing, amazement, bare-faced, countless, dexterously, dislocate, dwindle, fancy-free, frugal, indistinguishable, lackluster, laughable, overawe, premeditated, sea change, star-crossed.* Among those that have not survived are the verb *convive,* meaning to feast together, and *smilet,* a little smile.

Less overtly troublesome than the technical words but more treacherous are the words that seem readily intelligible to us but whose Elizabethan meanings differ from their modern ones. When Horatio describes the Ghost as an "erring spirit," he is saying not that the ghost has sinned or made an error but that it is wandering. Here is a short list of some of the most common words in Shakespeare's plays that often (but not always) have a meaning other than their most usual modern meaning:

'a	he
abuse	deceive
accident	occurrence
advertise	inform
an, and	if
annoy	harm
appeal	accuse
artificial	skillful
brave	fine, splendid
censure	opinion
cheer	(1) face (2) frame of mind
chorus	a single person who comments on the events
closet	small private room
competitor	partner
conceit	idea, imagination
cousin	kinsman
cunning	skillful
disaster	evil astrological influence
doom	judgment
entertain	receive into service

envy	malice
event	outcome
excrement	outgrowth (of hair)
fact	evil deed
fancy	(1) love (2) imagination
fell	cruel
fellow	(1) companion (2) low person (often an insulting term if addressed to someone of approximately equal rank)
fond	foolish
free	(1) innocent (2) generous
glass	mirror
hap, haply	chance, by chance
head	army
humor	(1) mood (2) bodily fluid thought to control one's psychology
imp	child
intelligence	news
kind	natural, acting according to nature
let	hinder
lewd	base
mere(ly)	utter(ly)
modern	commonplace
natural	a fool, an idiot
naughty	(1) wicked (2) worthless
next	nearest
nice	(1) trivial (2) fussy
noise	music
policy	(1) prudence (2) stratagem
presently	immediately
prevent	anticipate
proper	handsome
prove	test
quick	alive
sad	serious
saw	proverb
secure	without care, incautious
silly	innocent

sensible	capable of being perceived by the senses
shrewd	sharp
so	provided that
starve	die
still	always
success	that which follows
tall	brave
tell	count
tonight	last night
wanton	playful, careless
watch	keep awake
will	lust
wink	close both eyes
wit	mind, intelligence

All glosses, of course, are mere approximations; sometimes one of Shakespeare's words may hover between an older meaning and a modern one, and as we have seen, his words often have multiple meanings.

3. Grammar. A few matters of grammar may be surveyed, though it should be noted at the outset that Shakespeare sometimes made up his own grammar. As E.A. Abbott says in *A Shakespearian Grammar,* "Almost any part of speech can be used as any other part of speech": a noun as a verb ("he childed as I fathered"); a verb as a noun ("She hath made compare"); or an adverb as an adjective ("a seldom pleasure"). There are hundreds, perhaps thousands, of such instances in the plays, many of which at first glance would not seem at all irregular and would trouble only a pedant. Here are a few broad matters.

Nouns: The Elizabethans thought the -*s* genitive ending for nouns (as in *man's*) derived from *his*; thus the line " 'gainst the count his galleys I did some service," for "the count's galleys."

Adjectives: By Shakespeare's time adjectives had lost the endings that once indicated gender, number, and case. About the only difference between Shakespeare's adjectives and ours is the use of the now redundant *more* or *most* with the comparative ("some more fitter place") or superlative

("This was the most unkindest cut of all"). Like double comparatives and double superlatives, double negatives were acceptable; Mercutio "will not budge for no man's pleasure."

Pronouns: The greatest change was in pronouns. In Middle English *thou, thy,* and *thee* were used among familiars and in speaking to children and inferiors; *ye, your,* and *you* were used in speaking to superiors (servants to masters, nobles to the king) or to equals with whom the speaker was not familiar. Increasingly the "polite" forms were used in all direct address, regardless of rank, and the accusative *you* displaced the nominative *ye.* Shakespeare sometimes uses *ye* instead of *you,* but even in Shakespeare's day *ye* was archaic, and it occurs mostly in rhetorical appeals.

Thou, thy, and *thee* were not completely displaced, however, and Shakespeare occasionally makes significant use of them, sometimes to connote familiarity or intimacy and sometimes to connote contempt. In *Twelfth Night* Sir Toby advises Sir Andrew to insult Cesario by addressing him as *thou:* "If thou thou'st him some thrice, it shall not be amiss" (3.2.46–47). In *Othello* when Brabantio is addressing an unidentified voice in the dark he says, "What are you?" (1.1.91), but when the voice identifies itself as the foolish suitor Roderigo, Brabantio uses the contemptuous form, saying, "I have charged thee not to haunt about my doors" (93). He uses this form for a while, but later in the scene, when he comes to regard Roderigo as an ally, he shifts back to the polite *you,* beginning in line 163, "What said she to you?" and on to the end of the scene. For reasons not yet satisfactorily explained, Elizabethans used *thou* in addresses to God—"O God, thy arm was here," the king says in *Henry V* (4.8.108)—and to supernatural characters such as ghosts and witches. A subtle variation occurs in *Hamlet.* When Hamlet first talks with the Ghost in 1.5, he uses *thou,* but when he sees the Ghost in his mother's room, in 3.4, he uses *you,* presumably because he is now convinced that the Ghost is not a counterfeit but is his father.

Perhaps the most unusual use of pronouns, from our point of view, is the neuter singular. In place of our *its, his* was often used, as in "How far that little candle throws *his* beams." But the use of a masculine pronoun for a neuter noun came to seem unnatural, and so _it_ was used for the possessive as well as the nominative: "The hedge-sparrow fed the cuckoo so long / That it had it head bit off by it young." In the late sixteenth century the possessive form _its_ developed, apparently by analogy with the _-s_ ending used to indicate a genitive noun, as in _book_'s, but _its_ was not yet common usage in Shakespeare's day. He seems to have used _its_ only ten times, mostly in his later plays. Other usages, such as "you have seen Cassio and she together" or the substitution of _who_ for _whom,_ cause little problem even when noticed.

Verbs, Adverbs, and Prepositions: Verbs cause almost no difficulty: The third person singular present form commonly ends in _-s,_ as in modern English (e.g., "He blesses"), but sometimes in _-eth_ (Portia explains to Shylock that mercy "blesseth him that gives and him that takes"). Broadly speaking, the _-eth_ ending was old-fashioned or dignified or "literary" rather than colloquial, except for the words _doth, hath,_ and _saith._ The _-eth_ ending (regularly used in the King James Bible, 1611) is very rare in Shakespeare's dramatic prose, though not surprisingly it occurs twice in the rather formal prose summary of the narrative poem _Lucrece._ Sometimes a plural subject, especially if it has collective force, takes a verb ending in _-s,_ as in "My old bones aches." Some of our strong or irregular preterites (such as _broke_) have a different form in Shakespeare (_brake_); some verbs that now have a weak or regular preterite (such as _helped_) in Shakespeare have a strong or irregular preterite (_holp_). Some adverbs that today end in _-ly_ were not inflected: "grievous sick," "wondrous strange." Finally, prepositions often are not the ones we expect: "We are such stuff as dreams are made on," "I have a king here to my flatterer."

Again, none of the differences (except meanings that have substantially changed or been lost) will cause much difficulty. But it must be confessed that for some elliptical passages there is no widespread agreement on meaning. Wise editors resist saying more than they know, and when they are uncertain they add a question mark to their gloss.

Shakespeare's Theater

In Shakespeare's infancy, Elizabethan actors performed wherever they could—in great halls, at court, in the court-yards of inns. These venues implied not only different audiences but also different playing conditions. The innyards must have made rather unsatisfactory theaters: on some days they were unavailable because carters bringing goods to London used them as depots; when available, they had to be rented from the innkeeper. In 1567, presumably to avoid such difficulties, and also to avoid regulation by the Common Council of London, which was not well disposed toward theatricals, one John Brayne, brother-in-law of the carpenter turned actor James Burbage, built the Red Lion in an eastern suburb of London. We know nothing about its shape or its capacity; we can say only that it may have been the first building in Europe constructed for the purpose of giving plays since the end of antiquity, a thousand years earlier. Even after the building of the Red Lion theatrical activity continued in London in makeshift circumstances, in marketplaces and inns, and always uneasily. In 1574 the Common Council required that plays and playing places in London be licensed because

> sundry great disorders and inconveniences have been found to ensue to this city by the inordinate haunting of great multitudes of people, specially youth, to plays, interludes, and shows, namely occasion of frays and quarrels, evil practices of incontinency in great inns having chambers and secret places adjoining to their open stages and galleries.

The Common Council ordered that innkeepers who wished licenses to hold performance put up a bond and make contributions to the poor.

The requirement that plays and innyard theaters be licensed, along with the other drawbacks of playing at inns and presumably along with the success of the Red Lion, led James Burbage to rent a plot of land northeast of the city walls, on property outside the jurisdiction of the city. Here he built England's second playhouse, called simply the Theatre. About all that is known of its construction is that it was wood. It soon had imitators, the most famous being the Globe (1599), essentially an amphitheater built across the Thames (again outside the city's jurisdiction), constructed with timbers of the Theatre, which had been dismantled when Burbage's lease ran out.

Admission to the theater was one penny, which allowed spectators to stand at the sides and front of the stage that jutted into the yard. An additional penny bought a seat in a covered part of the theater, and a third penny bought a more comfortable seat and a better location. It is notoriously difficult to translate prices into today's money, since some things that are inexpensive today would have been expensive in the past and vice versa—a pipeful of tobacco (imported, of course) cost a lot of money, about three pennies, and an orange (also imported) cost two or three times what a chicken cost—but perhaps we can get some idea of the low cost of the penny admission when we realize that a penny could also buy a pot of ale. An unskilled laborer made about five or sixpence a day, an artisan about twelve pence a day, and the hired actors (as opposed to the sharers in the company, such as Shakespeare) made about ten pence a performance. A printed play cost five or sixpence. Of course a visit to the theater (like a visit to a baseball game today) usually cost more than the admission since the spectator probably would also buy food and drink. Still, the low entrance fee meant that the theater was available to all except the very poorest people, rather as movies and most athletic events are today. Evidence indicates that the audience ranged from apprentices who somehow managed to scrape together the minimum entrance fee and to escape from their masters for a few hours, to prosperous members of the middle class and aristocrats who paid the additional fee for admission to the galleries. The exact proportion of men to women cannot be determined, but women of all classes certainly were present. Theaters were open every afternoon but Sundays for much of the year, except in times of plague, when they were closed because of fear of infection. By the way, no evidence suggests the presence of toilet facilities. Presumably the patrons relieved themselves by making a quick trip to the fields surrounding the playhouses.

There are four important sources of information about the

structure of Elizabethan public playhouses—drawings, a contract, recent excavations, and stage directions in the plays. Of drawings, only the so-called de Witt drawing (c. 1596) of the Swan—really his friend Aernout van Buchell's copy of Johannes de Witt's drawing—is of much significance. The drawing, the only extant representation of the interior of an Elizabethan theater, shows an amphitheater of three tiers, with a stage jutting from a wall into the yard or

Johannes de Witt, a Continental visitor to London, made a drawing of the Swan theater in about the year 1596. The original drawing is lost; this is Aernout van Buchell's copy of it.

center of the building. The tiers are roofed, and part of the stage is covered by a roof that projects from the rear and is supported at its front on two posts, but the groundlings, who paid a penny to stand in front of the stage or at its sides, were exposed to the sky. (Performances in such a playhouse were held only in the daytime; artificial illumination was not used.) At the rear of the stage are two massive doors; above the stage is a gallery.

The second major source of information, the contract for the Fortune (built in 1600), specifies that although the Globe (built in 1599) is to be the model, the Fortune is to be square, eighty feet outside and fifty-five inside. The stage is to be forty-three feet broad, and is to extend into the middle of the yard, i.e., it is twenty-seven and a half feet deep.

The third source of information, the 1989 excavations of the Rose (built in 1587), indicate that the Rose was fourteen-sided, about seventy-two feet in diameter with an inner yard almost fifty feet in diameter. The stage at the Rose was about sixteen feet deep, thirty-seven feet wide at the rear, and twenty-seven feet wide downstage. The relatively small dimensions and the tapering stage, in contrast to the rectangular stage in the Swan drawing, surprised theater historians and have made them more cautious in generalizing about the Elizabethan theater. Excavations at the Globe have not yielded much information, though some historians believe that the fragmentary evidence suggests a larger theater, perhaps one hundred feet in diameter.

From the fourth chief source, stage directions in the plays, one learns that entrance to the stage was by the doors at the rear (*"Enter one citizen at one door, and another at the other"*). A curtain hanging across the doorway—or a curtain hanging between the two doorways—could provide a place where a character could conceal himself, as Polonius does, when he wishes to overhear the conversation between Hamlet and Gertrude. Similarly, withdrawing a curtain from the doorway could "discover" (reveal) a character or two. Such discovery scenes are very rare in Elizabethan drama, but a good example occurs in *The Tempest* (5.1.171), where a stage direction tells us, *"Here Prospero discovers Ferdinand and Miranda playing at chess."* There was also some sort of playing space "aloft" or "above" to represent, for instance, the top of a city's walls or a room above the street. Doubtless each theater had its own peculiarities, but perhaps we can talk about a "typical" Elizabethan theater if we realize that no theater need exactly fit the description, just as no mother is the average mother with 2.7 children.

This hypothetical theater is wooden, round, or polygonal (in *Henry V* Shakespeare calls it a "wooden *O*") capable of holding some eight hundred spectators who stood in the yard around the projecting elevated stage—these spectators were the "groundlings"—and some fifteen hundred additional spectators who sat in the three roofed galleries. The stage, protected by a "shadow" or "heavens" or roof, is entered from two doors; behind the doors is the "tiring house" (attiring house, i.e., dressing room), and above the stage is some sort of gallery that may sometimes hold spectators but can be used (for example) as the bedroom from which Romeo—according to a stage direction in one text—"goeth down." Some evidence suggests that a throne can be lowered onto the platform stage, perhaps from the "shadow"; certainly characters can descend from the stage through a trap or traps into the cellar or "hell." Sometimes this space beneath the stage accommodates a sound-effects man or musician (in *Antony and Cleopatra "music of the hautboys* [oboes] *is under the stage"*) or an actor (in *Hamlet* the *"Ghost cries under the stage"*). Most characters simply walk on and off through the doors, but because there is no curtain in front of the platform, corpses will have to be carried off (Hamlet obligingly clears the stage of Polonius's corpse, when he says, "I'll lug the guts into the neighbor room"). Other characters may have fallen at the rear, where a curtain on a doorway could be drawn to conceal them.

Such may have been the "public theater," so called because its inexpensive admission made it available to a wide range of the populace. Another kind of theater has been called the "private theater" because its much greater admission charge (sixpence versus the penny for general admission at the public theater) limited its audience to the wealthy or the prodigal. The private theater was basically a large room, entirely roofed and therefore artificially illuminated, with a stage at one end. The theaters thus were distinct in two ways: One was essentially an amphitheater that catered to the general public; the other was a hall that catered to the wealthy. In 1576 a hall theater was established in Blackfriars, a Dominican priory in London that had been suppressed in 1538 and confiscated by the Crown and thus was not under the city's jurisdiction. All the actors in this Blackfriars theater were boys about eight to thirteen years old (in the public theaters similar boys played female parts; a boy Lady Macbeth played to a man Macbeth). Near the end of this section on Shakespeare's theater we will talk at some length about possible implications in this convention of using boys to play female roles, but for the moment we should say that it doubtless accounts for the relative lack of female roles in Elizabethan drama. Thus, in *A Midsummer Night's Dream*, out of twenty-one named roles, only four are female; in *Hamlet*, out of twenty-four, only two (Gertrude and Ophelia) are female. Many of Shakespeare's characters have fathers but no mothers—for instance, King Lear's daughters. We need not bring in Freud to explain the disparity; a dramatic company had only a few boys in it.

To return to the private theaters, in some of which all of the performers were children—the "eyrie of . . . little eyases" (nest of unfledged hawks—2.2.347–48) which Rosencrantz mentions when he and Guildenstern talk with Hamlet. The theater in Blackfriars had a precarious existence, and ceased operations in 1584. In 1596 James Burbage, who had already made theatrical history by building the Theatre, began to construct a second Blackfriars theater. He died in 1597, and for several years this second Blackfriars theater was used by a troupe of boys, but in 1608 two of Burbage's sons and five other actors (including Shakespeare) became joint operators of the theater, using it in the winter when the open-air Globe was unsuitable. Perhaps such a smaller theater, roofed, artificially illuminated, and with a tradition of a wealthy audience, exerted an influence in Shakespeare's late plays.

Performances in the private theaters may well have had intermissions during which music was played, but in the public theaters the action was probably uninterrupted, flowing from scene to scene almost without a break. Actors would enter, speak, exit, and others would immediately enter and establish (if necessary) the new locale by a few properties and by words and gestures. To indicate that the scene took place at night, a player or two would carry a torch. Here are some samples of Shakespeare establishing the scene:

This is Illyria, lady.   (*Twelfth Night*, 1.2.2)

Well, this is the Forest of Arden.   (*As You Like It*, 2.4.14)

This castle has a pleasant seat; the air
Nimbly and sweetly recommends itself
Unto our gentle senses.   (*Macbeth*, 1.6.1–3)

The west yet glimmers with some streaks of day.
                                                                        (*Macbeth*, 3.3.5)

Sometimes a speech will go far beyond evoking the minimal setting of place and time, and will, so to speak, evoke the social world in which the characters move. For instance, early in the first scene of *The Merchant of Venice* Salerio suggests an explanation for Antonio's melancholy. (In the following passage, *pageants* are decorated wagons, floats, and *cursy* is the verb "to curtsy," or "to bow.")

Your mind is tossing on the ocean,
There where your argosies with portly sail—
Like signiors and rich burghers on the flood,
Or as it were the pageants of the sea—
Do overpeer the petty traffickers
That cursy to them, do them reverence,
As they fly by them with their woven wings.   (1.1.8–14)

Late in the nineteenth century, when Henry Irving produced the play with elaborate illusionistic sets, the first scene showed a ship moored in the harbor, with fruit vendors and dock laborers, in an effort to evoke the bustling and exotic life of Venice. But Shakespeare's words give us this exotic, rich world of commerce in his highly descriptive language when Salerio speaks of "argosies with portly sail" that fly with "woven wings"; equally important, through Salerio Shakespeare conveys a sense of the orderly, hierarchical society in which the lesser ships, "the petty traffickers," curtsy and thereby "do . . . reverence" to their superiors, the merchant prince's ships, which are "Like signiors and rich burghers."

On the other hand, it is a mistake to think that except for verbal pictures the Elizabethan stage was bare. Although Shakespeare's Chorus in *Henry V* calls the stage an "unworthy scaffold" (Prologue 1.10) and urges the spectators to "eke out our performance with your mind" (Prologue 3.35), there was considerable spectacle. The last act of *Macbeth*, for instance, has five stage directions calling for *"drum and colors,"* and another sort of appeal to the eye is indicated by the stage direction *"Enter Macduff, with Macbeth's head."* Some scenery and properties may have been substantial; doubtless a throne was used, but the pillars supporting the roof would have served for the trees on which Orlando pins his poems in *As You Like It*.

Having talked about the public theater—"this wooden *O*"—at some length, we should mention again that Shakespeare's plays were performed also in other locales. Alvin Kernan, in *Shakespeare, the King's Playwright: Theater in the Stuart Court 1603–1613* (1995) points out that "several of [Shakespeare's] plays contain brief theatrical performances, set always in a court or some noble house. When Shakespeare portrayed a theater, he did not, except for the choruses in *Henry V*, imagine a public theater" (p. 195). (Examples include episodes in *The Taming of the Shrew*, *A Midsummer Night's Dream*, *Hamlet*, and *The Tempest*.)

A Note on the Use of Boy Actors in Female Roles

Until fairly recently, scholars were content to mention that the convention existed; they sometimes also mentioned that it continued the medieval practice of using males in female roles, and that other theaters, notably in ancient Greece and in China and Japan, also used males in female roles. (In classical Noh drama in Japan, males still play the female roles.) Prudery may have been at the root of the academic failure to talk much about the use of boy actors, or maybe there really is not much more to say than that it was a convention of a male-centered culture (Stephen Greenblatt's view, in *Shakespearean Negotiations* [1988]). Further, the very nature of a convention is that it is not thought about: Hamlet is a Dane and Julius Caesar is a Roman, but in Shakespeare's plays they speak English, and we in the audience never give this odd fact a thought. Similarly, a character may speak in the presence of others and we understand, again without thinking about it, that he or she is not heard by the figures on the stage (the aside); a character alone on the stage may speak (the soliloquy), and we do not take the character to be unhinged; in a realistic (box) set, the fourth wall, which allows us to see what is going on, is miraculously missing. The no-nonsense view, then, is that the boy actor was an accepted convention, accepted unthinkingly—just as today we know that Kenneth Branagh is not Hamlet, Al Pacino is not Richard III, and Denzel Washington is not the Prince of Aragon. In this view, the audience takes the performer for the role, and that is that; such is the argument we now make for race-free casting, in which African-Americans and Asians can play roles of persons who lived in medieval Denmark and ancient Rome. But gender perhaps is different, at least today. It is a matter of abundant academic study: The Elizabethan theater is now sometimes called a transvestite theater, and we hear much about cross-dressing.

Shakespeare himself in a very few passages calls attention to the use of boys in female roles. At the end of *As You Like It* the boy who played Rosalind addresses the audience, and says, "O men, . . . if I were a woman, I would kiss as many of you as had beards that pleased me." But this is in the Epilogue; the plot is over, and the actor is stepping out of the play and into the audience's everyday world. A second reference to the practice of boys playing female roles occurs in *Antony and Cleopatra*, when Cleopatra imagines that she and Antony will be the subject of crude plays, her role being performed by a boy:

> The quick comedians
> Extemporally will stage us, and present
> Our Alexandrian revels: Antony
> Shall be brought drunken forth, and I shall see
> Some squeaking Cleopatra boy my greatness.   (5.2.216–20)

In a few other passages, Shakespeare is more indirect. For instance, in *Twelfth Night* Viola, played of course by a boy, disguises herself as a young man and seeks service in the house of a lord. She enlists the help of a Captain, and (by way of explaining away her voice and her beardlessness) says,

> I'll serve this duke
> Thou shalt present me as an eunuch to him.   (1.2.55–56)

In *Hamlet*, when the players arrive in 2.2, Hamlet jokes with the boy who plays a female role. The boy has grown since Hamlet last saw him: "By'r Lady, your ladyship is nearer to heaven than when I saw you last by the altitude of a chopine" (a lady's thick-soled shoe). He goes on: "Pray God your voice . . . be not cracked" (434–38).

Exactly how sexual, how erotic, this material was and is, is now much disputed. Again, the use of boys may have been unnoticed, or rather not thought about—an unexamined convention—by most or all spectators most of the time, perhaps *all* of the time, except when Shakespeare calls the convention to the attention of the audience, as in the passages just quoted. Still, an occasional bit seems to invite erotic thoughts. The clearest example is the name that Rosalind takes in *As You Like It*, Ganymede—the beautiful youth whom Zeus abducted. Did boys dressed to play female roles carry homoerotic appeal for straight men (Lisa Jardine's view, in *Still Harping on Daughters* [1983]), or for gay men, or for some or all women in the audience? Further, when the boy actor played a woman who (for the purposes of the plot) disguised herself as a male, as Rosalind, Viola, and Portia do—so we get a boy playing a woman playing a man—what sort of appeal was generated, and for what sort of spectator?

Some scholars have argued that the convention empowered women by letting female characters display a freedom unavailable in Renaissance patriarchal society; the convention, it is said, undermined rigid gender distinctions. In this view, the convention (along with plots in which female characters for a while disguised themselves as young men) allowed Shakespeare to say what some modern gender

critics say: Gender is a constructed role rather than a bio-
logical given, something we make, rather than a fixed binary
opposition of male and female (see Juliet Dusinberre, in
Shakespeare and the Nature of Women [1975]). On the other
hand, some scholars have maintained that the male disguise
assumed by some female characters serves only to reaffirm
traditional social distinctions since female characters who
don male garb (notably Portia in *The Merchant of Venice*
and Rosalind in *As You Like It*) return to their female garb
and at least implicitly (these critics say) reaffirm the status
quo. (For this last view, see Clara Claiborne Park, in an
essay in *The Woman's Part*, ed. Carolyn Ruth Swift Lenz et
al. [1980].) Perhaps no one answer is right for all plays; in
As You Like It cross-dressing empowers Rosalind, but in
Twelfth Night cross-dressing comically traps Viola.

Shakespeare's Dramatic Language: Costumes, Gestures and Silences; Prose and Poetry

Because Shakespeare was a dramatist, not merely a poet,
he worked not only with language but also with costume,
sound effects, gestures, and even silences. We have already
discussed some kinds of spectacle in the preceding section,
and now we will begin with other aspects of visual language;
a theater, after all, is literally a "place for seeing." Consider
the opening stage direction in *The Tempest*, the first play in
the first published collection of Shakespeare's plays: *"A
tempestuous noise of thunder and Lightning heard: Enter a
Ship-master, and a Boteswain."*

Costumes: What did that shipmaster and that boatswain
wear? Doubtless they wore something that identified them
as men of the sea. Not much is known about the costumes
that Elizabethan actors wore, but at least three points are
clear: (1) many of the costumes were splendid versions of
contemporary Elizabethan dress; (2) some attempts were
made to approximate the dress of certain occupations and of
antique or exotic characters such as Romans, Turks, and
Jews; (3) some costumes indicated that the wearer was

supernatural. Evidence for elaborate Elizabethan clothing can be found in the plays themselves and in contemporary comments about the "sumptuous" players who wore the discarded clothing of noblemen, as well as in account books that itemize such things as "a scarlet cloak with two broad gold laces, with gold buttons down the sides."

The attempts at approximation of the dress of certain occupations and nationalities also can be documented from the plays themselves, and it derives additional confirmation from a drawing of the first scene of Shakespeare's *Titus Andronicus*—the only extant Elizabethan picture of an identifiable episode in a play. (See pp. xxxviii–xxxix.) The drawing, probably done in 1594 or 1595, shows Queen Tamora pleading for mercy. She wears a somewhat medieval-looking robe and a crown; Titus wears a toga and a wreath, but two soldiers behind him wear costumes fairly close to Elizabethan dress. We do not know, however, if the drawing represents an actual stage production in the public theater, or perhaps a private production, or maybe only a reader's visualization of an episode. Further, there is some conflicting evidence: In *Julius Caesar* a reference is made to Caesar's doublet (a close-fitting jacket), which, if taken literally, suggests that even the protagonist did not wear Roman clothing; and certainly the lesser characters, who are said to wear hats, did not wear Roman garb.

It should be mentioned, too, that even ordinary clothing can be symbolic: Hamlet's "inky cloak," for example, sets him apart from the brightly dressed members of Claudius's court and symbolizes his mourning; the fresh clothes that are put on King Lear partly symbolize his return to sanity. Consider, too, the removal of disguises near the end of some plays. For instance, Rosalind in *As You Like It* and Portia and Nerissa in *The Merchant of Venice* remove their male attire, thus again becoming fully themselves.

Gestures and Silences: Gestures are an important part of a dramatist's language. King Lear kneels before his daughter Cordelia for a benediction (4.7.57–59), an act of humility that contrasts with his earlier speeches banishing her and that contrasts also with a comparable gesture, his ironic kneeling before Regan (2.4.153–55). Northumberland's failure to kneel before King Richard II (3.3.71–72) speaks volumes. As for silences, consider a moment in *Coriolanus*: Before the protagonist yields to his mother's entreaties (5.3.182), there is this stage direction: *"Holds her by the hand, silent."* Another example of "speech in dumbness" occurs in *Macbeth*, when Macduff learns that his wife and children have been murdered. He is silent at first, as Malcolm's speech indicates: "What, man! Ne'er pull your hat upon your brows. Give sorrow words" (4.3.208–09). (For a discussion of such moments, see Philip C. McGuire's *Speechless Dialect: Shakespeare's Open Silences* [1985].)

Of course when we think of Shakespeare's work, we think primarily of his language, both the poetry and the prose.

Prose: Although two of his plays (*Richard II* and *King John*) have no prose at all, about half the others have at least one quarter of the dialogue in prose, and some have notably more: *1 Henry IV* and *2 Henry IV*, about half; *As You Like It* and *Twelfth Night*, a little more than half; *Much Ado About Nothing*, more than three quarters; and *The Merry Wives of Windsor*, a little more than five sixths. We should remember that despite Molière's joke about M. Jourdain, who was amazed to learn that he spoke prose, most of us do not speak prose. Rather, we normally utter repetitive, shapeless, and often ungrammatical torrents; prose is something very different—a sort of literary imitation of speech at its most coherent.

Today we may think of prose as "natural" for drama; or even if we think that poetry is appropriate for high tragedy we may still think that prose is the right medium for comedy. Greek, Roman, and early English comedies, however, were written in verse. In fact, prose was not generally considered a literary medium in England until the late fifteenth century; Chaucer tells even his bawdy stories in verse. By the end of the 1580s, however, prose had established itself on the English comic stage. In tragedy, Marlowe made some use of prose, not simply in the speeches of clownish servants but even in the speech of a tragic hero, Doctor Faustus. Still, before Shakespeare, prose normally was used in the theater only for special circumstances: (1) letters and proclamations, to set them off from the poetic dialogue; (2) mad characters, to indicate that normal thinking has become disordered; and (3) low comedy, or speeches uttered by clowns even when they are not being comic. Shakespeare made use of these conventions, but he also went far beyond them. Sometimes he begins a scene in prose and then shifts into verse as the emotion is heightened; or conversely, he may shift from verse to prose when a speaker is lowering the emotional level, as when Brutus speaks in the Forum.

Shakespeare's prose usually is not prosaic. Hamlet's prose includes not only small talk with Rosencrantz and Guildenstern but also princely reflections on "What a piece of work is a man" (2.2.312). In conversation with Ophelia, he shifts from light talk in verse to a passionate prose denunciation of women (3.1.103), though the shift to prose here is perhaps also intended to suggest the possibility of madness. (Consult Brian Vickers, *The Artistry of Shakespeare's Prose* [1968].)

Poetry: Drama in rhyme in England goes back to the Middle Ages, but by Shakespeare's day rhyme no longer dominated poetic drama; a finer medium, blank verse (strictly speaking, unrhymed lines of ten syllables, with the stress on every second syllable) had been adopted. But before looking at unrhymed poetry, a few things should be said about the chief uses of rhyme in Shakespeare's plays. (1) A couplet (a pair of rhyming lines) is sometimes used to convey emotional heightening at the end of a blank verse speech; (2) characters sometimes speak a couplet as they leave the stage, suggesting closure; (3) except in the latest plays, scenes fairly often conclude with a couplet, and sometimes, as in *Richard II*, 2.1.145–46, the entrance of a new character within a scene is preceded by a couplet, which wraps up the earlier portion of that scene; (4) speeches of two characters occasionally are linked by rhyme, most notably in *Romeo and Juliet*, 1.5.95–108, where the lovers speak a sonnet between them; elsewhere a taunting reply occasionally rhymes with the previous speaker's last line; (5) speeches with sententious or gnomic remarks are sometimes in rhyme, as in the duke's speech in *Othello* (1.3.199–206); (6) speeches of sardonic mockery are sometimes in rhyme—for example, Iago's speech on women in *Othello* (2.1.146–58)—and they sometimes conclude with an emphatic couplet, as in Bolingbroke's speech on comforting words in *Richard II* (1.3.301–2); (7) some characters are associated with rhyme, such as the fairies in *A Midsummer Night's Dream*; (8) in the early plays, especially *The Comedy of Errors* and *The Taming of the Shrew*, comic scenes that in later plays would be in prose are in jingling rhymes; (9) prologues, choruses, plays-within-the-play, inscriptions, vows, epilogues, and so on are often in rhyme, and the songs in the plays are rhymed.

Neither prose nor rhyme immediately comes to mind when we first think of Shakespeare's medium: It is blank verse, unrhymed iambic pentameter. (In a mechanically exact line there are five iambic feet. An iambic foot consists of two syllables, the second accented, as in *away*; five feet make a pentameter line. Thus, a strict line of iambic pentameter contains ten syllables, the even syllables being stressed more heavily than the odd syllables. Fortunately, Shakespeare usually varies the line somewhat.) The first speech in *A Midsummer Night's Dream*, spoken by Duke Theseus to his betrothed, is an example of blank verse:

> Now, fair Hippolyta, our nuptial hour
> Draws on apace. Four happy days bring in
> Another moon; but, O, methinks, how slow
> This old moon wanes! She lingers my desires,
> Like to a stepdame, or a dowager,
> Long withering out a young man's revenue.   (1.1.1–6)

As this passage shows, Shakespeare's blank verse is not mechanically unvarying. Though the predominant foot is the iamb (as in *apace* or *desires*), there are numerous variations. In the first line the stress can be placed on "fair," as the regular metrical pattern suggests, but it is likely that "Now" gets almost as much emphasis; probably in the second line "Draws" is more heavily emphasized than "on," giving us a trochee (a stressed syllable followed by an unstressed one); and in the fourth line each word in the phrase "This old moon wanes" is probably stressed fairly heavily, conveying by two spondees (two feet, each of two stresses) the oppressive tedium that Theseus feels.

In Shakespeare's early plays much of the blank verse is end-stopped (that is, it has a heavy pause at the end of each line), but he later developed the ability to write iambic pentameter verse paragraphs (rather than lines) that give the illusion of speech. His chief techniques are (1) enjambing, i.e., running the thought beyond the single line, as in the first three lines of the speech just quoted; (2) occasionally replacing an iamb with another foot; (3) varying the position of the chief pause (the caesura) within a line; (4) adding an occasional unstressed syllable at the end of a line, traditionally called a feminine ending; (5) and beginning or ending a speech with a half line.

Shakespeare's mature blank verse has much of the rhythmic flexibility of his prose; both the language, though richly figurative and sometimes dense, and the syntax seem natural. It is also often highly appropriate to a particular character. Consider, for instance, this speech from *Hamlet*, in which Claudius, King of Denmark ("the Dane"), speaks to Laertes:

> And now, Laertes, what's the news with you?
> You told us of some suit. What is't, Laertes?
> You cannot speak of reason to the Dane
> And lose your voice. What wouldst thou beg, Laertes,
> That shall not be my offer, not thy asking?   (1.2.42–46)

Notice the short sentences and the repetition of the name "Laertes," to whom the speech is addressed. Notice, too, the shift from the royal "us" in the second line to the more intimate "my" in the last line, and from "you" in the first three lines to the more intimate "thou" and "thy" in the last two lines. Claudius knows how to ingratiate himself with Laertes.

For a second example of the flexibility of Shakespeare's blank verse, consider a passage from *Macbeth*. Distressed by the doctor's inability to cure Lady Macbeth and by the imminent battle, Macbeth addresses some of his remarks to the doctor and others to the servant who is arming him. The entire speech, with its pauses, interruptions, and irresolution (in "Pull't off, I say," Macbeth orders the servant to remove the armor that the servant has been putting on him), catches Macbeth's disintegration. (In the first line, *physic* means "medicine," and in the fourth and fifth lines, *cast the water* means "analyze the urine.")

> Throw physic to the dogs, I'll none of it.
> Come, put mine armor on. Give me my staff.
> Seyton, send out.—Doctor, the thanes fly from me.—
> Come, sir, dispatch. If thou couldst, doctor, cast
> The water of my land, find her disease
> And purge it to a sound and pristine health,
> I would applaud thee to the very echo,
> That should applaud again.—Pull't off, I say.—
> What rhubarb, senna, or what purgative drug,
> Would scour these English hence? Hear'st thou of them?
>
> (5.3.47–56)

Blank verse, then, can be much more than unrhymed iambic pentameter, and even within a single play Shakespeare's blank verse often consists of several styles, depending on the speaker and on the speaker's emotion at the moment.

The Play Text as a Collaboration

Shakespeare's fellow dramatist Ben Jonson reported that the actors said of Shakespeare, "In his writing, whatsoever he penned, he never blotted out line," i.e., never crossed out material and revised his work while composing. None of Shakespeare's plays survives in manuscript (with the possible exception of a scene in *Sir Thomas More*), so we cannot fully evaluate the comment, but in a few instances the published work clearly shows that he revised his manuscript. Consider the following passage (shown here in facsimile) from the best early text of *Romeo and Juliet*, the Second Quarto (1599):

Ro. Would I were sleepe and peace so sweet to rest
The grey eyde morne smiles on the frowning night,
Checkring the Easterne Clouds with streaks of light,
And darknesse fleckted like a drunkard reeles,
From forth daies pathway, made by *Tytans* wheeles.
Hence will I to my ghostly Friers close cell,
His helpe to craue, and my deare hap to tell.

Exit.

Enter Frier alone with a basket.   (night,
Fri. The grey-eyed morne smiles on the frowning
Checking the Easterne clowdes with streaks of light:
And fleckeld darknesse like a drunkard reeles,
From forth daies path, and *Titans* burning wheeles:
Now ere the sun aduance his burning eie,

Romeo rather elaborately tells us that the sun at dawn is dispelling the night (morning is smiling, the eastern clouds are checked with light, and the sun's chariot—Titan's wheels—advances), and he will seek out his spiritual father, the Friar. He exits and, oddly, the Friar enters and says pretty much the same thing about the sun. Both speakers say that "the gray-eyed morn smiles on the frowning night," but there are small differences, perhaps having more to do with the business of printing the book than with the author's composition: For Romeo's "checkring," "fleckted," and "pathway," we get the Friar's "checking," "fleckeld," and "path." (Notice, by the way, the inconsistency in Elizabethan spelling: Romeo's "clouds" become the Friar's "clowdes.")

Both versions must have been in the printer's copy, and it seems safe to assume that both were in Shakespeare's manuscript. He must have written one version—let's say he first wrote Romeo's closing lines for this scene—and then he decided, no, it's better to give this lyrical passage to the Friar, as the opening of a new scene, but he neglected to delete the first version. Editors must make a choice, and they may feel that the reasonable thing to do is to print the text as Shakespeare intended it. But how can we know what he intended? Almost all modern editors delete the lines from

Romeo's speech, and retain the Friar's lines. They don't do this because they know Shakespeare's intention, however. They give the lines to the Friar because the first published version (1597) of *Romeo and Juliet* gives only the Friar's version, and this text (though in many ways inferior to the 1599 text) is thought to derive from the memory of some actors, that is, it is thought to represent a performance, not just a script. Maybe during the course of rehearsals Shakespeare—an actor as well as an author—unilaterally decided that the Friar should speak the lines; if so (remember that we don't know this to be a fact) his final intention was to give the speech to the Friar. Maybe, however, the actors talked it over and settled on the Friar, with or without Shakespeare's approval. On the other hand, despite the 1597 version, one might argue (if only weakly) on behalf of giving the lines to Romeo rather than to the Friar, thus: (1) Romeo's comment on the coming of the daylight emphasizes his separation from Juliet, and (2) the figurative language seems more appropriate to Romeo than to the Friar. Having said this, in the Signet edition we have decided in this instance to draw on the evidence provided by earlier text and to give the lines to the Friar, on the grounds that since Q1 reflects a production, in the theater (at least on one occasion) the lines were spoken by the Friar.

A playwright sold a script to a theatrical company. The script thus belonged to the company, not the author, and author and company alike must have regarded this script not as a literary work but as the basis for a play that the actors would create on the stage. We speak of Shakespeare as the author of the plays, but readers should bear in mind that the texts they read, even when derived from a single text, such as the First Folio (1623), are inevitably the collaborative work not simply of Shakespeare with his company—doubtless during rehearsals the actors would suggest alterations—but also with other forces of the age. One force was governmental censorship. In 1606 parliament passed "an Act to restrain abuses of players," prohibiting the utterance of oaths and the name of God. So where the earliest text of *Othello* gives us "By heaven" (3.3.106), the first Folio gives "Alas," presumably reflecting the compliance of stage practice with the law. Similarly, the 1623 version of *King Lear* omits the oath "Fut" (probably from "By God's foot") at 1.2.142, again presumably reflecting the line as it was spoken on the stage. Editors who seek to give the reader the play that Shakespeare initially conceived—the "authentic" play conceived by the solitary Shakespeare—probably will restore the missing oaths and references to God. Other editors, who see the play as a collaborative work, a construction made not only by Shakespeare but also by actors and compositors and even government censors, may claim that what counts is the play as it was actually performed. Such editors regard the censored text as legitimate, since it is the play that was (presumably) finally put on. A performed text, they argue, has more historical reality than a text produced by an editor who has sought to get at what Shakespeare initially wrote. In this view, the text of a play is rather like the script of a film; the script is not the film, and the play text is not the performed play. Even if we want to talk about the play that Shakespeare "intended," we will find ourselves talking about a script that he handed over to a company with the intention that it be implemented by actors. The "intended" play is the one that the actors—we might almost say "society"—would help to construct.

Further, it is now widely held that a play is also the work of readers and spectators, who do not simply receive meaning, but who create it when they respond to the play. This idea is fully in accord with contemporary post-structuralist critical thinking, notably Roland Barthes's "The Death of the Author," in *Image-Music-Text* (1977) and Michel Foucault's "What Is an Author?," in *The Foucault Reader* (1984). The gist of the idea is that an author is not an isolated genius; rather, authors are subject to the politics and other social structures of their age. A dramatist especially is a worker in a collaborative project, working most obviously with actors—parts may be written for particular actors—but working also with the audience. Consider the words of Samuel Johnson, written to be spoken by the actor David Garrick at the opening of a theater in 1747:

> The stage but echoes back the public voice;
> The drama's laws, the drama's patrons give,
> For we that live to please, must please to live.

The audience—the public taste as understood by the playwright—helps to determine what the play is. Moreover, even members of the public who are not part of the playwright's immediate audience may exert an influence through censorship. We have already glanced at governmental censorship, but there are also other kinds. Take one of Shakespeare's most beloved characters, Falstaff, who appears in three of Shakespeare's plays, the two parts of *Henry IV* and *The Merry Wives of Windsor*. He appears with this name in the earliest printed version of the first of these plays, *1 Henry IV*, but we know that Shakespeare originally called him (after an historical figure) Sir John Oldcastle. Oldcastle appears in Shakespeare's source (partly reprinted in the Signet edition of *1 Henry IV*), and a trace of the name survives in Shakespeare's play, 1.2.43–44, where Prince Hal punningly addresses Falstaff as "my old lad of the castle." But for some reason—perhaps because the family of the historical Oldcastle complained—Shakespeare had to change the name. In short, the play as we have it was (at least in this detail) subject to some sort of censorship. If we think that a text should present what we take to be the author's intention, we probably will want to replace *Falstaff* with *Oldcastle*. But if we recognize that a play is a collaboration, we may welcome the change, even if it was forced on Shakespeare. Somehow *Falstaff*, with its hint of *false-staff*, i.e., inadequate prop, seems just right for this fat knight who, to our delight, entertains the young prince with untruths. We can go as far as saying that, at least so far as a play is concerned, an insistence on the author's original intention (even if we could know it) can sometimes impoverish the text.

The tiny example of Falstaff's name illustrates the point that the text we read is inevitably only a version—something in effect produced by the collaboration of the playwright with his actors, audiences, compositors, and editors—of a fluid text that Shakespeare once wrote, just as the *Hamlet* that we see on the screen starring Kenneth Branagh is not the *Hamlet* that Shakespeare saw in an open-air playhouse starring Richard Burbage. *Hamlet* itself, as we shall note in a moment, also exists in several versions. It is not surprising that there is now much talk about the *instability* of Shakespeare's texts.

Because he was not only a playwright but was also an actor and a shareholder in a theatrical company, Shakespeare probably was much involved with the translation of the play from a manuscript to a stage production. He may or may not have done some rewriting during rehearsals, and he may or may not have been happy with cuts that were made. Some plays, notably *Hamlet* and *King Lear*, are so long that it is most unlikely that the texts we read were acted in their entirety. Further, for both of these plays we have more than one early text that demands consideration. In *Hamlet*, the Second Quarto (1604) includes some two hundred lines not found in the Folio (1623). Among the passages missing from the Folio are two of Hamlet's reflective speeches, the "dram of evil" speech (1.4.13–38) and "How all occasions do inform against me" (4.4.32–66). Since the Folio has more numerous and often fuller stage directions, it certainly looks as though in the Folio we get a theatrical version of the play, a text whose cuts were probably made—this is only a hunch, of course—not because Shakespeare was changing his conception of Hamlet but because the playhouse demanded a modified play. (The problem is complicated, since the Folio not only cuts some of the Quarto but adds some material. Various explanations have been offered.)

Or take an example from *King Lear*. In the First and Second Quarto (1608, 1619), the final speech of the play is given to Albany, Lear's surviving son-in-law, but in the First Folio version (1623), the speech is given to Edgar. The Quarto version is in accord with tradition—usually the highest-ranking character in a tragedy speaks the final words. Why does the Folio give the speech to Edgar? One possible answer is this: The Folio version omits some of Albany's speeches in earlier scenes, so perhaps it was decided (by Shakespeare? by the players?) not to give the final lines to so pale a character. In fact, the discrepancies are so many between the two texts, that some scholars argue we do not simply have texts showing different theatrical productions. Rather, these scholars say, Shakespeare substantially revised the play, and we really have two versions of *King Lear* (and of *Othello* also, say some)—two different plays—not simply two texts, each of which is in some ways imperfect.

In this view, the 1608 version of *Lear* may derive from Shakespeare's manuscript, and the 1623 version may derive from his later revision. The Quartos have almost three hundred lines not in the Folio, and the Folio has about a hundred lines not in the Quartos. It used to be held that all the texts were imperfect in various ways and from various causes— some passages in the Quartos were thought to have been set from a manuscript that was not entirely legible, other passages were thought to have been set by a compositor who was new to setting plays, and still other passages were thought to have been provided by an actor who misremembered some of the lines. This traditional view held that an editor must draw on the Quartos and the Folio in order to get Shakespeare's "real" play. The new argument holds (although not without considerable strain) that we have two authentic plays, Shakespeare's early version (in the Quarto) and Shakespeare's—or his theatrical company's—revised version (in the Folio). Not only theatrical demands but also Shakespeare's own artistic sense, it is argued, called for extensive revisions. Even the titles vary: Q1 is called *True Chronicle Historie of the life and death of King Lear and his three Daughters*, whereas the Folio text is called *The Tragedie of King Lear*. To combine the two texts in order to produce what the editor thinks is the play that Shakespeare intended to write is, according to this view, to produce a text that is false to the history of the play. If the new view is correct, and we do have texts of two distinct versions of *Lear* rather than two imperfect versions of one play, it supports in a textual way the poststructuralist view that we cannot possibly have an unmediated vision of (in this case) a play by Shakespeare; we can only recognize a plurality of visions.

Editing Texts

Though eighteen of his plays were published during his lifetime, Shakespeare seems never to have supervised their publication. There is nothing unusual here; when a playwright sold a play to a theatrical company he surrendered his ownership to it. Normally a company would not publish the play, because to publish it meant to allow competitors to acquire the piece. Some plays did get published: Apparently hard-up actors sometimes pieced together a play for a publisher; sometimes a company in need of money sold a play; and sometimes a company allowed publication of a play that no longer drew audiences. That Shakespeare did not concern himself with publication is not remarkable; of his contemporaries, only Ben Jonson carefully supervised the publication of his own plays.

In 1623, seven years after Shakespeare's death, John Heminges and Henry Condell (two senior members of Shakespeare's company, who had worked with him for about twenty years) collected his plays—published and unpublished—into a large volume, of a kind called a folio. (A folio is a volume consisting of large sheets that have been folded once, each sheet thus making two leaves, or four pages. The size of the page of course depends on the size of the sheet—a folio can range in height from twelve to sixteen inches, and in width from eight to eleven; the pages in the 1623 edition of Shakespeare, commonly called the First Folio, are approximately thirteen inches tall and eight inches wide.) The eighteen plays published during Shakespeare's lifetime had been issued one play per volume in small formats called quartos. (Each sheet in a quarto has been folded twice, making four leaves, or eight pages, each page being about nine inches tall and seven inches wide, roughly the size of a large paperback.)

Heminges and Condell suggest in an address "To the great variety of readers" that the republished plays are presented in better form than in the quartos:

> Before you were abused with diverse stolen and surreptitious copies, maimed and deformed by the frauds and stealths of injurious impostors that exposed them; even those, are now offered to your view cured and perfect of their limbs, and all the rest absolute in their numbers, as he [i.e., Shakespeare] conceived them.

There is a good deal of truth to this statement, but some of the quarto versions are better than others; some are in fact preferable to the Folio text.

Whoever was assigned to prepare the texts for publication

in the first Folio seems to have taken the job seriously and yet not to have performed it with uniform care. The sources of the texts seem to have been, in general, good unpublished copies or the best published copies. The first play in the collection, *The Tempest*, is divided into acts and scenes, has unusually full stage directions and descriptions of spectacle, and concludes with a list of the characters, but the editor was not able (or willing) to present all of the succeeding texts so fully dressed. Later texts occasionally show signs of carelessness: in one scene of *Much Ado About Nothing* the names of actors, instead of characters, appear as speech prefixes, as they had in the Quarto, which the Folio reprints; proofreading throughout the Folio is spotty and apparently was done without reference to the printer's copy; the pagination of *Hamlet* jumps from 156 to 257. Further, the proofreading was done while the presses continued to print, so that each play in each volume contains a mix of corrected and uncorrected pages.

Modern editors of Shakespeare must first select their copy; no problem if the play exists only in the Folio, but a considerable problem if the relationship between a Quarto and the Folio—or an early Quarto and a later one—is unclear. In the case of *Romeo and Juliet*, the First Quarto (Q1), published in 1597, is vastly inferior to the Second (Q2), published in 1599. The basis of Q1 apparently is a version put together from memory by some actors. Not surprisingly, it garbles many passages and is much shorter than Q2. On the other hand, occasionally Q1 makes better sense than Q2. For instance, near the end of the play, when the parents have assembled and learned of the deaths of Romeo and Juliet, in Q2 the Prince says (5.3.208–9),

Come, *Montague;* for thou art early vp
To see thy sonne and heire, now earling downe.

The last three words of this speech surely do not make sense, and many editors turn to Q1, which instead of "now earling downe" has "more early downe." Some modern editors take only "early" from Q1, and print "now early down"; others take "more early," and print "more early down." Further, Q1 (though, again, quite clearly a garbled and abbreviated text) includes some stage directions that are not found in Q2, and today many editors who base their text on Q2 are glad to add these stage directions, because the directions help to give us a sense of what the play looked like on Shakespeare's stage. Thus, in 4.3.58, after Juliet drinks the potion, Q1 gives us this stage direction, not in Q2: *"She falls upon her bed within the curtains."*

In short, an editor's decisions do not end with the choice of a single copy text. First of all, editors must reckon with Elizabethan spelling. If they are not producing a facsimile, they probably modernize the spelling, but ought they to preserve the old forms of words that apparently were pronounced quite unlike their modern forms—*lanthorn, alablaster*? If they preserve these forms are they really preserving Shakespeare's forms or perhaps those of a compositor in the printing house? What is one to do when one finds *lanthorn* and *lantern* in adjacent lines? (The editors of this series in general, but not invariably, assume that words should be spelled in their modern form, unless, for instance, a rhyme is involved.) Elizabethan punctuation, too, presents problems. For example, in the First Folio, the only text for the play, Macbeth rejects his wife's idea that he can wash the blood from his hand (2.2.60–62):

> No: this my Hand will rather
> The multitudinous Seas incarnardine,
> Making the Greene one, Red.

Obviously an editor will remove the superfluous capitals, and will probably alter the spelling to "incarnadine," but what about the comma before "Red"? If we retain the comma, Macbeth is calling the sea "the green one." If we drop the comma, Macbeth is saying that his bloody hand will make the sea ("the Green") *uniformly* red.

An editor will sometimes have to change more than spelling and punctuation. Macbeth says to his wife (1.7.46–47):

> I dare do all that may become a man,
> Who dares no more, is none.

For two centuries editors have agreed that the second line is unsatisfactory, and have emended "no" to "do": "Who dares do more is none." But when in the same play (4.2.21–22) Ross says that fearful persons

> Floate vpon a wilde and violent Sea
> Each way, and moue,

need we emend the passage? On the assumption that the compositor misread the manuscript, some editors emend "each way, and move" to "and move each way"; others emend "move" to "none" (i.e., "Each way and none"). Other editors, however, let the passage stand as in the original. The editors of the Signet Classic Shakespeare have restrained themselves from making abundant emendations. In their minds they hear Samuel Johnson on the dangers of emendation: "I have adopted the Roman sentiment, that it is more honorable to save a citizen than to kill an enemy." Some departures (in addition to spelling, punctuation, and lineation) from the copy text have of course been made, but the original readings are listed in a note following the play, so that readers can evaluate the changes for themselves.

Following tradition, the editors of the Signet Classic Shakespeare have prefaced each play with a list of characters, and throughout the play have regularized the names of the speakers. Thus, in our text of *Romeo and Juliet*, all speeches by Juliet's mother are prefixed "Lady Capulet," although the 1599 Quarto of the play, which provides our copy text, uses at various points seven speech tags for this one character: *Capu. Wi.* (i.e., Capulet's wife), *Ca. Wi., Wi., Wife, Old La.* (i.e., Old Lady), *La.,* and *Mo.* (i.e., Mother). Similarly, in *All's Well That Ends Well*, the character whom we regularly call "Countess" is in the Folio (the copy text) variously identified as *Mother, Countess, Old Countess, Lady,* and *Old Lady*. Admittedly there is some loss in regularizing, since the various prefixes may give us a hint of the way Shakespeare (or a scribe who copied Shakespeare's manuscript) was thinking of the character in a particular scene—for instance, as a mother, or as an old lady. But too much can be made of these differing prefixes, since the social relationships implied are *not* always relevant to the given scene.

We have also added line numbers and in many cases act and scene divisions as well as indications of locale at the beginning of scenes. The Folio divided most of the plays into acts and some into scenes. Early eighteenth-century editors increased the divisions. These divisions, which provide a convenient way of referring to passages in the plays, have been retained, but when not in the text chosen as the basis for the Signet Classic text they are enclosed within square brackets, [ ], to indicate that they are editorial additions. Similarly, though no play of Shakespeare's was equipped with indications of the locale at the heads of scene divisions, locales have here been added in square brackets for the convenience of readers, who lack the information that costumes, properties, gestures, and scenery afford to spectators. Spectators can tell at a glance they are in the throne room, but without an editorial indication the reader may be puzzled for a while. It should be mentioned, incidentally, that there are a few authentic stage directions—perhaps Shakespeare's, perhaps a prompter's—that suggest locales, such as *"Enter Brutus in his orchard,"* and *"They go up into the Senate house."* It is hoped that the bracketed additions in the Signet text will provide readers with the sort of help provided by these two authentic directions, but it is equally hoped that the reader will remember that the stage was not loaded with scenery.

Shakespeare on the Stage

Each volume in the Signet Classic Shakespeare includes a brief stage (and sometimes film) history of the play. When we read about earlier productions, we are likely to find them eccentric, obviously wrongheaded—for instance, Nahum Tate's version of *King Lear*, with a happy ending, which held the stage for about a century and a half, from the late seventeenth century until the end of the first quarter of the nineteenth. We see engravings of David Garrick, the greatest actor of the eighteenth century, in eighteenth-century garb as King Lear, and we smile, thinking how absurd the production must have been. If we are more thoughtful, we say, with the English novelist L. P. Hartley, "The past is a foreign country: they do things differently there." But if the eighteenth-century staging is a foreign country, what of the plays of the late sixteenth and seventeenth centuries? A foreign language, a foreign theater, a foreign audience.

Probably all viewers of Shakespeare's plays, beginning with Shakespeare himself, at times have been unhappy with the plays on the stage. Consider three comments about production that we find in the plays themselves, which suggest Shakespeare's concerns. The Chorus in *Henry V* complains that the heroic story cannot possibly be adequately staged:

> But pardon, gentles all,
> The flat unraisèd spirits that hath dared
> On this unworthy scaffold to bring forth
> So great an object. Can this cockpit hold
> The vasty fields of France? Or may we cram
> Within this wooden *O* the very casques
> That did affright the air at Agincourt?
>
> . . . .
>
> Piece out our imperfections with your thoughts.
>   (Prologue 1.8–14,23)

Second, here are a few sentences (which may or may not represent Shakespeare's own views) from Hamlet's longish lecture to the players:

> Speak the speech, I pray you, as I pronounced it to you, trippingly on the tongue. But if you mouth it, as many of our players do, I had as lief the town crier spoke my lines. . . . O, it offends me to the soul to hear a robustious periwig-pated fellow tear a passion to tatters, to very rags, to split the ears of the groundlings. . . . And let those that play your clowns speak no more than is set down for them, for there be of them that will themselves laugh, to set on some quantity of barren spectators to laugh too, though in the meantime some necessary question of the play be then to be considered. That's villainous and shows a most pitiful ambition in the fool that uses it. (3.2.1–47)

Finally, we can quote again from the passage cited earlier in this introduction, concerning the boy actors who played the female roles. Cleopatra imagines with horror a theatrical version of her activities with Antony:

> The quick comedians
> Extemporally will stage us, and present
> Our Alexandrian revels: Antony
> Shall be brought drunken forth, and I shall see
> Some squeaking Cleopatra boy my greatness
> I' th' posture of a whore.   (5.2.216–21)

It is impossible to know how much weight to put on such passages—perhaps Shakespeare was just being modest about his theater's abilities—but it is easy enough to think that he was unhappy with some aspects of Elizabethan production. Probably no production can fully satisfy a playwright, and for that matter, few productions can fully satisfy *us;* we regret this or that cut, this or that way of costuming the play, this or that bit of business.

One's first thought may be this: Why don't they just do "authentic" Shakespeare, "straight" Shakespeare, the play as Shakespeare wrote it? But as we read the plays—words written to be performed—it sometimes becomes clear that we do not know *how* to perform them. For instance, in *Antony and Cleopatra* Antony, the Roman general who has succumbed to Cleopatra and to Egyptian ways, says, "The nobleness of life / Is to do thus" (1.1.36–37). But what is "thus"? Does Antony at this point embrace Cleopatra? Does he embrace and kiss her? (There are, by the way, very few scenes of kissing on Shakespeare's stage, possibly because boys played the female roles.) Or does he make a sweeping gesture, indicating the Egyptian way of life?

This is not an isolated example; the plays are filled with lines that call for gestures, but we are not sure what the gestures should be. *Interpretation* is inevitable. Consider a passage in *Hamlet*. In 3.1, Polonius persuades his daughter, Ophelia, to talk to Hamlet while Polonius and Claudius eavesdrop. The two men conceal themselves, and Hamlet encounters Ophelia. At 3.1.131 Hamlet suddenly says to her, "Where's your father?" Why does Hamlet, apparently out of nowhere—they have not been talking about Polonius—ask this question? Is this an example of the "antic disposition" (fantastic behavior) that Hamlet earlier (1.5.172) had told Horatio and others—including us—he would display? That is, is the question about the whereabouts of her father a seemingly irrational one, like his earlier question (3.1.103) to Ophelia, "Ha, ha! Are you honest?" Or, on the other hand, has Hamlet (as in many productions) suddenly glimpsed Polonius's foot protruding from beneath a drapery at the rear? That is, does Hamlet ask the question because he has suddenly seen something suspicious and now is testing Ophelia? (By the way, in productions that do give Hamlet a physical cue, it is almost always Polonius rather than Claudius who provides the clue. This itself is an act of inter-pretation on the part of the director.) Or (a third possibility) does Hamlet get a clue from Ophelia, who inadvertently betrays the spies by nervously glancing at their place of hiding? This is the interpretation used in the BBC television version, where Ophelia glances in fear toward the hiding place just after Hamlet says "Why wouldst thou be a breeder of sinners?" (121–22). Hamlet, realizing that he is being ob-served, glances here and there *before* he asks "Where's your father?" The question thus is a climax to what he has been doing while speaking the preceding lines. Or (a fourth inter-pretation) does Hamlet suddenly, without the aid of any clue whatsoever, intuitively (insightfully, mysteriously, wonder-fully) sense that someone is spying? Directors must decide, of course—and so must readers.

Recall, too, the preceding discussion of the texts of the plays, which argued that the texts—though they seem to be before us in permanent black on white—are unstable. The Signet text of *Hamlet*, which draws on the Second Quarto (1604) and the First Folio (1623) is considerably longer than any version staged in Shakespeare's time. Our version, even if spoken very briskly and played without any intermission, would take close to four hours, far beyond "the two hours' traffic of our stage" mentioned in the Prologue to *Romeo and Juliet*. (There are a few contemporary references to the dura-tion of a play, but none mentions more than three hours.) Of Shakespeare's plays, only *The Comedy of Errors*, *Macbeth*, and *The Tempest* can be done in less than three hours without cutting. And even if we take a play that exists only in a short text, *Macbeth*, we cannot claim that we are experiencing the very play that Shakespeare conceived, partly because some of the Witches' songs almost surely are non-Shakespearean additions, and partly because we are not willing to watch the play performed without an intermission and with boys in the female roles.

Further, as the earlier discussion of costumes mentioned, the plays apparently were given chiefly in contemporary, that is, in Elizabethan dress. If today we give them in the costumes that Shakespeare probably saw, the plays seem not contemporary but curiously dated. Yet if we use our own dress, we find lines of dialogue that are at odds with what we see; we may feel that the language, so clearly not our own, is inappropriate coming out of people in today's dress. A common solution, incidentally, has been to set the plays in the nineteenth century, on the grounds that this attractively distances the plays (gives them a degree of foreignness, allowing for interesting costumes) and yet doesn't put them into a museum world of Elizabethan England.

Inevitably our productions are adaptations, *our* adaptations, and inevitably they will look dated, not in a century but in twenty years, or perhaps even in a decade. Still, we cannot escape from our own conceptions. As the director Peter Brook has said, in *The Empty Space* (1968):

> It is not only the hair-styles, costumes and make-ups that look dated. All the different elements of staging—the shorthands of behavior that stand for emotions; gestures, gesticulations and tones of voice—are all fluctuating on an invisible stock exchange all the time. . . . A living theatre that thinks it can stand aloof from anything as trivial as fashion will wilt. (p. 16)

As Brook indicates, it is through today's hairstyles, costumes, makeup, gestures, gesticulations, tones of voice—this includes our *conception* of earlier hairstyles, costumes, and so forth if we stage the play in a period other than our own—that we inevitably stage the plays.

It is a truism that every age invents its own Shakespeare, just as, for instance, every age has invented its own classical world. Our view of ancient Greece, a slave-holding society

in which even free Athenian women were severely circumscribed, does not much resemble the Victorians' view of
ancient Greece as a glorious democracy, just as, perhaps, our
view of Victorianism itself does not much resemble theirs.
We cannot claim that the Shakespeare on our stage is the
true Shakespeare, but in our stage productions we find a
Shakespeare that speaks to us, a Shakespeare that our ances-
tors doubtless did not know but one that seems to us to be the
true Shakespeare—at least for a while.

Our age is remarkable for the wide variety of kinds of
staging that it uses for Shakespeare, but one development
deserves special mention. This is the now common practice
of race-blind or color-blind or nontraditional casting, which
allows persons who are not white to play in Shakespeare.
Previously blacks performing in Shakespeare were limited
to a mere three roles, Othello, Aaron (in *Titus Andronicus*),
and the Prince of Morocco (in *The Merchant of Venice*),
and there were no roles at all for Asians. Indeed, African-
Americans rarely could play even one of these three roles,
since they were not welcome in white companies. Ira
Aldridge (c.1806–1867), a black actor of undoubted talent,
was forced to make his living by performing Shakespeare
in England and in Europe, where he could play not only
Othello but also—in whiteface—other tragic roles such as
King Lear. Paul Robeson (1898–1976) made theatrical history when he played Othello in London in 1930, and there
was some talk about bringing the production to the United
States, but there was more talk about whether American
audiences would tolerate the sight of a black man—a real
black man, not a white man in blackface—kissing and then
killing a white woman. The idea was tried out in summer
stock in 1942, the reviews were enthusiastic, and in the following year Robeson opened on Broadway in a production
that ran an astounding 296 performances. An occasional all-
black company sometimes performed Shakespeare's plays,
but otherwise blacks (and other minority members) were in
effect shut out from performing Shakespeare. Only since
about 1970 has it been common for nonwhites to play major
roles along with whites. Thus, in a 1996–97 production of
Antony and Cleopatra, a white Cleopatra, Vanessa Redgrave, played opposite a black Antony, David Harewood.

Multiracial casting is now especially common at the New York Shakespeare Festival, founded in 1954 by Joseph Papp, and in England, where even siblings such as Claudio and Isabella in *Measure for Measure* or Lear's three daughters may be of different races. Probably most viewers today soon stop worrying about the lack of realism, and move beyond the color of the performers' skin to the quality of the performance.

Nontraditional casting is not only a matter of color or race; it includes sex. In the past, occasionally a distinguished woman of the theater has taken on a male role—Sarah Bernhardt (1844–1923) as Hamlet is perhaps the most famous example—but such performances were widely regarded as eccentric. Although today there have been some performances involving cross-dressing (a drag *As You Like It* staged by the National Theatre in England in 1966 and in the United States in 1974 has achieved considerable fame in the annals of stage history), what is more interesting is the casting of women in roles that traditionally are male but that need not be. Thus, a 1993–94 English production of *Henry V* used a woman—*not* cross-dressed—in the role of the governor of Harfleur. According to Peter Holland, who reviewed the production in *Shakespeare Survey* 48 (1995), "having a female Governor of Harfleur feminized the city and provided a direct response to the horrendous threat of rape and murder that Henry had offered, his language and her body in direct connection and opposition" (p. 210). Ten years from now the device may not play so effectively, but today it speaks to us. Shakespeare, born in the Elizabethan Age, has been dead nearly four hundred years, yet he is, as Ben Jonson said, "not of an age but for all time." We must understand, however, that he is "for all time" precisely because each age finds in his abundance something for itself and something of itself.

And here we come back to two issues discussed earlier in this introduction—the instability of the text and, curiously, the Bacon/Oxford heresy concerning the authorship of the plays. *Of course* Shakespeare wrote the plays, and we should daily fall on our knees to thank him for them—and yet there is something to the idea that he is not their only author. Every editor, every director and actor, and every reader to some degree shapes them, too, for when we edit, direct, act, or read, we inevitably become Shakespeare's collaborator and re-create the plays. The plays, one might say, are so cunningly contrived that they guide our responses, tell us how we ought to feel, and make a mark on us, but (for better or for worse) we also make a mark on them.

—SYLVAN BARNET
Tufts University

Introduction

Antony and Cleopatra was written in 1607, or a little earlier. That is, it probably followed immediately after the four great tragedies, *Hamlet, Othello, King Lear*, and *Macbeth*, all of which were written in the half-dozen years after the turn of the century—the period at which Shakespeare's genius was at its most assured, mature, and profound. And *Antony and Cleopatra* itself witnesses to this authoritative mastery of an artistic maturity: Coleridge, in a fine phrase, spoke of the play as being "in all exhibitions of a giant power in its strength and vigor of maturity, a formidable rival of the *Macbeth, Lear, Othello*, and *Hamlet*." But whether the play is, in reality, a tragedy, is a more open question: its uniqueness of form and mood is a part of its power, and unique things are not easy to classify. When the Folio's editors came to collect the plays together after Shakespeare's death, they named this *The Tragedie of Anthonie, and Cleopatra* (unless the title was Shakespeare's own) and placed it in the "Tragedies" section that closed the Folio. But the play is, in its total effect, so unlike the tragedies that preceded it, that for long now critics have hesitated to group it with them. The words with which Coleridge praises the play are in themselves suggestive of a distinction; Bradley, later, did not include it in his *Shakespearean Tragedy*, and G. Wilson Knight similarly excludes it from his study of the tragedies, *The Wheel of Fire*—though both discuss it elsewhere. New classifications of the play have been made in the attempt to specify its highly individual quality. It is most usually referred to, now, as a "Roman Play" and grouped as such with *Julius Caesar* and *Coriolanus*: on the grounds that all three, in taking their materials from North's Plutarch, take also from these "Lives of the Noble Grecians and Romans" an interest that is at least as historical and political as it is tragical, and an ethos that is at least as classical as it is Christian. A recent study has classified it anew, as a "Problem Play," and grouped it as such with *Julius Caesar* and *Measure for Measure*, arguing that all three are alike, and unusual, in presenting a specifically moral problem in such a way as to leave radical indecision as to the rights and wrongs of the case. And lastly, though no critic has ever gone so far as to group the play with the Comedies, several have pointed out—and with good reason—how comic its effect sometimes is.

Obviously, categorizing a play is not vital to understanding it. Moreover, the exercise of classifying a thing can only aim at the comparative, and hope to create some limited definition within which unlike things may be compared and contrasted, and so throw light on one another. However, the attempts to classify *Antony and Cleopatra*— and the difficulties met with in the process—do have an unusual interest. For it is "uncategorizable" in a new and special way. There are one or two plays of Shakespeare— *Troilus and Cressida* and *Measure for Measure* are probably the best examples—which are similarly hard to classify, but which remain much simpler propositions. Though brilliant and full of interest, they are far from perfect or coherent works of art; and it is therefore easier to see in them (or to imagine one sees) the marks of changing purpose, or of discordances within the given materials, that make the act of classification so difficult. It is possible to suggest that *Measure for Measure* was intended to be a comedy on a not unfamiliar pattern, though in an unfamiliar milieu, but that the development in Shakespeare's artistic vision broke apart the preconceived notion on which the play began. Similarly, it is possible to suggest that *Troilus and Cressida* may have begun as a love tragedy on the same design as *Romeo and Juliet*, but that a greatly changed mood and insight destroyed that simpler romantic formula. Both plays at least offer materials for such hesitant suggestions with their sudden changes of mood, their strange discordances in characterization, their awkward or seemingly patched-up endings. *Antony and Cleopatra*, by contrast, suggests no such change of purpose or uncertainty in handling materials. It is, in final poetic and dramatic effect, one of the most triumphantly harmonious, coherent, and "finished" plays that Shakespeare ever wrote, from first to last line bearing the impress of a unified purpose powerfully carried out. Coleridge, again, seizes on this dominant effect of the play when he points out the degree to which Shakespeare "impresses the notion of giant strength. . . . This [is] owing to the manner in which it is sustained throughout—that he *lives* in and through the play." And yet, though the impression of a unified purpose is so strong, it is far from easy to decide what that unified purpose is.

One of the reasons for this is that the play "works" at many different levels and in many different ways. In it, many different—and even contradictory—kinds of experience are fused together; with the result that the play is continually suggestive of different kinds and categories of drama. Diversity and complexity of experience are of course a part of the strength and power of the preceding tragedies: but in them all diversities are subsumed under a dominating tragic discipline, by which the play moves steadily to its catastrophic climax. Hamlet's Gravedigger, Lear's Fool, Macbeth's Porter do not provide "comic relief," though this phrase is sometimes used of them: rather, they substantiate the tragic experience from a point of view at a large distance from the heroic—and therefore substantiate it the more impressively. In *Antony and Cleopatra*, the tragic and the comic experience coexist, among others. It is tragic not only in the sense of containing the "sad" and the "serious" (for many of Shakespeare's best and truest comedies also do that) but also in the expression of an irremediable loss, incurred consciously and borne responsibly: Antony reaches "the very heart of loss," and knows it. And yet it is also comic, not only in the sense of containing the satirical or the farcical (for Shakespeare's tragedies also do that) but also in the expression of an ineffaceable lightheartedness: As when Cleopatra, preparing for death, says:

go fetch
My best attires. I am again for Cydnus,
To meet Mark Antony.   (5.2.227–29)

and, to the asp that kills her:

O, couldst thou speak,
That I might hear thee call great Caesar ass
Unpolicied!   (306–8)

"Lighthearted" is not, admittedly, a complete enough word for this: the somewhat old-fashioned word "high-hearted" is perhaps closer to it. But however it is named, the mood evoked here, and elsewhere in the play, is nearer to the experience evoked in the mature comedies than it is to the gravely responsible tone of Hamlet at his death, Othello's solemn bravura, Lear's agonized questioning, or Macbeth's desperate obduracy. The tone and presentation throughout the play are thus so compounded of strangely blended elements as to be elusive of a final classification. The play can be described from several different points of view, and in the terms of several different categories, and each would point to elements really present in it: but none would describe it quite completely enough.

There is, for instance, good reason to call *Antony and Cleopatra* a "Roman Play," and to point out the historical and political interest that distinguishes it from the earlier tragedies. As in *Julius Caesar*, which had been written some eight years earlier (that is, just before *Hamlet*, the first of the mature tragedies), Shakespeare has taken his materials from well-known history—so well-known, in fact, as in part to circumscribe his treatment of it. The basis of *Hamlet*, *King Lear*, and *Macbeth* is also of course historical, but presented Shakespeare with nothing as radically unalterable as the murder of Julius Caesar, the fate of Antony, or the coming to power of Octavius Caesar. Shakespeare's Octavius—Caesar, as he is always called in *Antony and Cleopatra*—was to become Augustus, perhaps greatest of Roman emperors, creator of the Pax Romana that closed the long period of unrest, revolution, and war, with the time of peace in which Christ was to be born. Thus, in the war with Antony, when Antony's allies have deserted and sympathy for him is at its strongest, Caesar redresses the balance by a brief but significant reminder of his future role in history:

> The time of universal peace is near.
> Prove this a prosp'rous day, the three-nooked world
> Shall bear the olive freely.   (4.6.5–7)

Antony's course is as much a "given factor" as Caesar's. Plutarch's life of Antony (perhaps somewhat romanticizing the case) had established the cause of Antony's downfall: he had lost the world because of his love for Cleopatra. Whether that love were treated with some severity (as Plutarch treated it) or with tender admiration (as Chaucer and many others had treated it) its fatality had become an historical fact.

The political battle, then, is between two men sharply distinguished in their roles: Caesar, the young, sober, peace-loving imperial administrator, and Antony, the middle-aged soldier, orator, and lover, a hardened campaigner in war, politics, and love. And the battle is fought for a large enough issue: the rule of the whole civilized world some forty years before the birth of Christ. For Antony and Caesar are two of the triumvirs who rule the Empire between them, and early in the play it becomes clear that the third, Lepidus, is an insignificant go-between. The scale of the prize that the two men are fighting for is also established at once in the play. Philo bitterly sees Antony as

> The triple pillar of the world transformed
> Into a strumpet's fool.   (1.1.12–13)

And Antony himself turns an exhilarated affirmation of his love into a rejection of the whole Empire:

> Let Rome in Tiber melt, and the wide arch
> Of the ranged empire fall! Here is my space.
>
> (1.1.33–34)

On Antony's second appearance in the play, he is
presented in a scene all the more sharply effective for its
contrast with the immediately preceding scene of the fortunetelling, which is slow, sleepy, and casual: he appears as
a man facing a rapid and cumulatively urgent succession of
news from all over the Empire—the wars of his wife Fulvia
and his brother Lucius, their conjunct war against Caesar,
the swift and victorious invasions of the Parthian Labienus,
Fulvia's death, the threats of Pompey, and the dangerously
shifting sympathies of the Roman people. Caesar, in his
turn, is presented on his first appearance in an exactly comparable way, as a man habituated to an enormous and
urgent sphere of action. Both these scenes are brilliantly
effective in their conversion of necessary exposition to
purely dramatic purposes: they move with an almost
breathless speed and energy, and establish Antony and
Caesar as men of affairs at a very high level indeed. This
effect is maintained, though by less concentrated means,
throughout the play. The action moves rapidly from place
to place in the great Empire, from Alexandria to Rome,
from Misenum to "a plain in Syria," from Athens to Rome
again. The characters think and plan—sometimes rhetori-
cally, sometimes merely with an easy and businesslike pre-
cision—in terms of the whole world:

> [his] quality, going on,
> The sides o' th' world may danger.   (1.2.193–94)
>
> ... thou, the greatest soldier of the world.   (1.3.38)
>
> The demi-Atlas of this earth.   (1.5.23)
>
> The third o' th' world is yours.   (2.2.67)
>
> To you all three,
> The senators alone of this great world ...   (2.6.8–9)
>
> Wilt thou be lord of all the world?   (2.7.63)

These three world-sharers.   (2.7.72)

    Wars 'twixt you twain would be
As if the world should cleave.   (3.4.30–31)

The greater cantle of the world is lost
With very ignorance.   (3.10.6–7)

Such language (of which this is only a selection) is the medium of the play, and it establishes the size of the battle-field—real and metaphorical—on which the contest for power is being fought.

The course of this battle for power is simple in outline. The first appearance of Antony and Caesar—Antony in his "Egyptian fetters," though still able to throw them off: Caesar revealing in clear, precise terms his cool disgust at a political associate—presents them as personally incompatible and potentially rivals. As Caesar says:

                    [it] cannot be
We shall remain in friendship, our conditions
So diff'ring in their acts.   (2.2.117–19)

The two are reconciled under the pressure of Pompey's threat to the triumvirate and seal their peace by Antony's marriage to Octavia, Caesar's sister. The desertion of Octavia by Antony gives Caesar the pretext for war, once he has himself gained some advantage in power. After the ruinous defeat at Actium, Antony's fall is rapid: his allies and his armies desert to the more powerful man, and he is lost. Through an apparently leisurely and circuitous stream of events that keeps closely to the historical sequence, there emerges into prominence the political theme: the maneuvers and manipulations, the honors and dishonors, of a battle between incompatible standards for the government of the whole Roman world.

To describe the play in these terms is to give it something of the discipline, and something of the limitation, of any game of power—say, a game of chess played out on the board of the world. And such an image would not be entirely alien to the mood of the play: Antony, for instance, accuses Cleopatra in similar terms, in a moment of despairing anger:

> she, Eros, has
> Packed cards with Caesar, and false-played my glory
> Unto an enemy's triumph.   (4.14.18–20)

And yet to use this image of the game is to realize how much in the play it does not comprehend: indeed, even as Antony uses this image, there is a sudden and significant sense that he has lost even his imaginative command of the full weight of the situation. If the play presents a game of history and politics, it presents also something deeper and more important: a tragedy of human experience. When Antony finds himself at "the very heart of loss," he is maddened at both the loss of the world and the loss of all trust in Cleopatra: but in losing both, he is also crying out at the loss of himself.

It is not enough to say, simply, that Shakespeare is far more interested in the loser, Antony, than he is in the winner, Caesar; or even to say that his interest is with that relation between Antony and Cleopatra that caused the loss of the world. It is rather that the whole situation is presented so that the historical and political interest—the gain or loss of world power—becomes a part or facet of another and greater subject: the ruin of two people, and with them, of a whole sphere of human experience. Any political history may have its "human interest"; Plutarch's "Life of Antony" is vivid, shrewd, and alive in its portraiture, and Shakespeare is largely and unusually indebted to Plutarch's characterization of Antony. What differentiates *Antony and Cleopatra* is not merely a livelier, or even a deeper characterization, but a transformation of all action and event into a process of tragic and individual experience.

This touches several characters besides the hero and heroine. The mere opportunist, Pompey, soon to disappear from the play, has a moment of sudden importance, seriousness, and dignity in the galley scene, when he rejects the chance of world power on a point of honor. The tough, cynical, common-sense soldier, Enobarbus (who in Plutarch dies of an ague) dies of a broken heart at his desertion of Antony, and the scene has, again, a weight of dignity and solemnity. Caesar himself, on hearing of the death of Antony, is moved—for the first time in the play—by a sudden access of personal feeling, in the awareness of what of himself he has lost by that death. None of these incidents could have any historical or political importance, though they might, perhaps, be shown as having historical and political effects; their significance and their weight lie in a different sphere of value. It is significant that each of these small incidents has the effect of isolating the person concerned, so that he appears for a moment as detached from, or even alien to, the world around him; for tragedy deals with the experience of a man, or of Man, rather than of men.

The greatest individuals in the play are, of course, Antony and Cleopatra: it is on their absolute selfhood that they base their glory. "We stand up peerless." And it is this arrogant and obdurate sense of themselves that distinguishes them from Caesar—though all three are, in fact, engaged on a quite similar quest for power that makes them, on a detached view, remarkably alike. Caesar can speak as nobly, as authoritatively, and as impressively as the other two; but he speaks a different language. His words have, at their best, the stature of judgment: of a rational social wisdom that takes its force from its generality. To him, Antony is

> A man who is th' abstract of all faults
> That all men follow.   (1.4.9–10)

He surveys Antony with a level detachment that reduces his actions to caricature, and gives the final condemnation a rigorous justice:

> to confound such time
> That drums him from his sport and speaks as loud
> As his own state and ours, 'tis to be chid
> As we rate boys who, being mature in knowledge,
> Pawn their experience to their present pleasure
> And so rebel to judgment.   (28–33)

This is powerfully spoken, and its effect is largely that of
the judicial and weighty summary of a situation from outside; it is the voice of common judgment and social
wisdom. This voice interposes its realities throughout the
play, and is not confirmed to Caesar alone: Antony too can
speak with the voice of "Rome." But the language that
Antony and Cleopatra make their own is something very
different, and challenges the sober judgment of Rome. It is
a language expressive of a whole radically different way of
living and feeling: a language of immediate individual
experience, sensory in its apprehension, exalted or intense
in its tone, and arrogant in its claims. Love or desolation,
exhilaration or rage become their own argument, and the
intense experience of an exceptional individual becomes its
own rationale. So Antony, proclaiming his love for
Cleopatra, converts his profession into a challenge of Rome
and all that Rome stands for:

> Let Rome in Tiber melt, and the wide arch
> Of the ranged empire fall! Here is my space,
> Kingdoms are clay: our dungy earth alike
> Feeds beast as man. The nobleness of life
> Is to do thus; when such a mutual pair
> And such a twain can do't, in which I bind,
> On pain of punishment, the world to weet
> We stand up peerless.   (1.1.33–40)

So also Cleopatra, exquisitely lamenting the death of
Antony, transforms her desolation into a vision of an empty
world:

> O, see, my women,
> The crown o' th' earth doth melt. My lord!
> O, withered is the garland of the war,
> The soldier's pole is fall'n: young boys and girls
> Are level now with men. The odds is gone,
> And there is nothing left remarkable
> Beneath the visiting moon.   (4.15.62–68)

Both these speeches reveal an element vital to the characterization of Antony and Cleopatra. The first is more than

a profession of love—whether we choose to regard that love as the glorification of sensual excitement or as the affirmation of a noble passion; the second is more than a woman's lament for a dead man—whether we choose to regard that lament as profound insight or as delusion. Each is an affirmation of selfhood, and a proclamation that this self is "peerless," "remarkable," incomparable, in its love and in its loss and in its very existence. Antony and Cleopatra are—to put the matter at its simplest—proud: proud of being themselves, and proud of being greater than anyone else in the world. Nor are they monstrous in this, for the whole world of the play is governed by the ideal of pride, and in it "honor" and "nobility," "greatness" and "reputation" are the very fabric of existence. Antony's fame, eminence, and power; Cleopatra's royalty; their love for each other; the admiration of their followers—all these things feed their pride and are fed by it. And all their great and good qualities serve it: Antony's courage and generosity and largeness of spirit, Cleopatra's wit and charm and enormous abundance of life. When their "greatness" is destroyed, the world is empty to them, for the loss of pride is a death:

> The soul and body rive not more in parting
> Than greatness going off.　　　　　　(4.13.5–6)

The tragedy of Antony and Cleopatra, then, is not simply their loss of the world, nor even their death, but the destruction of pride that accompanies both. All that makes them admirable is inextricably confused with its own corruptions: their energy, vitality, and power are self-defeating. Antony is caught between the dual and mutually destructive sources of his pride, power in Rome and pleasure in Egypt; Cleopatra discovers or proves at Actium her full power over Antony, and in doing so loses both him and the world. Cleopatra fights to hold Antony, and Antony fights to hold the world, and in the process all Antony's courage reveals itself as inextricable from blind and irrational violence, and his generosity from sensual obsession; all Cleopatra's vitality and self-possession reveals itself as wayward, demanding, and treacherous. Caesar sees clearly when he calls Antony "the old ruffian," and Antony knows Cleopatra for a "boggler ever." In defeat—a defeat which is the loss of an ideal, as well as the loss of the world—both grow, paradoxically, more gentle, more human, and more wholly sympathetic. But both choose the "Roman" death of suicide, which is itself a last affirmation of pride in themselves and a refusal of the humiliation of walking in Caesar's triumph. Cleopatra places on her head the crown of a country she no longer rules, prepares to join a husband she never had, and rejects with contempt a world which has humiliated her, dying a death

> fitting for a princess
> Descended of so many royal kings.   (5.2.326–27)

This tragic subject Shakespeare has created out of his historical and political materials; and it is a subject that merits Caesar's words at the close of the play:

> High events as these
> Strike those that make them; and their story is
> No less in pity, than his glory which
> Brought them to be lamented.   (359–62)

Yet there can be a large difference between a play's "subject," summarized in detachment, and the full effect of the play itself; and this is true of *Antony and Cleopatra*. It certainly contains the "high events," the "pity" and "glory" that Caesar suggests as he closes the play on a fittingly high and sober note. But to leave the account of the play here would be as partial as to describe it, simply, as a historical and political drama.

In the first place, Antony's and Cleopatra's fates and fortunes are not presented with the kind of tragic or dramatic intensity that such an outline might suggest. Rather, they and their world are presented in a series of leisurely—at first sight, almost casual—insights, that include in their range the great and the small, the significant and the insignificant: a fortunetelling and a great battle, a political conference and a wild party, a memory of the lovers' first meeting and a death in a monument, a woman slapping a messenger and a countryman giving a lecture on the nature of asps. Instead of the cumulative intensity of the earlier tragedies, which speed and slacken and speed again to their catastrophic climaxes, the play presents something more leisurely, more spacious, and more impassive; its structure lies in the panoramic or kaleidoscopic display of diverse aspects of a world, seen in all its variety. At one moment, we watch a conference of world leaders, attempting with some dignity and seriousness to come to terms with each other—an attempt that justifies Antony's earlier bitter self-accusations; after the briefest of pauses, they are all celebrating in a farcical party that ends with a Bacchic version of ring-a-ring-a-roses. Cleopatra speaks, over the dead Antony, her exquisite lament for the loss of all that is valuable in the world; shortly after, she is doing her best to cheat Caesar of her jewels. The whole play is constructed, in this manner, out of a pattern of juxtapositions and contrasts, with the point of view continually shifting and changing; and the effect is something very different from "tragic" intensity, though full of a complex and absorbing life.

Closely related to this fluid and changing dramatic vision is the presentation of the characters themselves; indeed, it might be more proper to say that the concept of "character" itself is transformed. The earlier tragic heroes change, where they change at all in the course of the play, by a process of development; inner potentialities for good and evil are gradually brought to the view as the play proceeds. This is only very partially true of Antony and Cleopatra. They display, rather, a succession of different moods and impulses, continually changing. This is, of course, most true of Cleopatra, who is "infinite variety" itself; but there is hardly a character in the play who is not capable, to some degree, of being and doing the unexpected. The result is that a quick fluidity and changeableness of character becomes the norm, almost the rule: And in such a world, tragic motivation becomes impossible, and tragic responsibility is largely absent. Men seem to be moved by impulse and instinct, chance and expediency; and the guilts and terrors, shames and miseries of the earlier tragedies are very largely absent.

This is to suggest a world that relatively lacks psychological and metaphysical depth. It would be truer to say that *Antony and Cleopatra* creates a physical rather than a metaphysical world and that its density of substance rather than its depth of treatment commands the attention. It creates a world that is triumphantly "natural" rather than "supernatural"—although the natural is not, in this play, without its mysteries. The soothsayer reads, and reads correctly, in "Nature's infinite book of secrecy" (1.2.9); and when the soldiers, on guard by night in the streets of Alexandria, hear "Music i' th' air," they recognize it as the departure of a god from a defeated man:

> 'Tis the god Hercules, whom Antony loved,
> Now leaves him.   (4.3.15–16)

To say that the world of *Antony and Cleopatra* is "natural" is to say that it presents all experiences and all events as rooted in the "dungy earth" or the "varying tide" of physical existence. And that physical existence is itself a "varying shore," subject to continual change in the battle of the elements. In politics as in love, the procession of time moves in a continual destruction; so Antony, in the proclamation of his love that challenges the power of the great Roman Empire, is making a proclamation and a challenge that time itself will silently verify:

> Let Rome in Tiber melt, and the wide arch
> Of the ranged empire fall! Here is my space:
> Kingdoms are clay.   (1.1.33–35)

The great lyrical image for the triumph of time is the image of the setting of the sun and the coming on of night; and this image fittingly colors the close of the play. The suicide of both Antony and Cleopatra is prefaced by the same echoing image:

> Unarm, Eros. The long day's task is done,
> And we must sleep.   (4.14.35–36)

> Finish, good lady, the bright day is done,
> And we are for the dark.   (5.2.193–94)

Wherever such imagery occurs in the play, it has an effect that is undoubtedly complex. One of the many things it does is to suggest that Antony's political defeat and his and Cleopatra's individual tragedy are both set within the context of a larger process, simpler and more universal. All that happens in the play—the reversals of fortune, the victories and defeats, the alienations and reconciliations—all are a part of the "interchange of state" that rules the whole natural world,

> Increasing store with loss, and loss with store.
>   (Sonnet 64)

Antony, in his "dotage," and Cleopatra, "wrinkled deep in time," suffer a defeat at the hands of a power greater than Caesar; and the cold politician Caesar himself has fought his way to the possession of an empire that will crumble in his hands to "dungy earth."

This fact Antony and Cleopatra know, and Caesar does not; their wisdom and their folly derives from their knowledge of it, and Caesar's power and his limitations derive from his ignorance or denial of it. Caesar's ambition is to "possess the time," by possessing the world for a while; Antony and Cleopatra live only in the present instant, and lose the world for good:

> There's not a minute of our lives should stretch
> Without some pleasure now.   (1.1.46–47)

To give up the battle with Time and live intensely in the present instant; to create a small and circumscribed area in which to exist, in an exhilarated moment of freedom and vitality—this is a way or vision of life more native to comedy than to tragedy. And it is the way of life that Cleopatra, above all, represents.

> That time—O, times!—
> I laughed him out of patience; and that night
> I laughed him into patience; and next morn,
> Ere the ninth hour, I drunk him to his bed;
> Then put my tires and mantles on him, whilst
> I wore his sword Philippan.   (2.5.18–23)

Cleopatra's world is essentially a world of "play": a world, that is, that studies to find fit expression for the exuberance of natural energies and needs no justification for what it does. Her world is self-justifying, self-delighting, perhaps self-destroying; as such it is a perpetual challenge and threat to Caesar's vision of universal power and universal peace. The two cannot coexist: and in any battle between Cleopatra's devious wits and Caesar's steady will-to-power, the latter must triumph. Yet Cleopatra will live out even defeat on her own terms, as though it were an exuberant and triumphant game, the rules of which are her own and no one else's; her image of the dead Antony is of a god who had eluded, by the play of his intense natural energies, the restraining world of time:

> For his bounty,
> There was no winter in't: an autumn 'twas
> That grew the more by reaping. His delights
> Were dolphinlike, they showed his back above
> The element they lived in. . . .   (5.2.86–90)

Just such an image she makes of her own death: she "plays till doomsday," secure and free within the limited dream she has created.

Certainly that dream is a limited one, always circumscribed by the opposed realities of Caesar and of Time:

> Think you there was or might be such a man
> As this I dreamt of?
>   Gentle madam, no.   (93–94)

In presenting these realities side by side, and involved with each other—the comic and tragic deeply interfused—*Antony and Cleopatra* creates a world that is as complex as it is profoundly original. One phrase of Cleopatra's—her "Here's sport indeed," as she draws the dying Antony to her—bears all the profound comic pathos and tragic irony that fills and characterizes the play. Yet this mingled experience is as strong as it is complex; it has a power and vitality that is Antony's when, in defeat, he "mocks the midnight bell":

> Let's have one other gaudy night: call to me
> All my sad captains; fill our bowls once more;
> Let's mock the midnight bell.   (3.13.183–85)

—BARBARA EVERETT
Somerville College
Oxford

The Tragedy of
Antony
and
Cleopatra

[*Dramatis Personae*

Mark Antony
Octavius Caesar   } triumvirs
M. Aemilius Lepidus
Sextus Pompeius
Domitius Enobarbus
Ventidius
Eros
Scarus   } friends to Antony
Decretas
Demetrius
Philo
Canidius, lieutenant general to Antony
Silius, an officer in Ventidius' army
Maecenas
Agrippa
Dolabella
Proculeius   } friends to Caesar
Thidias
Gallus
Taurus, lieutenant general to Caesar
Menas
Menecrates   } friends to Pompey
Varrius
Roman Officer under Ventidius
An Ambassador from Antony to Caesar
Alexas
Mardian
Seleucus   } attendants on Cleopatra
Diomedes
A Soothsayer
A Clown
Cleopatra, Queen of Egypt
Octavia, sister to Caesar and wife to Antony
Charmian   } attendants on Cleopatra
Iras
Officers, Soldiers, Messengers, Attendants

Scene: several parts of the Roman Empire]

The Tragedy of Antony and Cleopatra

ACT 1

Scene 1. [*Alexandria. Cleopatra's palace.*]

Ignore stage directions

Enter Demetrius and Philo.

Philo. Nay, but this dotage of our general's.
O'erflows the measure. Those his goodly eyes
That o'er the files and musters of the war
Have glowed like plated°1 Mars, now bend, now
    turn
The office° and devotion of their view   5
Upon a tawny front.° His captain's heart,
Which in the scuffles of great fights hath burst
The buckles on his breast, reneges all temper°
And is become the bellows and the fan
To cool a gypsy's° lust.

    *Flourish.° Enter Antony, Cleopatra, her Ladies,
        the Train, with Eunuchs fanning her.*

                      Look where they come: 10

---

¹The degree sign (°) indicates a footnote, which is keyed to the text by
line number. Text references are printed in **boldface** type; the annotation
follows in roman type.
1.1.4 **plated** armored   5 **office** service   6 **tawny front** dark face (with a
pun on the military sense of *front,* "first line of battle")   8 **reneges all
temper** gives up all self-control   10 **gypsy's** (gypsies were believed to
have come from Egypt, hence " 'gyptians"; they had a reputation for
trickery, sorcery, and lechery)   10 s.d. **Flourish** fanfare of trumpets

Take but good note, and you shall see in him
The triple pillar° of the world transformed
Into a strumpet's fool. Behold and see.

Cleopatra. If it be love indeed, tell me how much.

Antony. There's beggary in the love that can be
15   reckoned.

Cleopatra. I'll set a bourn° how far to be beloved.

Antony. Then must thou needs find out new heaven,
new earth.

Enter a Messenger.

Messenger. News, my good lord, from Rome.

Antony.   Grates me! The sum.°

Cleopatra. Nay, hear them, Antony.
20   Fulvia° perchance is angry; or who knows
If the scarce-bearded Caesar° have not sent
His pow'rful mandate to you, "Do this, or this;
Take in° that kingdom, and enfranchise° that.
Perform't, or else we damn thee."

Antony.   How,° my love?

25   *Cleopatra.* Perchance? Nay, and most like:
You must not stay here longer, your dismission°
Is come from Caesar; therefore hear it, Antony.
Where's Fulvia's process?° Caesar's I would say?
Both?
Call in the messengers. As I am Egypt's Queen,
30   Thou blushest, Antony, and that blood of thine
Is Caesar's homager:° else so° thy cheek pays shame
When shrill-tongued Fulvia scolds. The messengers!

---

12 **The triple pillar** i.e., one of the triumvirs who ruled the world
16 **bourn** limit   18 **Grates me! The sum** It's irritating! Be brief
20 **Fulvia** Antony's wife   21 **scarce-bearded Caesar** (Octavius, then
twenty-three, was some twenty years younger than Antony)   23 **Take
in** occupy   23 **enfranchise** set free from slavery   24 **How** (a common
exclamation, like "What!")   26 **dismission** dismissal 28 **process** summons (i.e., to appear in court)   31 **homager** vassal   31 **else so** or else

Antony. Let Rome in Tiber melt, and the wide arch
 Of the ranged empire fall! Here is my space,
 Kingdoms are clay: our dungy earth alike   *35*
 Feeds beast as man. The nobleness of life
 Is to do thus;° when such a mutual pair
 And such a twain can do't, in which I bind,
 On pain of punishment, the world to weet°
 We stand up peerless.

Cleopatra.   Excellent falsehood!   *40*
 Why did he marry Fulvia, and not love her?
 I'll seem the fool I am not. Antony
 Will be—himself.°

Antony.   But stirred° by Cleopatra.
 Now for the love of Love and her soft hours,
 Let's not confound° the time with conference harsh. *45*
 There's not a minute of our lives should stretch
 Without some pleasure now. What sport tonight?

Cleopatra. Hear the ambassadors.

Antony.   Fie, wrangling queen!
 Whom everything becomes—to chide, to laugh,
 To weep; whose every passion fully° strives   *50*
 To make itself, in thee, fair and admired.
 No messenger but thine; and all alone
 Tonight we'll wander through the streets and note
 The qualities of people. Come, my queen;
 Last night you did desire it. [*To Attendants*] Speak
  not to us.   *55*
   Exeunt [*Antony and Cleopatra*] *with the Train.*

Demetrius. Is Caesar with° Antonius prized so slight?

Philo. Sir, sometimes, when he is not Antony,
 He comes too short of that great property°
 Which still° should go with Antony.

---

37 **thus** (perhaps they embrace, but perhaps **thus** alludes to their way of
life) 39 **weet** know 43 **himself** (1) the peerless Antony (2) the fool he
is 43 **stirred** (1) angered (2) inspired, inflamed 45 **confound** waste
50 **fully** absolutely and successfully 56 **with** by 58 **property** quality
59 **still** always

Demetrius.   I am full sorry
60   That he approves° the common liar, who
     Thus speaks of him at Rome; but I will hope
     Of better deeds tomorrow. Rest you happy! *Exeunt.*

[Scene 2. *Alexandria. Cleopatra's palace.*]

Enter Enobarbus, Lamprius, a Soothsayer, Ran-
nius, Lucillius, Charmian, Iras, Mardian the
Eunuch, and Alexas.

Charmian. Lord Alexas, sweet Alexas, most anything
     Alexas, almost most absolute Alexas, where's the
     soothsayer that you praised so to th' Queen? O, that
     I knew this husband, which, you say, must charge
5   his horns with garlands!°

Alexas. Soothsayer!

Soothsayer. Your will?

Charmian. Is this the man? Is't you, sir, that know
     things?

Soothsayer. In Nature's infinite book of secrecy
     A little I can read.

10   *Alexas.*   Show him your hand.

Enobarbus. Bring in the banquet° quickly: wine enough
     Cleopatra's health to drink.

Charmian. Good sir, give me good fortune.

---

60 **approves** corroborates   1.2.4–5 **charge his horns with garlands** be
a blindly happy cuckold of a husband (*charge* = load; *horns* = symbol
of a cuckold; *garlands* = bridegroom's chaplet, and sign of happy prosperity)   11 **banquet** light refreshment of fruit and wine

Soothsayer. I make not, but foresee.

Charmian. Pray then, foresee me one.   15

Soothsayer. You shall be yet far fairer° than you are.

Charmian. He means in flesh.

Iras. No, you shall paint when you are old.

Charmian. Wrinkles forbid!

Alexas. Vex not his prescience; be attentive.   20

Charmian. Hush!

Soothsayer. You shall be more beloving than beloved.

Charmian. I had rather heat my liver° with drinking.

Alexas. Nay, hear him.

Charmian. Good now, some excellent fortune! Let me   25
be married to three kings in a forenoon and widow
them all; let me have a child at fifty, to whom Herod
of Jewry° may do homage; find me to marry me
with Octavius Caesar, and companion me with my
mistress.   30

Soothsayer. You shall outlive the lady whom you
serve.

Charmian. O excellent! I love long life better than
figs.°

Soothsayer. You have seen and proved a fairer former
fortune
Than that which is to approach.   35

Charmian. Then belike my children shall have no
names.° Prithee, how many boys and wenches must
I have?

---

16 **fairer** more beautiful (though in the next line Charmian pretends
to take it another way, "plumper")   23 **liver** (believed to be the seat
of sexual desire)   27–28 **Herod of Jewry** i.e., even that blustering
tyrant who slaughtered the innocents of Judea   33 **figs** (phallic allusion)
36–37 **have no names** be bastards

Soothsayer. If every of your wishes had a womb,
40   And fertile every wish, a million.

Charmian. Out, fool! I forgive thee for a witch.°

Alexas. You think none but your sheets are privy to your wishes.

Charmian. Nay, come, tell Iras hers.

45   *Alexas.* We'll know all our fortunes.

Enobarbus. Mine, and most of our fortunes, tonight, shall be—drunk to bed.

Iras. There's a palm presages chastity, if nothing else.

Charmian. E'en as the o'erflowing Nilus presageth
50   famine.

Iras. Go, you wild bedfellow, you cannot soothsay.

Charmian. Nay, if an oily palm° be not a fruitful prognostication,° I cannot scratch mine ear. Prithee, tell her but a workyday° fortune.

55   *Soothsayer.* Your fortunes are alike.

Iras. But how, but how? Give me particulars.

Soothsayer. I have said.

Iras. Am I not an inch of fortune better than she?

Charmian. Well, if you were but an inch of fortune
60   better than I, where would you choose it?

Iras. Not in my husband's nose.°

Charmian. Our worser thoughts Heavens mend! Alexas—come, his fortune, his fortune! O, let him marry a woman that cannot go,° sweet Isis,° I

41 **I forgive thee for a witch** (1) you have no power of prophecy, so I absolve you from the charge of being a witch (2) a sorcerer like you is allowed to be outspoken   52 **oily palm** (sign of a lascivious nature) 52–53 **fruitful prognostication** omen of fertility   54 **workyday** commonplace   61 **husband's nose** (bawdy, hence **worser thoughts** in next line)   64 **go** satisfactorily copulate (?) bear children (?)   64 **Isis** goddess of fertility and the moon

beseech thee, and let her die too, and give him a   65
worse, and let worse follow worse till the worst of
all follow him laughing to his grave, fiftyfold a
cuckold! Good Isis, hear me this prayer, though
thou deny me a matter of more weight: good Isis,
I beseech thee!   70

Iras. Amen. Dear goddess, hear that prayer of the
people! For, as it is a heartbreaking to see a handsome man loose-wived,° so it is a deadly sorrow to
behold a foul° knave uncuckolded. Therefore, dear
Isis, keep decorum,° and fortune him accordingly!   75

Charmian. Amen.

Alexas. Lo, now, if it lay in their hands to make me a
cuckold, they would make themselves whores but
they'd do't.

Enobarbus. Hush, here comes Antony.

Charmian.   Not he, the Queen.   80

Enter Cleopatra.

Cleopatra. Saw you my lord?

Enobarbus.   No, lady.

Cleopatra.   Was he not here?

Charmian. No, madam.

Cleopatra. He was disposed to mirth; but on the sudden
A Roman thought° hath struck him. Enobarbus!

Enobarbus. Madam?   85

Cleopatra. Seek him, and bring him hither. Where's
Alexas?

Alexas. Here at your service. My lord approaches.

Enter Antony with a Messenger [and Attendants].

73 **loose-wived** with a faithless, lecherous wife   74 **foul** ugly   75 **keep
decorum** i.e., act like a just goddess   84 **Roman thought** (1) thought of
Rome (2) serious reflection

Cleopatra. We will not look upon him. Go with us.
                    Exeunt [all but Antony, Messenger, and
                                              Attendants].

Messenger. Fulvia thy wife first came into the field.

90   *Antony.* Against my brother Lucius?

Messenger. Ay.
      But soon that war had end, and the time's state
      Made friends of them, jointing their force 'gainst
            Caesar,
      Whose better issue° in the war, from Italy
      Upon the first encounter drave them.

95   *Antony.*   Well, what worst?

Messenger. The nature of bad news infects the teller.

Antony. When it concerns the fool or coward. On.
      Things that are past are done, with me. 'Tis thus:
      Who tells me true, though in his tale lie death,
      I hear him as° he flattered.

100 *Messenger.*   Labienus—
      This is stiff news—hath with his Parthian force
      Extended° Asia: from Euphrates°
      His conquering banner shook, from Syria
      To Lydia and to Ionia,
      Whilst——

Antony.   Antony, thou wouldst say——

105 *Messenger.*   O, my lord.

Antony. Speak to me home, mince not the general
            tongue:°
      Name Cleopatra as she is called in Rome;
      Rail thou in Fulvia's phrase, and taunt my faults
      With such full license as both truth and malice
110   Have power to utter. O, then we bring forth weeds

---

94 **better issue** greater success 100 **as** as if 102 **Extended** seized
upon 102 **Euphrates** (accented on first syllable) 106 **Speak . . .
tongue** be blunt, don't diminish what everyone is saying

When our quick winds° lie still, and our ills told us
Is as our earing.° Fare thee well awhile.

Messenger. At your noble pleasure.   *Exit Messenger.*

Antony. From Sicyon, ho, the news! Speak there!

First Attendant. The man from Sicyon—is there such
     an one?   115

Second Attendant. He stays upon your will.°

Antony.   Let him appear.
     These strong Egyptian fetters I must break
     Or lose myself in dotage.

             Enter another Messenger, with a letter.

                              What are you?

Messenger. Fulvia thy wife is dead.

Antony.   Where died she?

Messenger. In Sicyon.   120
     Her length of sickness, with what else more serious
     Importeth thee to know, this bears. [*Gives a letter.*]

Antony.   Forbear me.° [*Exit Messenger.*]
     There's a great spirit gone! Thus did I desire it:
     What our contempts doth often hurl from us,
     We wish it ours again. The present pleasure,   125
     By revolution low'ring,° does become
     The opposite of itself: she's good, being gone;
     The hand could° pluck her back that shoved her on.
     I must from this enchanting° queen break off:
     Ten thousand harms, more than the ills I know,   130
     My idleness doth hatch. Ho now, Enobarbus!

---

111 **quick winds** lively winds (that ventilate the soil)   111–12 **our ills
. . . earing** i.e., when our faults are told to us, it is like plowing (that
makes the ground fertile)   116 **stays upon your will** awaits your
pleasure   122 **Forbear me** leave me   126 **By revolution low'ring**
sinking in our estimation (as the wheel of time turns and spins the
present moment downward)   128 **could** would like to   129 **enchanting**
spellbinding

Enter Enobarbus.

Enobarbus. What's your pleasure, sir?

Antony. I must with haste from hence.

Enobarbus. Why, then we kill all our women. We see
135   how mortal an unkindness is to them. If they suffer
our departure, death's the word.

Antony. I must be gone.

Enobarbus. Under a compelling occasion let women
die.° It were pity to cast them away for nothing,
140   though between them and a great cause they should
be esteemed nothing. Cleopatra, catching but the
least noise of this, dies instantly; I have seen her
die twenty times upon far poorer moment.° I do
think there is mettle° in death, which commits some
145   loving act upon her, she hath such a celerity in
dying.

Antony. She is cunning past man's thought.

Enobarbus. Alack, sir, no; her passions are made of
nothing but the finest part of pure love. We cannot
150   call her winds and waters sighs and tears; they are
greater storms and tempests than almanacs can report. This cannot be cunning in her; if it be, she
makes a show'r of rain as well as Jove.

Antony. Would I had never seen her!

155 *Enobarbus.* O, sir, you had then left unseen a wonderful piece of work, which not to have been blest
withal would have discredited your travel.

Antony. Fulvia is dead.

Enobarbus. Sir?

160 *Antony.* Fulvia is dead.

Enobarbus. Fulvia?

139 **die** (throughout this speech Enobarbus puns on a second meaning of
die, "to experience sexual orgasm")   143 **moment** cause   144 **mettle**
strength

Antony. Dead.

Enobarbus. Why, sir, give the gods a thankful sacrifice. When it pleaseth their deities to take the wife
of a man from him, it shows to man the tailors of   *165*
the earth; comforting therein, that when old robes
are worn out, there are members to make new. If
there were no more women but Fulvia, then had
you indeed a cut,° and the case to be lamented.
This grief is crowned with consolation: your old   *170*
smock brings forth a new petticoat, and indeed the
tears live in an onion that should water this sorrow.

Antony. The business she hath broachèd in the state
    Cannot endure my absence.

Enobarbus. And the business you have broached here   *175*
cannot be without you; especially that of Cleopatra's, which wholly depends on your abode.°

Antony. No more light° answers. Let our° officers
    Have notice what we purpose. I shall break°
    The cause of our expedience° to the Queen   *180*
    And get her leave to part. For not alone
    The death of Fulvia, with more urgent touches,°
    Do strongly speak to us, but the letters too
    Of many our contriving friends° in Rome
    Petition us at home. Sextus Pompeius   *185*
    Hath given the dare to Caesar and commands
    The empire of the sea. Our slippery people,
    Whose love is never linked to the deserver
    Till his deserts are past, begin to throw
    Pompey the Great and all his dignities   *190*
    Upon° his son; who, high in name and power,

169 **cut** (1) severe blow (2) pudendum (the entire speech infuses bawdy
meanings [e.g., of **tailors** and **members**] into the conceit of the world as
a tailor's shop, with the gods as tailors cutting new clothes out of
old, replacing old people with new; the tailor's shop is where men make
love and breed)   175–77 **And the business . . . abode** (bawdy again)
178 **light** indecent   178 **our** (royal plural)   179 **break** tell   180 **expe-
dience** (1) haste (2) expedition   182 **more urgent touches** more press-
ing reasons   184 **many our contriving friends** many who plot on my
behalf   189–91 **throw . . . /Upon** transfer . . . to

Higher than both in blood and life,° stands up
For the main soldier;° whose quality, going on,
The sides o' th' world may danger.° Much is breed-
　　ing,
195　Which, like the courser's hair,° hath yet but life
And not a serpent's poison. Say our pleasure,
To such whose places under us require,
Our quick remove from hence.

Enobarbus. I shall do't.   [*Exeunt.*]

[Scene 3. *Alexandria. Cleopatra's palace.*]

Enter Cleopatra, Charmian, Alexas, and Iras.

Cleopatra. Where is he?

Charmian.   I did not see him since.°

Cleopatra. See where he is, who's with him, what he
　　does:
I did not send you. If you find him sad,°
Say I am dancing; if in mirth, report
5　That I am sudden sick. Quick, and return.
                                    [*Exit Alexas.*]

Charmian. Madam, methinks, if you did love him
　　dearly,
You do not hold the method to enforce
The like from him.

Cleopatra.   What should I do, I do not?

---

192 **blood and life** courage and energy   192–93 **stands ... soldier**
sets himself up as the greatest soldier in the world   193–94 **whose
quality ... danger** whose character may, if his fortunes prosper, threaten
the structure of the world   195 **courser's hair** (a horse's hair placed in
water was thought to turn into a serpent)   1.3.1 **since** recently   3 **sad**
serious

Charmian. In each thing give him way, cross him in
nothing.

Cleopatra. Thou teachest like a fool: the way to lose
him!   10

Charmian. Tempt° him not so too far. I wish, forbear.
In time we hate that which we often fear.

Enter Antony.

But here comes Antony.

Cleopatra.   I am sick and sullen.

Antony. I am sorry to give breathing° to my purpose—

Cleopatra. Help me away, dear Charmian! I shall fall.   15
It cannot be thus long; the sides of nature
Will not sustain it.°

Antony.   Now, my dearest queen—

Cleopatra. Pray you, stand farther from me.

Antony.   What's the matter?

Cleopatra. I know by that same eye there's some good
news.
What, says the married woman you may go?   20
Would she had never given you leave to come!
Let her not say 'tis I that keep you here.
I have no power upon you; hers you are.

Antony. The gods best know——

Cleopatra.   O, never was there queen
So mightily betrayed! Yet at the first   25
I saw the treasons planted.°

Antony.   Cleopatra—

Cleopatra. Why should I think you can be mine, and
true

---

11 **Tempt** try   14 **breathing** utterance   16–17 **the sides ... it** the
human frame will not stand it   26 **planted** (like seeds, and like mines)

(Though you in swearing shake the thronèd gods)
Who have been false to Fulvia? Riotous madness,
To be entangled with those mouth-made vows
Which break themselves in swearing.°

Antony.   Most sweet queen—

Cleopatra. Nay, pray you seek no color° for your
    going,
But bid farewell, and go. When you sued staying,°
Then was the time for words: no going then;
Eternity was in our lips and eyes,
Bliss in our brows' bent,° none our parts so poor
But was a race of heaven;° they are so still,
Or thou, the greatest soldier of the world,
Art turned the greatest liar.

Antony.   How now, lady?

Cleopatra. I would I had thy inches; thou shouldst
    know
There were a heart in Egypt.°

Antony.   Hear me, Queen:
The strong necessity of time commands
Our services awhile; but my full heart
Remains in use with you.° Our Italy
Shines o'er with civil swords;° Sextus Pompeius
Makes his approaches to the port of Rome;
Equality of two domestic powers
Breed scrupulous faction;° the hated, grown to
    strength,
Are newly grown to love;° the condemned Pompey,
Rich in his father's honor, creeps apace

30

35

40

45

50

---

31 **Which . . . swearing** which are broken the second they are
uttered   32 **color** pretext   33 **sued staying** pleaded to stay   36 **brows'
bent** eyebrows' arch   37 **a race of heaven** (1) of heavenly favor (2) of
heavenly origin, rooted in heaven   41 **Egypt** (here, as elsewhere, Cleopatra as well as the country)   44 **in use with you** for you to possess   45 **civil swords** swords drawn in civil war   47–48 **Equality . . .
faction** where the rule at home is equally divided between two, parties
grow up, quarreling over tiny points   48–49 **the hated . . . to love** the
hated begin to be loved as they gain power

Into the hearts of such as have not thrived
Upon the present state, whose numbers threaten;
And quietness, grown sick of rest, would purge
By any desperate change.° My more particular,°
And that which most with you should safe my
    going,   55
Is Fulvia's death.

Cleopatra. Though age from folly could not give me
    freedom,
It does from childishness. Can Fulvia die?

Antony. She's dead, my queen.
Look here, and at thy sovereign leisure read   60
The garboils° she awaked. At the last, best,°
See when and where she died.

Cleopatra.   O most false love!
Where be the sacred vials° thou shouldst fill
With sorrowful water? Now I see, I see,
In Fulvia's death, how mine received shall be.   65

Antony. Quarrel no more, but be prepared to know
The purposes I bear; which are, or cease,
As you shall give th' advice. By the fire
That quickens Nilus' slime,° I go from hence
Thy soldier-servant, making peace or war   70
As thou affects.°

Cleopatra.   Cut my lace,° Charmian, come—
But let it be: I am quickly ill, and well,
So Antony loves.°

Antony.   My precious queen, forbear,

53–54 **quietness ... change** i.e., a long peace has developed disease
in the body politic, which demands to be made well by the bloodletting
of war and revolution   54 **My more particular** my own more personal reason   61 **garboils** commotion   61 **best** i.e., best news of all
63 **sacred vials** (the bottles of tears supposedly placed by Romans in
friends' tombs)   68–69 **By the fire ... slime** by the sun that generates
life in the Nile's mud   71 **affects** choosest   71 **Cut my lace** (of her
tight bodice, i.e., "Give me air")   73 **So Antony loves** (1) if Antony
loves me (2) in just such a changeable way does Antony love me

And give true evidence to his love, which stands°
An honorable trial.

75   *Cleopatra.*   So Fulvia told me.
I prithee turn aside and weep for her;
Then bid adieu to me, and say the tears
Belong to Egypt. Good now, play one scene
Of excellent dissembling, and let it look
Like perfect honor.

80   *Antony.*   You'll heat my blood: no more.

Cleopatra. You can do better yet; but this is meetly.°

Antony. Now by my sword—

Cleopatra.   And target.° Still he mends.
But this is not the best. Look, prithee, Charmian,
How this Herculean Roman does become
The carriage of his chafe.°

85   *Antony.*   I'll leave you, lady.

Cleopatra. Courteous lord, one word.
Sir, you and I must part, but that's not it:
Sir, you and I have loved, but there's not it:
That you know well. Something it is I would—
90   O, my oblivion is a very Antony,
And I am all forgotten.°

Antony.   But that your royalty
Holds idleness your subject,° I should take you
For idleness itself.

Cleopatra.   'Tis sweating labor
To bear° such idleness so near the heart
95   As Cleopatra this. But, sir, forgive me,
Since my becomings° kill me when they do not

74 **stands** sustains 81 **meetly** suitable 82 **target** small shield 84–85
How this . . . his chafe how gracefully this descendant of Hercules acts
out his rage 90–91 **my oblivion . . . forgotten** (1) my forgetful memory
is like Antony and has deserted me (2) my forgetfulness even, like my
memory, is consumed by the image of Antony, and my mind is empty of
all else 91–92 **But that . . . subject** if you were not queen over
trifling 93–94 **labor/To bear** (pun on childbirth) 96 **becomings** graces

　Eye well to you. Your honor calls you hence;
　Therefore be deaf to my unpitied folly,
　And all the gods go with you. Upon your sword
　Sit laurel victory, and smooth success　　　　　　　*100*
　Be strewed before your feet!

Antony.　　　　　　　　　Let us go. Come:
　Our separation so abides and flies
　That thou residing here goes yet with me,
　And I hence fleeting here remain with thee.
　Away!　　　　　　　　　　　　*Exeunt.*　　*105*

[Scene 4. *Rome. Caesar's house.*]

Enter Octavius [Caesar], reading a letter,
Lepidus, and their Train.

Caesar. You may see, Lepidus, and henceforth know
　It is not Caesar's natural vice to hate
　Our great competitor.° From Alexandria
　This is the news: he fishes, drinks, and wastes
　The lamps of night in revel; is not more manlike　　*5*
　Than Cleopatra, nor the queen of Ptolemy°
　More womanly than he; hardly gave audience, or
　Vouchsafed to think he had partners. You shall
　　find there
　A man who is th' abstract of all faults
　That all men follow.°

Lepidus.　　　　　　I must not think there are　　*10*
　Evils enow° to darken all his goodness;
　His faults, in him, seem as the spots of heaven,
　More fiery by night's blackness, hereditary

1.4.3 **competitor** partner　6 **queen of Ptolemy** (Cleopatra had nomi-
nally married her brother Ptolemy, who was only a child, at the command
of Julius Caesar)　9–10 **abstract . . . follow** symbol of universal weakness　11 **enow** enough

Rather than purchased,° what he cannot change
15 Than what he chooses.

   Caesar. You are too indulgent. Let's grant it is not
      Amiss to tumble on the bed of Ptolemy,
      To give a kingdom for a mirth, to sit
      And keep the turn of tippling° with a slave,
20   To reel the streets at noon, and stand the buffet
      With knaves that smells of sweat. Say this becomes
         him
      (As his composure° must be rare indeed
      Whom these things cannot blemish); yet must An-
         tony
      No way excuse his foils° when we do bear
25   So great weight in his lightness.° If he filled
      His vacancy° with his voluptuousness,
      Full surfeits and the dryness of his bones
      Call on him for't.° But to confound° such time
      That drums him from his sport and speaks as loud
30   As his own state and ours, 'tis to be chid
      As we rate boys who, being mature in knowledge,
      Pawn their experience to their present pleasure
      And so rebel to judgment.°

                  Enter a Messenger.

   Lepidus.   Here's more news.

   Messenger. Thy biddings have been done, and every
         hour,
35   Most noble Caesar, shalt thou have report
      How 'tis abroad. Pompey is strong at sea,
      And it appears he is beloved of those
      That only have feared Caesar: to the ports

---

14 **purchased** acquired   19 **keep the turn of tippling** exchange toasts
22 **composure** character   24 **foils** stains   24–25 **when we . . . lightness**
when his triviality throws such a burden on us   26 **vacancy** leisure
27–28 **Full . . . for't** let him pay the price in sickness and syphilis
28 **confound** waste   30–33 **'tis to be . . . judgment** deserves the considered rebuke we give to boys who, though old enough to know better, give
up all the wisdom they have learned in exchange for a moment's pleasure

The discontents° repair, and men's reports
Give him° much wronged.

Caesar.   I should have known no less.   *40*
    It hath been taught us from the primal state°
    That he which is was wished until he were;°
    And the ebbed man, ne'er loved till ne'er worth
      love,
    Comes deared by being lacked. This common
      body,°
    Like to a vagabond flag° upon the stream,   *45*
    Goes to and back, lackeying the varying tide,
    To rot itself with motion.

Messenger.   Caesar, I bring thee word
    Menecrates and Menas, famous pirates,
    Makes the sea serve them, which they ear° and
      wound
    With keels of every kind. Many hot inroads   *50*
    They make in Italy; the borders maritime
    Lack blood to think on't, and flush° youth revolt.
    No vessel can peep forth but 'tis as soon
    Taken as seen; for Pompey's name strikes more
    Than could his war resisted.

Caesar.   Antony,   *55*
    Leave thy lascivious wassails.° When thou once
    Was beaten from Modena,° where thou slew'st
    Hirtius and Pansa, consuls, at thy heel
    Did famine follow, whom thou fought'st against
    (Though daintily brought up) with patience more   *60*
    Than savages could suffer.° Thou didst drink
    The stale° of horses and the gilded° puddle
    Which beasts would cough at. Thy palate then did
      deign°

---

39 discontents malcontents **40 Give him** say he is **41 from the primal state** since government began **42 That he . . . were** that a man in power had supporters until he gained power **44 common body** populace **45 vagabond flag** aimlessly drifting iris **49 ear** plow **52 flush** vigorous, lusty **56 wassails** revelry **57 Modena** (accented on second syllable) **61 suffer** summon up **62 stale** urine **62 gilded** i.e., yellow with scum **63 deign** not disdain

The roughest berry on the rudest hedge.
65   Yea, like the stag when snow the pasture sheets,
      The barks of trees thou browsed. On the Alps
      It is reported thou didst eat strange flesh,
      Which some did die to look on. And all this
      (It wounds thine honor that I speak it now)
70   Was borne so like a soldier that thy cheek
      So much as lanked° not.

Lepidus.   'Tis pity of him.

Caesar. Let his shames quickly
      Drive him to Rome. 'Tis time we twain
      Did show ourselves i' th' field; and to that end
75   Assemble we immediate council. Pompey
      Thrives in our idleness.

Lepidus.   Tomorrow, Caesar,
      I shall be furnished to inform you rightly
      Both what by sea and land I can be able°
      To front° this present time.

Caesar.   Till which encounter,
80   It is my business too. Farewell.

Lepidus. Farewell, my lord. What you shall know
            meantime
      Of stirs abroad, I shall beseech you, sir,
      To let me be partaker.

Caesar.   Doubt not, sir;
      I knew it for my bond.°   *Exeunt.*

---

71 **lanked** thinned   78 **I can be able** my powers can be   79 **front** confront   84 **bond** duty

[Scene 5. *Alexandria. Cleopatra's palace.*]

Enter Cleopatra, Charmian, Iras, and Mardian.

Cleopatra. Charmian!

Charmian. Madam?

Cleopatra. [*Yawning*] Ha, ha.
  Give me to drink mandragora.°

Charmian.   Why, madam?

Cleopatra. That I might sleep out this great gap of time   5
  My Antony is away.

Charmian.   You think of him too much.

Cleopatra. O, 'tis treason!

Charmian.   Madam, I trust, not so.

Cleopatra. Thou, eunuch Mardian!

Mardian.   What's your Highness' pleasure?

Cleopatra. Not now to hear thee sing. I take no
    pleasure
  In aught an eunuch has: 'tis well for thee   10
  That, being unseminared,° thy freer thoughts
  May not fly forth of Egypt. Hast thou affections?°

Mardian. Yes, gracious madam.

Cleopatra. Indeed?

Mardian. Not in deed, madam; for I can do nothing   15
  But what indeed is honest° to be done:

1.5.4 **mandragora** mandrake (a strong narcotic) 11 **unseminared**
unsexed 12 **affections** passions 16 **honest** chaste

Yet have I fierce affections, and think
What Venus did with Mars.°

Cleopatra.   O, Charmian,
Where think'st thou he is now? Stands he, or sits he?
20   Or does he walk? Or is he on his horse?
O happy horse, to bear the weight of Antony!
Do bravely, horse, for wot'st° thou whom thou
    mov'st?
The demi-Atlas° of this earth, the arm
And burgonet° of men. He's speaking now,
25   Or murmuring, "Where's my serpent of old Nile?"
(For so he calls me.) Now I feed myself
With most delicious poison. Think on me,
That am with Phoebus'° amorous pinches black
And wrinkled deep in time. Broad-fronted Caesar,°
30   When thou wast here above the ground, I was
A morsel for a monarch; and great Pompey°
Would stand and make his eyes grow in my brow;
There would he anchor his aspect,° and die
With looking on his life.

Enter Alexas from Antony.

Alexas.   Sovereign of Egypt, hail!

35   *Cleopatra.* How much unlike art thou Mark Antony!
Yet, coming from him, that great med'cine hath
With his tinct gilded thee.°
How goes it with my brave Mark Antony?

Alexas. Last thing he did, dear Queen,
40   He kissed—the last of many doubled kisses—
This orient° pearl. His speech sticks in my heart.

18 **Venus ... Mars** (Venus, goddess of love, and Mars, god of war, were lovers)   22 **wot'st** knowest   23 **demi-Atlas** (the Titan Atlas supported the heavens on his shoulders)   24 **burgonet** visored helmet   28 **Phoebus'** the sun's   29 **Broad-fronted Caesar** wide-browed Caesar (i.e., Julius Caesar, whose mistress she had been in youth)   31 **great Pompey** Cneius Pompeius (son of Pompey the Great)   33 **aspect** gaze (accented on second syllable)   36–37 **that great med'cine ... thee** (alchemists long tried to make or discover the "philosopher's stone" or **elixir vitae**—known as the "great medicine" and the "tincture"—which had the property of turning base metals to gold, and of restoring youth)   41 **orient** eastern, bright

Cleopatra. Mine ear must pluck it thence.

Alexas.   "Good friend," quoth he,
  "Say the firm° Roman to great Egypt sends
  This treasure of an oyster; at whose foot,
  To mend the petty present, I will piece°   45
  Her opulent throne with kingdoms. All the East
  (Say thou) shall call her mistress." So he nodded,
  And soberly did mount an arm-gaunt° steed,
  Who neighed so high that what I would have spoke
  Was beastly dumbed° by him.

Cleopatra.   What was he, sad or merry?   50

Alexas. Like to the time o' th' year between the ex-
      tremes
  Of hot and cold, he was nor sad nor merry.

Cleopatra. O well-divided disposition!° Note him,
  Note him, good Charmian, 'tis the man;° but note
      him.
  He was not sad, for he would shine on those   55
  That make their looks by his; he was not merry,
  Which seemed to tell them his remembrance lay
  In Egypt with his joy; but between both.
  O heavenly mingle! Be'st thou sad or merry,
  The violence of either thee becomes,   60
  So does it no man else. —Met'st thou my posts?°

Alexas. Ay, madam, twenty several° messengers.
  Why do you send so thick?

Cleopatra.   Who's born that day
  When I forget to send to Antony
  Shall die a beggar. Ink and paper, Charmian.   65
  Welcome, my good Alexas. Did I, Charmian,
  Ever love Caesar so?

Charmian.   O, that brave° Caesar!

43 **firm** constant 45 **piece** add to 48 **arm-gaunt** battle-worn (?)
battle-hungry (?) 50 **beastly dumbed** silenced by a beast 53 **disposition** temperament 54 **'tis the man** that's exactly what he is like
61 **posts** messengers 62 **several** separate 67 **brave** splendid, fine

Cleopatra. Be choked with such another emphasis!°
    Say "the brave Antony."

Charmian.   The valiant Caesar!

70 *Cleopatra.* By Isis, I will give thee bloody teeth
    If thou with Caesar paragon° again
    My man of men.

Charmian.   By your most gracious pardon,
    I sing but after you.

Cleopatra.   My salad days,
    When I was green° in judgment, cold in blood,
75   To say as I said then. But come, away,
    Get me ink and paper.
    He shall have every day a several greeting,
    Or I'll unpeople Egypt.   *Exeunt.*

---

68 emphasis forceful statement **71 paragon** compare **74 green** young,
silly

[ACT 2

Scene 1. *Messina. Pompey's house.*]

Enter Pompey, Menecrates, and Menas, in war-like manner.

Pompey. If the great gods be just, they shall° assist
    The deeds of justest men.

Menecrates.   Know, worthy Pompey,
    That what they do delay, they not deny.°

Pompey. Whiles we are suitors to their throne, decays
    The thing we sue° for.

Menecrates.   We, ignorant of ourselves   5
    Beg often our own harms, which the wise pow'rs
    Deny us for our good; so find we profit
    By losing of our prayers.

Pompey.   I shall do well:
    The people love me, and the sea is mine;
    My powers are crescent,° and my auguring° hope   *10*

2.1.1 **shall** surely must   3 **what they . . . deny** i.e., delay in performing does not necessarily imply a refusal   5 **sue** beg   10 **crescent**
growing (i.e., waxing like the moon—hence the following image)
10 **auguring** prophesying

27

Says it will come to th' full. Mark Antony
In Egypt sits at dinner, and will make
No wars without doors.° Caesar gets money where
He loses hearts. Lepidus flatters both,
15 Of both is flattered, but he neither loves,
Nor either cares for him.

Menas.   Caesar and Lepidus
Are in the field;° a mighty strength they carry.

Pompey. Where have you this? 'Tis false.

Menas.   From Silvius, sir.

Pompey. He dreams: I know they are in Rome to-
gether,
20 Looking for Antony. But all the charms° of love,
Salt° Cleopatra, soften thy waned° lip!
Let witchcraft join with beauty, lust with both!
Tie up the libertine in a field of feasts,
Keep his brain fuming. Epicurean cooks
25 Sharpen with cloyless sauce his appetite,
That sleep and feeding may prorogue° his honor
Even till a Lethe'd° dullness—

Enter Varrius.

                                    How now, Varrius?

Varrius. This is most certain, that I shall deliver:
Mark Antony is every hour in Rome
30 Expected. Since he went from Egypt 'tis
A space for farther travel.°

Pompey.   I could have given less matter
A better ear. Menas, I did not think
This amorous surfeiter would have donned his helm
For such a petty war. His soldiership

---

13 **without doors** out-of-doors (contrasted with the indoor "wars" of
love)   17 **in the field** ready for battle   20 **charms** spells   21 **Salt**
lustful   21 **waned** pale and thin (like the old moon)   26 **prorogue** sus-
pend   27 **Lethe'd** oblivious (from Lethe, a river in Hades; those who
drank of the water forgot all)   30–31 **'tis . . . travel** there has been time
for an even longer journey

Is twice the other twain; but let us rear   35
The higher our opinion,° that our stirring
Can from the lap of Egypt's widow pluck
The ne'er-lust-wearied Antony.

Menas.   I cannot hope°
Caesar and Antony shall well greet° together;
His wife that's dead did trespasses to Caesar;   40
His brother warred upon him—although I think
Not moved° by Antony.

Pompey.   I know not, Menas,
How lesser enmities may give way to greater.
Were't not that we stand up against them all,
'Twere pregnant they should square between them-
     selves,°   45
For they have entertainèd cause enough
To draw their swords; but how the fear of us
May cement° their divisions and bind up
The petty difference, we yet not know.
Be't as our gods will have't! It only stands   50
Our lives upon,° to use our strongest hands.
Come, Menas.   *Exeunt.*

[Scene 2. *Rome. Lepidus' house.*]

Enter Enobarbus and Lepidus.

Lepidus. Good Enobarbus, 'tis a worthy deed,
     And shall become you well, to entreat your captain
     To soft and gentle speech.

Enobarbus.   I shall entreat him

35–36 **let us ... opinion** let us think all the better of ourselves   38 **hope**
believe   39 **well greet** meet amiably   42 **moved** encouraged   44–45
Were't not ... themselves had we not challenged them (and thus
united them) they would probably have quarreled among themselves
48 **cement** (accented on first syllable)   50–51 **It only ... upon** only, it
is a matter of life and death to us all

To answer like himself: if Caesar move° him,
5   Let Antony look over Caesar's head
And speak as loud as Mars. By Jupiter,
Were I the wearer of Antonio's beard,
I would not shave't today!°

Lepidus.   'Tis not a time
For private stomaching.°

Enobarbus.   Every time
10   Serves for the matter that is then born in't.

Lepidus. But small to greater matters must give way.

Enobarbus. Not if the small come first.

Lepidus.   Your speech is passion:
But pray you stir no embers up. Here comes
The noble Antony.

Enter Antony and Ventidius [in conversation].

Enobarbus.   And yonder, Caesar.

*Enter [from the other side] Caesar, Maecenas,
          and Agrippa [in conversation].*

15   *Antony.* If we compose° well here, to Parthia.
Hark, Ventidius.

Caesar.   I do not know,
Maecenas; ask Agrippa.

Lepidus.   Noble friends,
That which combined us was most great, and let not
A leaner action rend us. What's amiss,
20   May it be gently heard. When we debate
Our trivial difference loud, we do commit
Murder in healing wounds. Then, noble partners,
The rather for I earnestly beseech,

2.2.4 **move** irritate   8 **I would not shave't today** (1) I would not do
him the courtesy of clean-shaving   (2) I would not remove the tempta-
tion of plucking it (an incitement to fight)   9 **private stomaching** personal resentment   15 **compose** come to an agreement

Touch you the sourest points with sweetest terms,
Nor curstness grow to th' matter.°

Antony. 'Tis spoken well. 25
Were we before our armies, and to fight,
I should do thus.° *Flourish.*

Caesar. Welcome to Rome.

Antony. Thank you.

Caesar. Sit. 30

Antony. Sit, sir.

Caesar. Nay then. [*They sit.*]

Antony. I learn you take things ill which are not so,
Or being, concern you not.

Caesar. I must be laughed at
If, or for nothing or° a little, I 35
Should say myself offended, and with you
Chiefly i' th' world; more laughed at that I should
Once name you derogately,° when to sound your
name
It not concerned me.

Antony. My being in Egypt, Caesar,
What was't to you? 40

Caesar. No more than my residing here at Rome
Might be to you in Egypt: yet if you there
Did practice on my state,° your being in Egypt
Might be my question.

Antony. How intend you? Practiced?

Caesar. You may be pleased to catch at mine intent 45
By what did here befall me. Your wife and brother

---

25 **Nor ... matter** and do not let ill temper be added to the problem
at hand   27 **thus** (perhaps Antony embraces Caesar, but perhaps he
means his words would be temperate in any circumstance)   35 **or ... or**
either ... or   38 **derogately** disparagingly   43 **practice on my state**
plot against my rule

Made wars upon me, and their contestation
Was theme for you;° you were the word of war.°

Antony. You do mistake your business: my brother
        never
50 Did urge me° in his act. I did inquire it
And have my learning from some true reports°
That drew their swords with you. Did he not rather
Discredit my authority with yours,
And make the wars alike against my stomach,°
55 Having alike your cause? Of this, my letters
Before did satisfy you. If you'll patch a quarrel,
As matter whole you have to make it with,°
It must not be with this.

Caesar.   You praise yourself
By laying defects of judgment to me, but
You patched up your excuses.

60 *Antony.*   Not so, not so:
I know you could not lack, I am certain on't,
Very necessity of this thought, that I,
Your partner in the cause 'gainst which he fought,
Could not with graceful eyes attend° those wars
65 Which fronted° mine own peace. As for my wife,
I would you had her spirit in such another;°
The third o' th' world is yours, which with a snaffle
You may pace° easy, but not such a wife.

Enobarbus. Would we had all such wives, that the men
70   might go to wars with the women.

Antony. So much uncurbable, her garboils, Caesar,
    Made out of her impatience—which not wanted
    Shrewdness of policy too—I grieving grant

---

48 **Was theme for you** had you as root cause (?) provided you with
a pretext (?)   48 **you were the word of war** the war was about
you   50 **Did urge me** made use of my name   51 **reports** reporters
54 **stomach** desire   56–57 **If you'll . . . with** if you want to fabricate a
quarrel out of odds and ends, though in fact you have more substantial
materials for one   64 **with graceful eyes attend** look favorably on
65 **fronted** attacked   66 **I would . . . another** I wish you were married
to just such a wife   68 **pace** train (used of horses)

    Did you too much disquiet: for that you must
    But° say, I could not help it.

Caesar.   I wrote to you;   *75*
    When rioting in Alexandria you
    Did pocket up my letters, and with taunts
    Did gibe my missive° out of audience.

Antony.   Sir,
    He fell upon me, ere admitted, then:
    Three kings I had newly feasted, and did want   *80*
    Of what I was i' th' morning; but next day
    I told him of myself,° which was as much
    As to have asked him pardon. Let this fellow
    Be nothing of° our strife: if we contend,
    Out of our question wipe him.

Caesar.   You have broken   *85*
    The article° of your oath, which you shall never
    Have tongue to charge me with.

Lepidus.   Soft,° Caesar!

Antony.   No,
    Lepidus; let him speak.
    The honor is sacred which he talks on now,
    Supposing that I lacked it. But on, Caesar,   *90*
    The article of my oath—

Caesar. To lend me arms and aid when I required
      them,
    The which you both denied.

Antony.   Neglected rather:
    And then when poisonèd hours had bound me up
    From mine own knowledge. As nearly as I may,   *95*
    I'll play the penitent to you: but mine honesty
    Shall not make poor my greatness, nor my power
    Work without it.° Truth is, that Fulvia,
    To have me out of Egypt, made wars here,
    For which myself, the ignorant motive, do   *100*

75 **But** only   78 **missive** messenger   82 **myself** my condition   84 **Be nothing of** have no place in   86 **article** precise terms   87 **Soft** be careful   98 **it** honesty (?)

So far ask pardon as befits mine honor
To stoop in such a case.

Lepidus.   'Tis noble spoken.

Maecenas. If it might please you, to enforce no further
The griefs° between ye: to forget them quite
105   Were to remember that the present need
Speaks to atone you.°

Lepidus.   Worthily spoken, Maecenas.

Enobarbus. Or, if you borrow one another's love for
the instant, you may, when you hear no more words
of Pompey, return it again: you shall have time to
110   wrangle in when you have nothing else to do.

Antony. Thou art a soldier only; speak no more.

Enobarbus. That truth should be silent I had almost
forgot.

Antony. You wrong this presence;° therefore speak no
more.

115 *Enobarbus.* Go to, then; your considerate stone.°

Caesar. I do not much dislike the matter, but
The manner of his speech; for't cannot be
We shall remain in friendship, our conditions°
So diff'ring in their acts. Yet if I knew
120   What hoop should hold us stanch, from edge to edge
O' th' world I would pursue it.

Agrippa.   Give me leave, Caesar.

Caesar. Speak, Agrippa.

Agrippa. Thou hast a sister by the mother's side,°
Admired Octavia: great Mark Antony
Is now a widower.

---

104 **griefs** grievances   105 **Speaks to atone you** demands your reconciliation   114 **presence** dignified company   115 **your considerate
stone** I will be silent as stone about what I am thinking   118 **conditions**
temperaments   123 **by the mother's side** i.e., half sister (though actually Octavia was a full sister of Octavius)

Caesar.   Say not so, Agrippa: *125*
  If Cleopatra heard you, your reproof
  Were well deserved of rashness.°

Antony. I am not married, Caesar: let me hear
  Agrippa further speak.

Agrippa. To hold you in perpetual amity,   *130*
  To make you brothers, and to knit your hearts
  With an unslipping knot, take Antony
  Octavia to his wife; whose beauty claims
  No worse a husband than the best of men;
  Whose virtue and whose general graces speak   *135*
  That which none else can utter. By this marriage
  All little jealousies,° which now seem great,
  And all great fears, which now import° their
      dangers,
  Would then be nothing: truths would be tales,
  Where now half-tales be truths:° her love to both   *140*
  Would each to other, and all loves to both,
  Draw after her. Pardon what I have spoke;
  For 'tis a studied, not a present° thought,
  By duty ruminated.

Antony.   Will Caesar speak?

Caesar. Not till he hears how Antony is touched°   *145*
  With what is spoke already.

Antony.   What power is in Agrippa,
  If I would say, "Agrippa, be it so,"
  To make this good?

Caesar.   The power of Caesar, and
  His power unto Octavia.

Antony.   May I never
  To this good purpose, that so fairly shows,   *150*
  Dream of impediment! Let me have thy hand.

126–27 **your reproof ... rashness** you would get a deserved reproof
for being foolhardy 137 **jealousies** suspicions 138 **import** bring
139–40 **truths would ... truths** things true would be disbelieved, whereas
now half-truths are believed 143 **present** momentary 145 **touched**
affected

Further this act of grace,° and from this hour
The heart of brothers govern in our loves
And sway our great designs.

Caesar.   There's my hand.
155 A sister I bequeath you, whom no brother
Did ever love so dearly. Let her live
To join our kingdoms and our hearts; and never
Fly off our loves° again.

Lepidus.   Happily, amen.

Antony. I did not think to draw my sword 'gainst
     Pompey,
160 For he hath laid strange courtesies and great
Of late upon me. I must thank him only,
Lest my remembrance° suffer ill report:
At heel of that,° defy him.

Lepidus.   Time calls upon's.
Of us must Pompey presently° be sought,
Or else he seeks out us.

165 *Antony.*   Where lies he?

Caesar. About the Mount Mesena.°

Antony. What is his strength by land?

Caesar. Great and increasing; but by sea
He is an absolute master.

Antony.   So is the fame.°
170 Would we had spoke together! Haste we for it,
Yet, ere we put ourselves in arms, dispatch we
The business we have talked of.

Caesar.   With most gladness;
And do invite you to my sister's view,
Whither straight I'll lead you.

---

152 **grace** reconciliation   158 **Fly off our loves** may our love for
each other desert us   162 **remembrance** memory (of kindnesses
done)   163 **At heel of that** immediately after   164 **presently** at once
166 **Mesena** Misenum, an Italian port   169 **fame** report

Antony.　　　　　　　　　　Let us, Lepidus,
　Not lack your company

Lepidus.　　　　　　　　　Noble Antony,　　　　*175*
　Not sickness should detain me.

　　　　　　　　　　　Flourish. Exit [all but]
　　　　　　　　　　　Enobarbus, Agrippa, Maecenas.

Maecenas. Welcome from Egypt, sir.

Enobarbus. Half the heart° of Caesar, worthy Maece-
　nas. My honorable friend, Agrippa.

Agrippa. Good Enobarbus.　　　　　　　　　　*180*

Maecenas. We have cause to be glad that matters are
　so well disgested.° You stayed well by't° in Egypt.

Enobarbus. Ay, sir, we did sleep day out of counte-
　nance° and made the night light with drinking.

Maecenas. Eight wild boars roasted whole at a break-　*185*
　fast, and but twelve persons there; is this true?

Enobarbus. This was but as a fly by° an eagle: we
　had much more monstrous matter of feast, which
　worthily deserved noting.

Maecenas. She's a most triumphant lady, if report be　*190*
　square° to her.

Enobarbus. When she first met Mark Antony, she
　pursed up° his heart, upon the river of Cydnus.

Agrippa. There she appeared indeed; or my reporter
　devised° well for her.　　　　　　　　　　　　*195*

Enobarbus. I will tell you.
　The barge she sat in, like a burnished throne,
　Burned on the water: the poop was beaten gold;
　Purple the sails, and so perfumèd that

178 **Half the heart** dear friend (though possibly the idea is that Caesar is
equally devoted to Agrippa and to Maecenas)　182 **disgested** digested
182 **stayed well by't** "lived it up"　183–84 **we did . . . countenance** we
disconcerted the day by sleeping through it　187 **by** compared with
191 **square** just, true　193 **pursed up** put in her purse, took possession
of　195 **devised** invented

The winds were lovesick with them; the oars were
200   silver,
Which to the tune of flutes kept stroke and made
The water which they beat to follow faster,
As amorous of their strokes. For her own person,
It beggared all description: she did lie
205   In her pavilion, cloth-of-gold of tissue,°
O'erpicturing that Venus where we see
The fancy outwork nature:° on each side her
Stood pretty dimpled boys, like smiling Cupids,
With divers-colored fans, whose wind did seem
210   To glow the delicate cheeks which they did cool,
And what they undid did.°

Agrippa.   O, rare for Antony.

Enobarbus. Her gentlewomen, like the Nereides,°
So many mermaids, tended her i' th' eyes,
And made their bends adornings.° At the helm
215   A seeming mermaid steers: the silken tackle
Swell with the touches of those flower-soft hands,
That yarely frame the office.° From the barge
A strange invisible perfume hits the sense
Of the adjacent wharfs.° The city cast
220   Her people out upon her; and Antony,
Enthroned i' th' marketplace, did sit alone,
Whistling to th' air; which, but for vacancy,°
Had gone to gaze on Cleopatra too,
And made a gap in nature.

Agrippa.   Rare Egyptian!

225 *Enobarbus.* Upon her landing, Antony sent to her,
Invited her to supper. She replied,

---

205 **cloth-of-gold of tissue** a rich fabric interwoven with gold threads
206–07 **O'erpicturing ... nature** surpassing that painting of Venus
where we can see the imagination excelling nature itself in creative
ability   211 **And ... did** i.e., and seemed to produce the warm color
they were cooling   212 **Nereides** sea nymphs   213–14 **tended ...
adornings** stood before her and waited on her, their bowing movements
being works of art in themselves   217 **yarely frame the office** deftly
perform the task   219 **wharfs** banks   222 **but for vacancy** i.e., but for
the law that nature abhors a vacuum

It should be better he became her guest;
Which she entreated. Our courteous Antony,
Whom ne'er the word of "No" woman heard speak,
Being barbered ten times o'er, goes to the feast,   230
And, for his ordinary,° pays his heart
For what his eyes eat only.

Agrippa.   Royal wench!
She made great Caesar lay his sword to bed;
He plowed her, and she cropped.°

Enobarbus.   I saw her once
Hop forty paces through the public street;   235
And having lost her breath, she spoke, and panted,
That° she did make defect perfection,
And, breathless, pow'r breathe forth.

Maecenas. Now Antony must leave her utterly.

Enobarbus. Never; he will not: 240
Age cannot wither her, nor custom stale
Her infinite variety: other women cloy
The appetites they feed, but she makes hungry
Where most she satisfies; for vilest things
Become themselves° in her, that the holy priests   245
Bless her when she is riggish.°

Maecenas. If beauty, wisdom, modesty, can settle
The heart of Antony, Octavia is
A blessèd lottery° to him.

Agrippa.   Let us go.
Good Enobarbus, make yourself my guest   250
Whilst you abide here.

Enobarbus.   Humbly, sir, I thank you. *Exeunt.*

231 **ordinary** public dinner in a tavern   234 **she cropped** i.e., had a
child (Caesarion)   237 **That** so that   245 **Become themselves** are
becoming   246 **riggish** wanton   249 **lottery** allotment

[Scene 3. *Rome. Caesar's house.*]

Enter Antony, Caesar, Octavia between them.

Antony. The world and my great office will sometimes
 Divide me from your bosom.

Octavia.   All which time
 Before the gods my knee shall bow my prayers
 To them for you.

Antony.   Good night, sir. My Octavia,
5 Read not my blemishes in the world's report:
 I have not kept my square,° but that to come
 Shall all be done by th' rule. Good night, dear lady.
 Good night, sir.

Caesar. Good night.   *Exit [with Octavia].*

Enter Soothsayer.

10 *Antony.* Now, sirrah: you do wish yourself in Egypt?

Soothsayer. Would I had never come from thence, nor
 you thither.

Antony. If you can, your reason?

Soothsayer. I see it in my motion,° have it not in my
15 tongue, but yet hie you to Egypt again.

Antony. Say to me, whose fortunes shall rise higher,
 Caesar's, or mine?

Soothsayer. Caesar's.
 Therefore, O Antony, stay not by his side.
20 Thy daemon,° that thy spirit which keeps thee, is

2.3.6 **kept my square** kept straight 14 **motion** mind 20 **daemon**
guardian angel

Noble, courageous, high, unmatchable,
Where Caesar's is not. But near him thy angel
Becomes afeard, as being o'erpow'red: therefore
Make space enough between you.

Antony.   Speak this no more.

Soothsayer. To none but thee; no more but when to
thee.   25
If thou dost play with him at any game,
Thou art sure to lose; and of° that natural luck
He beats thee 'gainst the odds. Thy luster thickens°
When he shines by: I say again, thy spirit
Is all afraid to govern thee near him;   30
But he away, 'tis noble.

Antony.   Get thee gone.
Say to Ventidius I would speak with him.

                              Exit [*Soothsayer*].
He shall to Parthia. Be it art or hap,°
He hath spoken true. The very dice obey him,
And in our sports my better cunning faints   35
Under his chance:° if we draw lots, he speeds;°
His cocks do win the battle still° of mine
When it is all to naught,° and his quails ever
Beat mine, inhooped,° at odds. I will to Egypt:
And though I make this marriage for my peace,   40
I' th' East my pleasure lies.

                    Enter Ventidius.

                    O, come, Ventidius,
You must to Parthia. Your commission's ready:
Follow me, and receive't.   *Exeunt.*

---

27 **of** by   28 **thickens** dims   33 **art or hap** skill or chance   36 **chance**
luck   36 **speeds** is successful   37 **still** always   38 **it is all to naught**
the odds are all to nothing (against him)   39 **inhooped** confined within
a ring

[Scene 4. *Rome. A street.*]

Enter Lepidus, Maecenas, and Agrippa.

Lepidus. Trouble yourselves no further: pray you, hasten
  Your generals after.

Agrippa.   Sir, Mark Antony
  Will e'en but kiss Octavia, and we'll follow.

Lepidus. Till I shall see you in your soldier's dress,
  Which will become you both, farewell.

5 *Maecenas.*   We shall,
  As I conceive° the journey, be at Mount°
  Before you, Lepidus.

Lepidus.   Your way is shorter;
  My purposes do draw me much about:°
  You'll win two days upon me.

Both.   Sir, good success.

10 *Lepidus.* Farewell.   *Exeunt.*

2.4.6 **conceive** understand 6 **Mount** i.e., Misenum 8 **My purposes
... about** my plans take me the long way around

[Scene 5. *Alexandria. Cleopatra's palace.*]

Enter Cleopatra, Charmian, Iras, and Alexas.

Cleopatra. Give me some music: music, moody° food
  Of us that trade in love.

Omnes.°   The music, ho!

Enter Mardian the Eunuch.

Cleopatra. Let it alone, let's to billiards: come, Charmian.

Charmian. My arm is sore; best play with Mardian.

Cleopatra. As well a woman with an eunuch played   5
  As with a woman. Come, you'll play with me, sir?

Mardian. As well as I can, madam.

Cleopatra. And when good will is showed, though't
    come too short,
  The actor may plead pardon. I'll none now.
  Give me mine angle,° we'll to th' river: there,   10
  My music playing far off, I will betray
  Tawny-finned fishes. My bended hook shall pierce
  Their slimy jaws; and as I draw them up,
  I'll think them every one an Antony,
  And say, "Ah, ha! y' are caught!"

Charmian.   'Twas merry when   15
  You wagered on your angling, when your diver
  Did hang a salt° fish on his hook, which he
  With fervency drew up.

2.5.1 **moody** melancholy (with pun on musical "mood" or key)
2 **Omnes** all (Latin)   10 **angle** fishing tackle   17 **salt** dried

Cleopatra.*   That time—O times!—
I laughed him out of patience; and that night
20 I laughed him into patience; and next morn,
Ere the ninth hour, I drunk him to his bed;
Then put my tires° and mantles on him, whilst
I wore his sword Philippan.°

Enter a Messenger.

         O, from Italy!
Ram thou thy fruitful tidings in mine ears,
That long time have been barren.

25 *Messenger.*   Madam, madam—

Cleopatra. Antonio's dead! If thou say so, villain,
Thou kill'st thy mistress: but well and free,
If thou so yield him. There is gold and here
My bluest veins to kiss, a hand that kings
30 Have lipped, and trembled kissing.

Messenger. First, madam, he is well.

Cleopatra.   Why, there's more gold.
But, sirrah, mark, we use
To say the dead are well:° bring it to that,
The gold I give thee will I melt and pour
35 Down thy ill-uttering throat.

Messenger. Good madam, hear me.

Cleopatra.   Well, go to, I will:
But there's no goodness in thy face if Antony
Be free and healthful; so tart a favor°
To trumpet such good tidings? If not well,
Thou shouldst come like a Fury crowned with
40   snakes,
Not like a formal° man.

Messenger.   Will't please you hear me?

22 tires headdresses   **23 Philippan** (Antony's sword is named after Philippi, where he conquered Brutus and Cassius)   **33 well** i.e., in having gone to heaven   **38 tart a favor** sour an expression   **41 formal** (1) sane (2) normally shaped

Cleopatra. I have a mind to strike thee ere thou
    speak'st:
  Yet, if thou say Antony lives, is well,
  Or friends with Caesar, or not captive to him,
  I'll set thee in a shower of gold, and hail   *45*
  Rich pearls upon thee.

Messenger.   Madam, he's well.

Cleopatra.   Well said.

Messenger. And friends with Caesar.

Cleopatra.   Th' art an honest man.

Messenger. Caesar and he are greater friends than
    ever.

Cleopatra. Make thee a fortune from me.

Messenger.   But yet, madam—

Cleopatra. I do not like "But yet"; it does allay   *50*
  The good precedence:° fie upon "But yet";
  "But yet" is as a jailer to bring forth
  Some monstrous malefactor. Prithee, friend,
  Pour out the pack of matter to mine ear,
  The good and bad together: he's friends with
    Caesar,   *55*
  In state of health, thou say'st, and thou say'st, free.

Messenger. Free, madam, no: I made no such report;
  He's bound unto Octavia.

Cleopatra.   For what good turn?°

Messenger. For the best turn i' th' bed.

Cleopatra.   I am pale, Charmian.

Messenger. Madam, he's married to Octavia.   *60*

Cleopatra. The most infectious pestilence upon thee!
                        Strikes him down.

50–51 **allay/The good precedence** qualify the good news before
it   58 **For what good turn** (She takes his **bound** in the sense "indebted
to"; he then takes up her **turn**, or "act," in a sexual sense)

Messenger. Good madam, patience.

Cleopatra.   What say you?
                                              Strikes him.
                                                    Hence,
    Horrible villain! Or I'll spurn° thine eyes
    Like balls before me: I'll unhair thy head,
                        She hales him up and down.
    Thou shalt be whipped with wire and stewed in
65   brine,
    Smarting in ling'ring pickle.°

Messenger.   Gracious madam,
    I that do bring the news made not the match.

Cleopatra. Say 'tis not so, a province I will give thee,
    And make thy fortunes proud: the blow thou hadst
70   Shall make thy peace for moving me to rage,
    And I will boot thee° with what gift beside
    Thy modesty° can beg.

Messenger.   He's married, madam.

Cleopatra. Rogue, thou hast lived too long.
                                      Draws a knife.

Messenger.   Nay, then I'll run.
    What mean you, madam? I have made no fault.
                                              Exit.

Charmian. Good madam, keep yourself within your-
75   self,
    The man is innocent.

Cleopatra. Some innocents 'scape not the thunderbolt.
    Melt Egypt into Nile, and kindly creatures
    Turn all to serpents! Call the slave again:
80   Though I am mad, I will not bite him. Call!

Charmian. He is afeard to come.

Cleopatra.   I will not hurt him.
                                      [Exit Charmian.]

---

63 **spurn** kick   66 **pickle** pickling solution (of painful salt or acid)
71 **boot thee** compensate you   72 **modesty** humble rank

These hands do lack nobility, that they strike
A meaner than myself; since I myself
Have given myself the cause.°

Enter [Charmian and] the Messenger again.

                   Come hither, sir.
Though it be honest, it is never good   85
To bring bad news: give to a gracious message
An host of tongues, but let ill tidings tell
Themselves, when they be felt.

Messenger.   I have done my duty.

Cleopatra. Is he married?
I cannot hate thee worser than I do   90
If thou again say "Yes."

Messenger.   He's married, madam.

Cleopatra. The gods confound° thee! Dost thou hold
   there still?

Messenger. Should I lie, madam?

Cleopatra.   O, I would thou didst,
So° half my Egypt were submerged and made
A cistern for scaled snakes! Go get thee hence;   95
Hadst thou Narcissus in thy face,° to me
Thou wouldst appear most ugly. He is married?

Messenger. I crave your Highness' pardon.

Cleopatra.   He is married?

Messenger. Take no offense that I would not offend
   you:°
To punish me for what you make me do   100
Seems much unequal:° he's married to Octavia.

Cleopatra. O, that his fault should make a knave of
   thee,

---

84 **the cause** i.e., by loving Antony   92 **confound** destroy   94 **So** even
if   96 **Hadst . . . face** even if you were as handsome as Narcissus (Greek
youth of great beauty)   99 **Take . . . offend you** do not be angry at me
for hesitating to tell you what I know will anger you   101 **unequal**
unjust

That art not what th' art sure of!° Get thee hence,
The merchandise which thou hast brought from
    Rome
105 Are all too dear for me. Lie they upon thy hand,
And be undone° by 'em!   [*Exit Messenger.*]

Charmian.   Good your Highness, patience.

Cleopatra. In praising Antony I have dispraised
    Caesar.

Charmian. Many times, madam.

Cleopatra.   I am paid for't now.
Lead me from hence;
110 I faint. O, Iras, Charmian! 'Tis no matter.
Go to the fellow, good Alexas; bid him
Report the feature° of Octavia: her years,
Her inclination,° let him not leave out
The color of her hair. Bring me word quickly.
          [*Exit Alexas.*]
115 Let him forever go!—let him not!—Charmian,
Though he be painted one way like a Gorgon,
The other way's a Mars.° [*To Mardian*] Bid you
    Alexas
Bring me word how tall she is. —Pity me, Char-
    mian,
But do not speak to me. Lead me to my chamber.
                              Exeunt.

---

103 **That art ... sure of** who are not really as wicked as the
news you insist on   106 **undone** bankrupted   112 **feature** appearance
(not limited to facial characteristics)   113 **inclination** character
116–17 **Though he ... Mars** (alluding to "perspective" pictures, trick
paintings that showed contrasted figures—here a monstrous woman and
the god of war—when looked at from opposite sides)

[Scene 6. *Near Misenum.*]

*Flourish. Enter Pompey [and Menas] at one door,
with Drum and Trumpet: at another, Caesar, Lepidus, Antony, Enobarbus, Maecenas, Agrippa, with
Soldiers marching.*

Pompey. Your hostages I have, so have you mine;
And we shall talk before we fight.

Caesar.   Most meet°
That first we come to words, and therefore have we
Our written purposes before us sent;
Which, if thou hast considered, let us know   5
If 'twill tie up thy discontented sword
And carry back to Sicily much tall° youth
That else must perish here.

Pompey.   To you all three,
The senators alone of this great world,
Chief factors° for the gods: I do not know   10
Wherefore my father should revengers want,°
Having a son and friends, since Julius Caesar,
Who at Philippi the good Brutus ghosted,°
There saw you laboring for him. What was't
That moved pale Cassius to conspire? And what   15
Made all-honored, honest, Roman Brutus,
With the armed rest, courtiers of beauteous free-
dom,
To drench the Capitol—but that they would
Have one man but a man?° And that is it
Hath made me rig my navy, at whose burden   20

2.6.2 **meet** fit 7 **tall** brave 10 **factors** agents 11 **want** lack
13 **ghosted** haunted 19 **but a man** merely a man (and not a king or
demigod)

The angered ocean foams; with which I meant
To scourge th' ingratitude that despiteful Rome
Cast on my noble father.

Caesar.   Take your time.

Antony. Thou canst not fear° us, Pompey, with thy
   sails.
25   We'll speak with thee° at sea. At land thou know'st
How much we do o'ercount thee.

Pompey.   At land indeed
Thou dost o'ercount° me of my father's house:
But since the cuckoo builds not for himself,
Remain in't as thou mayst.°

Lepidus.   Be pleased to tell us
30   (For this is from the present)° how you take
The offers we have sent you.

Caesar.   There's the point.

Antony. Which do not be entreated to, but weigh
What it is worth embraced.°

Caesar.   And what may follow,
To try a larger fortune.°

Pompey.   You have made me offer
35   Of Sicily, Sardinia; and I must
Rid all the sea of pirates; then, to send
Measures of wheat to Rome; this 'greed upon,
To part with unhacked edges° and bear back
Our targes° undinted.

---

24 **fear** frighten   25 **speak with thee** meet you   27 **o'ercount** cheat
(Antony had used it in the sense of "outnumber," but Pompey punningly
alludes to a house Antony bought from the elder Pompey but did not pay
for)   28–29 **But since ... mayst** but since cuckoos can't build (and
therefore have to steal other birds' nests), keep it if you can hold on to it.
(Pompey includes in this sentence a jeering suggestion that Antony is a
cuckold, a lover of a faithless woman)   30 **from the present** beside the
point   33 **embraced** if accepted   33–34 **And what ... fortune** (1) and
what the result may be, if you try to do better for yourself (i.e., risk war)
(2) and the even greater things you may gain, if you join us and our
affairs prosper   38 **edges** swords   39 **targes** shields

Omnes.°   That's our offer.

Pompey.   Know then
  I came before you here a man prepared   40
  To take this offer. But Mark Antony
  Put me to some impatience. Though I lose
  The praise of it by telling, you must know,
  When Caesar and your brother were at blows,
  Your mother came to Sicily and did find   45
  Her welcome friendly.

Antony.   I have heard it, Pompey,
  And am well studied for a liberal thanks,
  Which I do owe you.°

Pompey.   Let me have your hand:
  I did not think, sir, to have met you here.

Antony. The beds i' th' East are soft; and thanks to
      you,   50
  That called me timelier° than my purpose hither;
  For I have gained by't.

Caesar.   Since I saw you last
  There's a change upon you.

Pompey.   Well, I know not
  What counts° harsh fortune casts° upon my face,
  But in my bosom shall she never come   55
  To make my heart her vassal.

Lepidus.   Well met here.

Pompey. I hope so, Lepidus. Thus we are agreed.
  I crave our composition° may be written,
  And sealed between us.

Caesar.   That's the next to do.

39 **Omnes** i.e., Caesar, Antony, Lepidus   47–48 **am well . . . you** I am
ready indeed to give you the free and full thanks that I owe you
51 **timelier** earlier   54 **counts** reckonings   54 **casts** (1) throws (2)
sums up (the lines and wrinkles resulting from a hard life are compared to
a bill of costs written out by a cruelly precise Fortune)   58 **composition**
agreement

60 *Pompey.* We'll feast each other ere we part, and let's
　　Draw lots who shall begin.

Antony.　　　　　　　　　　That will I, Pompey.

Pompey. No, Antony, take the lot:
　　But, first or last, your fine Egyptian cookery
　　Shall have the fame. I have heard that Julius Caesar
　　Grew fat with feasting there.

65 *Antony.*　　　　　　　　　You have heard much.

Pompey. I have fair meanings, sir.

Antony.　　　　　　　　And fair words to them.

Pompey. Then so much have I heard:
　　And I have heard Apollodorus carried—

Enobarbus. No more of that: he did so.

Pompey.　　　　　　　　　What, I pray you?

70 *Enobarbus.* A certain queen to Caesar in a mattress.

Pompey. I know thee now; how far'st thou, soldier?

Enobarbus.　　　　　　　　　　　Well;
　　And well am like to do, for I perceive
　　Four feasts are toward.°

Pompey.　　　　　　Let me shake thy hand;
　　I never hated thee: I have seen thee fight
　　When I have envied thy behavior.

75 *Enobarbus.*　　　　　　　　　　Sir,
　　I never loved you much; but I ha' praised ye
　　When you have well deserved ten times as much
　　As I have said you did.

Pompey.　　　　　　Enjoy thy plainness,
　　It nothing ill becomes thee.°
80 　　Aboard my galley I invite you all:
　　Will you lead, lords?

All.　　　　　　　Show's the way, sir.

73 **toward** in the offing (accented "tòward")　79 **It . . . thee** it suits you
very well

Pompey.   Come.
              Exeunt. Manet° Enobarbus and Menas

Menas. [*Aside*] Thy father, Pompey, would ne'er have
    made this treaty. —You and I have known,° sir.

Enobarbus. At sea, I think.

Menas. We have, sir.   85

Enobarbus. You have done well by water.

Menas. And you by land.

Enobarbus. I will praise any man that will praise me;
    though it cannot be denied what I have done by
    land.   90

Menas. Nor what I have done by water.

Enobarbus. Yes, something you can deny for your
    own safety: you have been a great thief by sea.

Menas. And you by land.

Enobarbus. There I deny my land service.° But give   95
    me your hand, Menas: if our eyes had authority,°
    here they might take two thieves kissing.°

Menas. All men's faces are true,° whatsome'er their
    hands are.

Enobarbus. But there is never a fair woman has a true 100
    face.

Menas. No slander; they steal hearts.

Enobarbus. We came hither to fight with you.

Menas. For my part, I am sorry it is turned to a drink-
    ing. Pompey doth this day laugh away his fortune.   105

Enobarbus. If he do, sure he cannot weep't back again.

81 s.d. **Manet** (Latin for "remains"; the plural is properly *manent*, but
the singular is often used for the plural, just as "exit" is often used for
"exeunt")   83 **known** met   95 **deny my land service** (a quibble: "I
claim exemption from military service" and "I deny that I have been a
thief")   96 **authority** authority to arrest   97 **two thieves kissing** (1)
two crooks fraternizing (2) two thieving hands clasping   98 **true** (1)
honest (2) natural, without make-up

Menas. Y' have said, sir. We looked not for Mark
Antony here. Pray you, is he married to Cleopatra?

Enobarbus. Caesar's sister is called Octavia.

110 *Menas.* True, sir, she was the wife of Caius Marcellus.

Enobarbus. But she is now the wife of Marcus Antonius.

Menas. Pray ye,° sir?

Enobarbus. 'Tis true.

115 *Menas.* Then is Caesar and he forever knit together.

Enobarbus. If I were bound to divine of this unity, I
would not prophesy so.

Menas. I think the policy° of that purpose made more
in the marriage than the love of the parties.

120 *Enobarbus.* I think so too. But you shall find the band
that seems to tie their friendship together will be
the very strangler of their amity: Octavia is of a
holy, cold, and still conversation.°

Menas. Who would not have his wife so?

125 *Enobarbus.* Not he that himself is not so; which is
Mark Antony. He will to his Egyptian dish again:
then shall the sighs of Octavia blow the fire up in
Caesar, and, as I said before, that which is the
strength of their amity shall prove the immediate
130 author of their variance. Antony will use his affection where it is. He married but his occasion° here.

Menas. And thus it may be. Come, sir, will you
aboard? I have a health for you.

Enobarbus. I shall take it, sir: we have used our
135 throats in Egypt.

Menas. Come, let's away.   *Exeunt.*

---

113 **Pray ye** pardon me (incredulous)   118 **policy** political expediency
123 **still conversation** quiet manner   131 **occasion** convenience

[Scene 7. *On board Pompey's galley, off Misenum.*]

Music plays. Enter two or three Servants,
with a banquet.

First Servant. Here they'll be, man. Some o' their
plants° are ill-rooted already; the least wind i' th'
world will blow them down.

Second Servant. Lepidus is high-colored.

First Servant. They have made him drink alms drink.°   5

Second Servant. As they pinch one another by the disposition, he cries out "No more";° reconciles them
to his entreaty, and himself to th' drink.

First Servant. But it raises the greater war between
him and his discretion.   10

Second Servant. Why, this it is to have a name in great
men's fellowship. I had as lief have a reed that will
do me no service, as a partisan° I could not heave.

First Servant. To be called into a huge sphere,° and
not to be seen to move° in't, are the holes where   15
eyes should be, which pitifully disaster° the cheeks.

A sennet° sounded. Enter Caesar, Antony, Pom-
pey, Lepidus, Agrippa, Maecenas, Enobarbus,
Menas, with other Captains.

2.7.2 **plants** (pun on foot or sole of foot)   5 **alms drink** (1) remains of
liquor usually saved for alms people (2) drinking done kindly, i.e., toasts
given to smooth over quarrels   7 **No more** (1) no more quarreling (2) no
more to drink   13 **partisan** great long-handled spear   14 **sphere** (1)
area of influence (2) revolving circle holding a star or planet, in the old
astronomy   15 **move** (1) be active, influential (2) circle, like a planet
16 **disaster** ruin (with a suggestion of a star's malignant influence)
16 s.d. **sennet** trumpet call signaling the entrance of a great man

Antony. Thus do they, sir: they take° the flow o' th'
    Nile
    By certain scales i'° th' pyramid. They know
    By th' height, the lowness, or the mean, if dearth
20   Or foison° follow. The higher Nilus swells,
    The more it promises; as it ebbs, the seedsman
    Upon the slime and ooze scatters his grain,
    And shortly comes to harvest.

Lepidus. Y' have strange serpents there.

25 *Antony.* Ay, Lepidus.

Lepidus. Your° serpent of Egypt is bred now of your
    mud by the operation of your sun: so is your croco-
    dile.

Antony. They are so.

30 *Pompey.* Sit—and some wine! A health to Lepidus!

Lepidus. I am not so well as I should be, but I'll ne'er
    out.°

Enobarbus. Not till you have slept; I fear me you'll be
    in° till then.

35 *Lepidus.* Nay, certainly, I have heard the Ptolemies'
    pyramises° are very goodly things; without contra-
    diction I have heard that.

Menas. [*Aside to Pompey*] Pompey, a word.

Pompey. [*Aside to Menas*] Say in mine ear: what is't?

Menas. [*Aside to Pompey*] Forsake thy seat, I do be-
    seech thee, captain,
    And hear me speak a word.

---

17 **take** measure 18 **scales i'** degree marks on 19–20 **dearth/Or
foison** famine or plenty 26 **Your** (a colloquialism suggesting casual
knowledgeableness) 31–32 **I'll ne'er out** I won't give in 34 **in** (1) in
the game (2) in liquor 36 **pyramises** (a false plural made up from the
Latin singular; Lepidus is pretentious and drunk)

Pompey.   [*Aside to Menas*] Forbear me till anon.°   40
                    [*Menas*] *whispers in's ear.*
  This wine for Lepidus!

Lepidus. What manner o' thing is your crocodile?

Antony. It is shaped, sir, like itself, and it is as broad
  as it hath breadth; it is just so high as it is, and
  moves with it° own organs. It lives by that which   45
  nourisheth it, and the elements once out of it, it
  transmigrates.

Lepidus. What color is it of?

Antony. Of it own color too.

Lepidus. 'Tis a strange serpent.   50

Antony. 'Tis so; and the tears of it are wet.

Caesar. Will this description satisfy him?

Antony. With the health that Pompey gives him; else
  he is a very epicure.

Pompey. [*Aside to Menas*] Go hang, sir, hang! Tell
  me of that? Away!   55
  Do as I bid you. —Where's this cup I called for?

Menas. [*Aside to Pompey*] If for the sake of merit
  thou wilt hear me,
  Rise from thy stool.

Pompey. [*Aside to Menas*] I think th' art mad. The
  matter?   [*Rises and walks aside.*]

Menas. I have ever held my cap off to° thy fortunes.

Pompey. Thou hast served me with much faith. What's
  else to say?   60
  Be jolly, lords.

Antony.   These quicksands, Lepidus,
  Keep off them, for you sink.

---

40 **Forbear me till anon** leave me alone for a minute   45 **it** its
59 **held my cap off to** treated respectfully

Menas. Wilt thou be lord of all the world?

Pompey.   What say'st thou?

Menas. Wilt thou be lord of the whole world? That's
     twice.

Pompey. How should that be?

65   *Menas.*   But entertain it,°
     And though thou think me poor, I am the man
     Will give thee all the world.

Pompey.   Hast thou drunk well?

Menas. No, Pompey, I have kept me from the cup.
     Thou art, if thou dar'st be, the earthly Jove:
70   Whate'er the ocean pales,° or sky inclips,°
     Is thine, if thou wilt ha't.

Pompey.   Show me which way.

Menas. These three world-sharers, these competitors,°
     Are in thy vessel. Let me cut the cable;
     And when we are put off, fall to their throats.
     All there is thine.

75   *Pompey.*   Ah, this thou shouldst have done,
     And not have spoke on't. In me 'tis villainy,
     In thee 't had been good service. Thou must know,
     'Tis not my profit that does lead mine honor;
     Mine honor, it. Repent that e'er thy tongue
80   Hath so betrayed thine act. Being done unknown,
     I should have found it afterwards well done,
     But must condemn it now. Desist, and drink.

Menas. [*Aside*] For this,
     I'll never follow thy palled° fortunes more.
85   Who seeks, and will not take when once 'tis offered,
     Shall never find it more.

Pompey.   This health to Lepidus!

65 **But entertain it** only accept it   70 **pales** fences in   70 **inclips** embraces   72 **competitors** partners   84 **palled** decayed

Antony. Bear him ashore. I'll pledge it for him,
    Pompey.

Enobarbus. Here's to thee, Menas!

Menas.   Enobarbus, welcome.

Pompey. Fill till the cup be hid.

Enobarbus. There's a strong fellow, Menas.   90
    [*Points to the Servant who carries off Lepidus.*]

Menas. Why?

Enobarbus. 'A° bears the third part of the world, man;
    seest not?

Menas. The third part then is drunk. Would it were all,
    That it might go on wheels!°   95

Enobarbus. Drink thou: increase the reels.°

Menas. Come.

Pompey. This is not yet an Alexandrian feast.

Antony. It ripens towards it. Strike the vessels,° ho!
    Here's to Caesar!

Caesar.   I could well forbear't.   100
    It's monstrous labor when I wash my brain
    And it grows fouler.

Antony.   Be a child o' th' time.

Caesar. Possess it, I'll make answer;°
    But I had rather fast from all, four days,
    Than drink so much in one.

Enobarbus.   Ha, my brave emperor!   105
    Shall we dance now the Egyptian bacchanals°
    And celebrate our drink?

---

92 **'A** he   95 **go on wheels** (1) go easily (2) spin wildly   96 **reels** (1)
revels (2) staggering movements   99 **Strike the vessels** broach the
casks   103 **Possess . . . answer** master the time (rather than be mastered
by it) is my answer   106 **bacchanals** riotous salute to Bacchus, god of
wine

Pompey.   Let's ha't, good soldier.

Antony. Come, let's all take hands
   Till that the conquering wine hath steeped our sense
   In soft and delicate Lethe.°

110 *Enobarbus.*   All take hands:
   Make battery to our ears with the loud music;
   The while I'll place you; then the boy shall sing.
   The holding° every man shall bear as loud
   As his strong sides can volley.

   Music plays. Enobarbus places them hand in hand.

        The Song

115   Come, thou monarch of the vine,
      Plumpy Bacchus with pink eyne!°
      In thy fats° our cares be drowned,
      With thy grapes our hairs be crowned.
        Cup us till the world go round,
120   Cup us till the world go round!

Caesar. What would you more? Pompey, good night.
   Good brother,
   Let me request you off:° our graver business
   Frowns at this levity. Gentle lords, let's part;
   You see we have burnt our cheeks: strong Enobarb
125 Is weaker than the wine, and mine own tongue
   Splits what it speaks: the wild disguise° hath almost
   Anticked° us all. What needs more words? Good
   night.
   Good Antony, your hand.

Pompey.   I'll try you° on the shore.

Antony. And shall, sir. Give's your hand.

110 **Lethe** forgetfulness   113 **holding** refrain   116 **pink eyne** half-
closed eyes   117 **fats** vats   122 **request you off** beg you leave the ship
with me   126 **disguise** drunken revelry   127 **Anticked** made fools of
128 **try you** test your power (to hold liquor)

Pompey.   O, Antony,
  You have my father's house. But what, we are
    friends!   *130*
  Come down into the boat.
            [*Exeunt all but Enobarbus and Menas.*]

Enobarbus. [*To Menas*]   Take heed you fall not.

Menas. I'll not on shore; no, to my cabin!
  These drums! These trumpets, flutes! What!
  Let Neptune hear we bid a loud farewell
  To these great fellows. Sound and be hanged, sound
    out!   *Sound a flourish, with drums.* *135*

Enobarbus. Hoo, says 'a. There's my cap.
              [*Throws his cap in the air.*]

Menas. Hoa! Noble captain, come.   *Exeunt.*

[ACT 3

Scene 1. *A plain in Syria.*]

*Enter Ventidius as it were in triumph, the dead
body of Pacorus borne before him; [with Silius
and other Romans].*

Ventidius. Now, darting° Parthia, art thou struck; and
    now
   Pleased fortune does of Marcus Crassus'° death
   Make me revenger. Bear the King's son's body
   Before our army. Thy Pacorus, Orodes,
   Pays this for Marcus Crassus.

5 *Silius.*   Noble Ventidius,
   Whilst yet with Parthian blood thy sword is warm,
   The fugitive Parthians follow. Spur through Media,
   Mesopotamia, and the shelters whither
   The routed fly. So thy grand captain, Antony,
10   Shall set thee on triumphant chariots, and
   Put garlands on thy head.

3.1.1 **darting** (the Parthians' method of attack was to fling darts and then
retreat swiftly, shooting arrows) 2 **Marcus Crassus** (treacherously
killed by Orodes, King of Parthia and father of Pacorus)

Ventidius.   O Silius, Silius,
   I have done enough: a lower place,° note well,
   May make too great an act. For learn this, Silius,
   Better to leave undone, than by our deed
   Acquire too high a fame when him we serve's away.   15
   Caesar and Antony have ever won
   More in their officer than person. Sossius,
   One of my place° in Syria, his° lieutenant,
   For quick accumulation of renown,
   Which he achieved by th' minute,° lost his favor.   20
   Who does i' th' wars more than his captain can
   Becomes his captain's captain; and ambition
   (The soldier's virtue) rather makes choice of loss
   Than gain which darkens him.
   I could do more to do Antonius good,   25
   But 'twould offend him, and in his offense
   Should my performance perish.°

Silius.   Thou hast, Ventidius, that
   Without the which a soldier and his sword
   Grants scarce distinction.° Thou wilt write to
      Antony?

Ventidius. I'll humbly signify what in his name,   30
   That magical word of war, we have effected;
   How, with his banners and his well-paid ranks,
   The ne'er-yet-beaten horse of Parthia
   We have jaded° out o' th' field.

Silius.   Where is he now?

Ventidius. He purposeth to Athens; whither, with what
      haste   35
   The weight we must convey with's will permit,
   We shall appear before him. —On, there; pass along.
                              Exeunt.

---

12 **lower place** subordinate   18 **place** rank   18 **his** i.e., Antony's
20 **by th' minute** every minute, incessantly   27 **perish** i.e., lose its
value to me   27–29 **that … distinction** that quality (i.e., discretion)
without which it is hard to see any difference between a soldier and his
sword   34 **jaded** driven like nags

[Scene 2. *Rome. Caesar's house.*]

Enter Agrippa at one door, Enobarbus at another.

Agrippa. What, are the brothers parted?°

Enobarbus. They have dispatched with Pompey; he is
    gone;
    The other three are sealing.° Octavia weeps
    To part from Rome; Caesar is sad, and Lepidus
5   Since Pompey's feast, as Menas says, is troubled
    With the green-sickness.°

Agrippa.   'Tis a noble Lepidus.

Enobarbus. A very fine one. O, how he loves Caesar!

Agrippa. Nay, but how dearly he adores Mark Antony!

Enobarbus. Caesar? Why, he's the Jupiter of men.

10 *Agrippa.* What's Antony? The god of Jupiter.

Enobarbus. Spake you of Caesar? How! The non-
    pareil!°

Agrippa. O Antony! O thou Arabian bird!°

Enobarbus. Would you praise Caesar, say "Caesar":
    go no further.

Agrippa. Indeed, he plied them both with excellent
    praises.

Enobarbus. But he loves Caesar best, yet he loves
15   Antony:

3.2.1 **parted** departed 3 **sealing** making the last arrangements
6 **green-sickness** anemia supposed to affect lovesick girls (Lepidus'
hangover is attributed to his love of Antony and Octavius) 11 **nonpareil**
unequaled thing 12 **Arabian bird** phoenix (unique and immortal)

Hoo! Hearts, tongues, figures, scribes, bards, poets,
  cannot
Think, speak, cast,° write, sing, number—hoo!—
His love to Antony. But as for Caesar,
Kneel down, kneel down, and wonder.

Agrippa.   Both he loves.

Enobarbus. They are his shards,° and he their beetle.
  [*Trumpet within.*] So—   20
  This is to horse. Adieu, noble Agrippa.

Agrippa. Good fortune, worthy soldier, and farewell!

  Enter Caesar, Antony, Lepidus, and Octavia.

Antony. No further, sir.

Caesar. You take from me a great part of myself;
  Use me well in't. Sister, prove such a wife   25
  As my thoughts make thee, and as my farthest band
  Shall pass on thy approof.° Most noble Antony,
  Let not the piece° of virtue which is set
  Betwixt us as the cement° of our love
  To keep it builded, be the ram to batter   30
  The fortress of it: for better might we
  Have loved without this mean,° if on both parts
  This be not cherished.

Antony.   Make me not offended
  In° your distrust.

Caesar.   I have said.

Antony.   You shall not find,
  Though you be therein curious,° the least cause   35
  For what you seem to fear. So the gods keep you
  And make the hearts of Romans serve your ends!
  We will here part.

Caesar. Farewell, my dearest sister, fare thee well.

17 **cast** count 20 **shards** wings 26–27 **As my thoughts … approof**
as I believe you to be, and such as I would give my utmost bond that
you will triumphantly prove to be 28 **piece** masterpiece 29 **cement**
(accented on first syllable) 32 **mean** intermediary 34 **In** by 35 **curious** overscrupulous

40   The elements be kind to thee, and make
      Thy spirits all of comfort. Fare thee well.

Octavia. My noble brother!

Antony. The April's in her eyes: it is love's spring,
      And these the showers to bring it on. Be cheerful.

Octavia. Sir, look well to my husband's house; and—

45 *Caesar.*   What,
      Octavia?

Octavia.   I'll tell you in your ear.

Antony. Her tongue will not obey her heart, nor can
      Her heart inform her tongue; the swan's-down
          feather
      That stands upon the swell at the full of tide,
50   And neither way inclines.°

Enobarbus. [*Aside to Agrippa*] Will Caesar weep?

Agrippa. [*Aside to Enobarbus*] He has a cloud in's
      face.

Enobarbus. [*Aside to Agrippa*] He were the worse for
      that, were he a horse;°
      So is he, being a man.

Agrippa. [*Aside to Enobarbus*] Why, Enobarbus,
      When Antony found Julius Caesar dead,
55   He cried almost to roaring; and he wept
      When at Philippi he found Brutus slain.

Enobarbus. [*Aside to Agrippa*] That year indeed he
      was troubled with a rheum.°
      What willingly he did confound° he wailed,
      Believe't, till I wept too.

Caesar.   No, sweet Octavia,

48–50 **the swan's . . . inclines** (pressure of feeling urges Octavia to
speak but prevents her from finding the words; she hesitates—like a
feather held immobile by cross-currents at the turn of the tide—between
husband and brother, love and sorrow, speech and silence)   52 **horse** (a
horse with a dark face, or without a white star on its face, was less prized)
57 **rheum** watering at the eyes   58 **confound** destroy

You shall hear from me still: the time shall not   60
Outgo my thinking on you.

Antony.   Come, sir, come,
  I'll wrestle with you in my strength of love:
  Look, here I have you; thus I let you go,
  And give you to the gods.

Caesar.   Adieu; be happy!

Lepidus. Let all the number of the stars give light   65
  To thy fair way!

Caesar.   Farewell, farewell! *Kisses Octavia.*

Antony.   Farewell!
                    Trumpets sound. Exeunt.

[Scene 3. *Alexandria. Cleopatra's palace.*]

Enter Cleopatra, Charmian, Iras, and Alexas.

Cleopatra. Where is the fellow?

Alexas.   Half afeard to come.

Cleopatra. Go to, go to.
          Enter the Messenger as before.°
                    Come hither, sir.

Alexas.   Good Majesty,
  Herod of Jewry° dare not look upon you
  But when you are well pleased.

Cleopatra.   That Herod's head
  I'll have: but how, when Antony is gone   5
  Through whom I might command it? Come thou
    near.

3.3.2 s.d. **as before** i.e., nervously, as he left her   3 **Herod of Jewry** i.e.,
even the fiercest of tyrants

Messenger. Most gracious Majesty!

Cleopatra. Didst thou behold Octavia?

Messenger. Ay, dread queen.

10 *Cleopatra.* Where?

Messenger. Madam, in Rome.
I looked her in the face, and saw her led
Between her brother and Mark Antony.

Cleopatra. Is she as tall as me?

Messenger.   She is not, madam.

Cleopatra. Didst hear her speak? Is she shrill-tongued
15   or low?

Messenger. Madam, I heard her speak; she is low-
     voiced.

Cleopatra. That's not so good.° He cannot like her
     long.

Charmian. Like her? O Isis! 'Tis impossible.

Cleopatra. I think so, Charmian. Dull of tongue, and
     dwarfish.
20   What majesty is in her gait? Remember,
     If e'er thou look'st on majesty.

Messenger.   She creeps:
     Her motion and her station are as one.°
     She shows a body rather than a life,
     A statue than a breather.

Cleopatra.   Is this certain?

Messenger. Or I have no observance.

25 *Charmian.*   Three in Egypt
     Cannot make better note.

Cleopatra.   He's very knowing,

---

17 **That's not so good** (1) that's a nuisance. Nevertheless . . . (2) that's a
bad thing to be   22 **Her motion . . . one** moving and standing still are
the same thing with her

I do perceive't. There's nothing in her yet.
The fellow has good judgment.

Charmian.   Excellent.

Cleopatra. Guess at her years, I prithee.

Messenger.   Madam,
She was a widow—

Cleopatra.   Widow? Charmian, hark.   30

Messenger. And I do think she's thirty.°

Cleopatra. Bear'st thou her face in mind? Is't long or
round?

Messenger. Round, even to faultiness.

Cleopatra. For the most part, too, they are foolish that
are so.
Her hair, what color?   35

Messenger. Brown, madam; and her forehead
As low as she would wish it.°

Cleopatra.   There's gold for thee.
Thou must not take my former sharpness ill;
I will employ thee back again: I find thee
Most fit for business. Go, make thee ready;   40
Our letters are prepared.   [*Exit Messenger.*]

Charmian.   A proper° man.

Cleopatra. Indeed he is so: I repent me much
That so I harried him. Why, methinks, by him,
This creature 's no such thing.°

Charmian.   Nothing, madam.

Cleopatra. The man hath seen some majesty, and
should know.   45

Charmian. Hath he seen majesty? Isis else defend,°
And serving you so long!

31 **thirty** (Cleopatra, being thirty-eight, lets this pass)   37 **As low . . . it**
(colloquial phrase: low enough, and I hope she's pleased with it)
41 **proper** excellent   44 **no such thing** nothing very much   46 **Isis else
defend** Isis forbid

Cleopatra. I have one thing more to ask him yet, good
    Charmian;
    But 'tis no matter, thou shalt bring him to me
50   Where I will write. All may be well enough.

Charmian. I warrant you, madam.   *Exeunt.*

[Scene 4. *Athens. Antony's house.*]

Enter Antony and Octavia.

Antony. Nay, nay, Octavia, not only that,
    That were excusable, that and thousands more
    Of semblable import°—but he hath waged
    New wars 'gainst Pompey; made his will, and read it
5   To public ear;°
    Spoke scantly of me: when perforce he could not
    But pay me terms of honor, cold and sickly
    He vented them, most narrow measure° lent me;
    When the best hint was given him, he not took't,
    Or did it from his teeth.°

10 *Octavia.*   O, my good lord,
    Believe not all; or, if you must believe,
    Stomach° not all. A more unhappy lady,
    If this division chance, ne'er stood between,
    Praying for both parts.
15   The good gods will mock me presently°
    When I shall pray "O, bless my lord and husband!"—
    Undo that prayer by crying out as loud
    "O, bless my brother!" Husband win, win brother,
    Prays, and destroys the prayer; no midway
    'Twixt these extremes at all.

3.4.3 **semblable import** similar significance 4–5 **made ... ear** i.e.,
like Julius Caesar, made a will benefiting the people and so worked up
popular support 8 **narrow measure** little credit 10 **from his teeth**
grudgingly 12 **Stomach** resent 15 **presently** immediately

Antony.　　　　　　　　Gentle Octavia,　　　20
Let your best love draw to that point which seeks
Best to preserve it. If I lose mine honor,
I lose myself: better I were not yours
Than yours so branchless.° But, as you requested,
Yourself shall go between's: the meantime, lady,　　25
I'll raise the preparation of a war
Shall stain° your brother. Make your soonest haste;
So your desires are yours.

Octavia.　　　　　　　Thanks to my lord.
The Jove of power make me, most weak, most weak,
Your reconciler! Wars 'twixt you twain would be　　30
As if the world should cleave, and that slain men
Should solder up the rift.

Antony. When it appears to you where this begins,
Turn your displeasure that way, for our faults
Can never be so equal that your love　　　35
Can equally move with them. Provide your going;
Choose your own company, and command what cost
Your heart has mind to.　　　　　　　*Exeunt.*

[Scene 5. *Athens. Antony's house.*]

Enter Enobarbus and Eros.

Enobarbus. How now, friend Eros?

Eros. There's strange news come, sir.

Enobarbus. What, man?

Eros. Caesar and Lepidus have made wars upon
　　Pompey.　　　　　　　　　　　　　　5

Enobarbus. This is old. What is the success?°

24 **branchless** mutilated　27 **stain** eclipse (the reputation of)　3.5.6
success sequel

Eros. Caesar, having made use of him in the wars
'gainst Pompey, presently denied him rivality,°
would not let him partake in the glory of the action;
10   and not resting here, accuses him of letters he had
formerly wrote to Pompey; upon his own appeal,°
seizes him; so the poor third is up,° till death enlarge
his confine.

Enobarbus. Then, world, thou hast a pair of chaps,°
no more;
15   And throw between them all the food thou hast,
They'll grind the one the other.° Where's Antony?

Eros. He's walking in the garden—thus, and spurns
The rush that lies before him; cries "Fool Lepidus!"
And threats the throat of that his officer
That murd'red Pompey.°

20   *Enobarbus.*   Our great navy's rigged.

Eros. For Italy and Caesar. More, Domitius:
My lord desires you presently. My news
I might have told hereafter.

Enobarbus.   'Twill be naught;
But let it be. Bring me to Antony.

Eros.   Come, sir.   *Exeunt.*

---

8 **rivality** partnership   11 **upon his own appeal** on his (Caesar's) own
accusation   12 **up** shut up, imprisoned   14 **chaps** jaws   15–16 **And
throw . . . other** and feed them with all the victims in the world, they
(Caesar and Antony) will nevertheless meet, and one consume the
other   20 **Pompey** (Pompey has by now been murdered, according to
Plutarch by Antony's command; Pompey would have proved useful to
Antony in the coming war)

[Scene 6. *Rome. Caesar's house.*]

Enter Agrippa, Maecenas, and Caesar.

Caesar. Contemning° Rome, he has done all this and
    more
  In Alexandria. Here's the manner of't:
  I' th' marketplace on a tribunal silvered,
  Cleopatra and himself in chairs of gold
  Were publicly enthroned; at the feet sat   5
  Caesarion, whom they call my father's° son,
  And all the unlawful issue that their lust
  Since then hath made between them. Unto her
  He gave the stablishment° of Egypt; made her
  Of lower Syria, Cyprus, Lydia,   10
  Absolute queen.

Maecenas.   This in the public eye?

Caesar. I' th' common showplace, where they exercise.
  His sons he there proclaimed the kings of kings:
  Great Media, Parthia, and Armenia
  He gave to Alexander; to Ptolemy he assigned   15
  Syria, Cilicia, and Phoenicia. She
  In th' habiliments of the goddess Isis
  That day appeared, and oft before gave audience,
  As 'tis reported, so.

Maecenas.   Let Rome be thus informed.

Agrippa. Who, queasy° with his insolence already,   20
  Will their good thoughts call from him.

3.6.1 **Contemning** despising   6 **my father** (Octavius had been adopted
by Julius Caesar)   9 **stablishment** possession   20 **queasy** disgusted

Caesar. The people knows it, and have now received
    His accusations.

Agrippa.   Who does he accuse?

Caesar. Caesar: and that, having in Sicily
25   Sextus Pompeius spoiled,° we had not rated° him
    His part o' th' isle. Then does he say he lent me
    Some shipping, unrestored. Lastly, he frets
    That Lepidus of the triumvirate
    Should be deposed; and, being, that we detain
    All his revenue.°

30 *Agrippa.*   Sir, this should be answered.

Caesar. 'Tis done already, and the messenger gone.
    I have told him Lepidus was grown too cruel,
    That he his high authority abused
    And did deserve his change; for what I have
        conquered,
35   I grant him part; but then in his Armenia,
    And other of his conquered kingdoms, I
    Demand the like.

Maecenas.   He'll never yield to that.

Caesar. Nor must not then be yielded to in this.

      Enter Octavia with her Train.

Octavia. Hail, Caesar, and my lord, hail, most dear
    Caesar!

40 *Caesar.* That ever I should call thee castaway!

Octavia. You have not called me so, nor have you
    cause.

Caesar. Why have you stol'n upon us thus? You come
    not
    Like Caesar's sister. The wife of Antony
    Should have an army for an usher, and
45   The neighs of horse to tell of her approach

---

25 **spoiled** despoiled   25 **rated** allotted   30 **revenue** (accented on
second syllable)

Long ere she did appear. The trees by th' way
Should have borne men, and expectation fainted,
Longing for what it had not. Nay, the dust
Should have ascended to the roof of heaven,
Raised by your populous troops. But you are come   50
A market maid to Rome, and have prevented
The ostentation° of our love; which, left unshown,
Is often left unloved.° We should have met you
By sea and land, supplying every stage
With an augmented greeting.

Octavia.   Good my lord,   55
To come thus was I not constrained, but did it
On my free will. My lord, Mark Antony,
Hearing that you prepared for war, acquainted
My grievèd ear withal; whereon I begged
His pardon for return.

Caesar.   Which soon he granted,   60
Being an abstract° 'tween his lust and him.

Octavia. Do not say so, my lord.

Caesar.   I have eyes upon him,
And his affairs come to me on the wind.
Where is he now?

Octavia.   My lord, in Athens.

Caesar. No, my most wrongèd sister, Cleopatra   65
Hath nodded him to her. He hath given his empire
Up to a whore, who now° are levying
The kings o' th' earth for war. He hath assembled
Bocchus, the King of Libya; Archelaus,
Of Cappadocia; Philadelphos, King   70
Of Paphlagonia; the Thracian king, Adallas;
King Mauchus of Arabia; King of Pont;
Herod of Jewry; Mithridates, King
Of Comagene; Polemon and Amyntas,

---

52 **ostentation** public display   53 **left unloved** (1) unrequited (2)
thought not to exist   61 **abstract** (1) immaterial, merely notional thing
(2) short cut (3) symbol (of what prevented him from indulging his lust)
67 **who now** and they now

75   The Kings of Mede and Lycaonia;
        With a more larger list of scepters.

        Octavia.   Ay me most wretched,
        That have my heart parted betwixt two friends
        That does afflict each other!

        Caesar.   Welcome hither.
        Your letters did withhold our breaking forth,
80   Till we perceived both how you were wrong led
        And we in negligent danger.° Cheer your heart:
        Be you not troubled with the time, which drives
        O'er your content these strong necessities;
        But let determined things to destiny
85   Hold unbewailed their way. Welcome to Rome,
        Nothing more dear to me. You are abused°
        Beyond the mark° of thought: and the high gods,
        To do you justice, makes his ministers
        Of us° and those that love you. Best of comfort,
        And ever welcome to us.

90 *Agrippa.*   Welcome, lady.

    Maecenas. Welcome, dear madam.
        Each heart in Rome does love and pity you.
        Only th' adulterous Antony, most large°
        In his abominations, turns you off
95   And gives his potent regiment to a trull°
        That noises it° against us.

        Octavia.   Is it so, sir?

    Caesar. Most certain. Sister, welcome. Pray you
        Be ever known to patience. My dear'st sister!
                                            Exeunt.

---

81 **in negligent danger** endangered by doing nothing   86 **abused**
deceived   87 **mark** reach   88–89 **makes . . . us** make us their agents to
justice   93 **large** loose, licentious   95 **potent regiment to a trull** powerful authority to a prostitute   96 **noises it** is clamorous

[Scene 7. *Near Actium. Antony's camp.*]

Enter Cleopatra and Enobarbus.

Cleopatra. I will be even with thee, doubt it not.

Enobarbus. But why, why, why?

Cleopatra. Thou hast forspoke° my being in these wars,
And say'st it is not fit.

Enobarbus.   Well, is it, is it?

Cleopatra. Is't not denounced against us?° Why should not we   5
Be there in person?

Enobarbus.   [*Aside*] Well, I could reply:
If we should serve with horse and mares together,
The horse were merely° lost; the mares would bear
A soldier and his horse.

Cleopatra.   What is't you say?

Enobarbus. Your presence needs must puzzle° Antony;   10
Take from his heart, take from his brain, from's time,
What should not then be spared. He is already
Traduced for levity; and 'tis said in Rome
That Photinus an eunuch and your maids
Manage this war.

Cleopatra.   Sink Rome, and their tongues rot   15
That speak against us! A charge we bear i' th' war,

3.7.3 **forspoke** spoken against   5 **denounced against us** (Caesar had declared, or denounced—the technical term—war on Cleopatra personally)   8 **merely** utterly   10 **puzzle** bewilder, bring to a standstill

And as the president of my kingdom will
Appear there for a man. Speak not against it,
I will not stay behind.

Enter Antony and Canidius.

Enobarbus.   Nay, I have done.
Here comes the Emperor.

20   *Antony.*   Is it not strange, Canidius,
That from Tarentum and Brundusium
He could so quickly cut the Ionian sea
And take in° Toryne?—You have heard on't,
    sweet?

Cleopatra. Celerity is never more admired
Than by the negligent.

25   *Antony.*   A good rebuke,
Which might have well becomed the best of men
To taunt at slackness. Canidius, we
Will fight with him by sea.

Cleopatra.   By sea; what else?

Canidius. Why will my lord do so?

Antony.   For that° he dares us to't.

30   *Enobarbus.* So hath my lord dared him to single fight.

Canidius. Ay, and to wage this battle at Pharsalia,
Where Caesar fought with Pompey: but these offers,
Which serve not for his vantage, he shakes off;
And so should you.

Enobarbus.   Your ships are not well manned;
35   Your mariners are muleters,° reapers, people
Ingrossed by swift impress.° In Caesar's fleet
Are those that often have 'gainst Pompey fought;
Their ships are yare,° yours, heavy: no disgrace
Shall fall you for refusing him at sea,
Being prepared for land.

23 **take in** conquer   29 **For that** because   35 **muleters** mule drivers
36 **Ingrossed by swift impress** collected by hasty conscription   38 **yare**
swift, nimble

Antony.   By sea, by sea.   40

Enobarbus. Most worthy sir, you therein throw away
   The absolute soldiership you have by land,
   Distract° your army, which doth most consist
   Of war-marked footmen, leave unexecuted
   Your own renownèd knowledge, quite forgo   45
   The way which promises assurance, and
   Give up yourself merely to chance and hazard
   From firm security.

Antony.   I'll fight at sea.

Cleopatra. I have sixty sails, Caesar none better.

Antony. Our overplus of shipping will we burn,   50
   And with the rest full-manned, from th' head of
     Actium
   Beat th' approaching Caesar. But if we fail,
   We then can do 't at land.

           Enter a Messenger.

            Thy business?

Messenger. The news is true, my lord, he is descried;
   Caesar has taken Toryne.   55

Antony. Can he be there in person? 'Tis impossible;
   Strange that his power° should be. Canidius,
   Our nineteen legions thou shalt hold by land
   And our twelve thousand horse. We'll to our ship.
   Away, my Thetis!°

           Enter a Soldier.

        How now, worthy soldier?   60

Soldier. O noble Emperor, do not fight by sea,
   Trust not to rotten planks. Do you misdoubt
   This sword and these my wounds? Let th' Egyptians
   And the Phoenicians go a-ducking:° we

---

43 Distract (1) divide (2) confuse   **57 power** army   **60 Thetis** sea goddess, mother of Achilles   **64 a-ducking** (1) swimming like ducks (2)
tipped underwater

65   Have used to conquer standing on the earth
     And fighting foot to foot.

Antony.   Well, well: away!
         Exit Antony, Cleopatra, and Enobarbus.

Soldier. By Hercules, I think I am i' th' right.

Canidius. Soldier, thou art; but his whole action grows
     Not in the power on't:° so our leader's led,
     And we are women's men.

70   *Soldier.*   You keep by land
     The legions and the horse whole, do you not?

Canidius. Marcus Octavius, Marcus Justeius,
     Publicola, and Caelius are for sea;
     But we keep whole by land. This speed of Caesar's
     Carries° beyond belief.

75   *Soldier.*   While he was yet in Rome,
     His power went out in such distractions° as
     Beguiled all spies.

Canidius.   Who's his lieutenant, hear you?

Soldier. They say, one Taurus.

Canidius.   Well I know the man.

         Enter a Messenger.

Messenger. The Emperor calls Canidius.

Canidius. With news the time's with labor, and throws
80   forth
     Each minute some.°   *Exeunt.*

68–69 **his whole ... power on't** his entire plan of action has developed
away from its sources of power   75 **Carries** shoots him forward
76 **distractions** divisions   80–81 **With news ... some** i.e., more news
is born every minute

[Scene 8. *A plain near Actium.*]

Enter Caesar, with his Army, marching.

Caesar. Taurus!

Taurus. My lord?

Caesar. Strike not by land; keep whole, provoke not
    battle
  Till we have done at sea. Do not exceed
  The prescript of this scroll. Our fortune lies   5
  Upon this jump.° *Exit [with Taurus and the Army].*

[Scene 9. *Another part of the plain.*]

Enter Antony and Enobarbus.

Antony. Set we our squadrons on yond side o' th' hill
  In eye of Caesar's battle;° from which place
  We may the number of the ships behold,
  And so proceed accordingly.   *Exit [with Enobarbus].*

3.8.6 **jump** risk   3.9.2 **battle** battle line

[Scene 10. *Another part of the plain.*]

*Canidius marcheth with his land army one way
over the stage, and Taurus, the lieutenant of
Caesar, [with his army,] the other way. After their
going in is heard the noise of a sea fight. Alarum.
Enter Enobarbus.*

Enobarbus. Naught,° naught, all naught! I can behold
   no longer.
Th' *Antoniad,* the Egyptian admiral,°
With all their sixty, fly and turn the rudder:
To see't mine eyes are blasted.

                    Enter Scarus.

Scarus.   Gods and goddesses,
   All the whole synod° of them!

5 *Enobarbus.*   What's thy passion?

Scarus. The greater cantle° of the world is lost
   With very ignorance;° we have kissed away
   Kingdoms and provinces.

Enobarbus.   How appears the fight?

Scarus. On our side like the tokened pestilence,°
   Where death is sure. Yon ribaudred° nag of
10   Egypt—
   Whom leprosy o'ertake!—i' th' midst o' th' fight,
   When vantage like a pair of twins appeared,

3.10.1 **Naught** i.e., all's come to nothing   2 **admiral** flagship   5 **synod**
assembly   6 **cantle** segment of a sphere   7 **With very ignorance** by
utter stupidity   9 **tokened pestilence** first fatal symptoms of the plague
10 **ribaudred** (apparently from "ribald," but of uncertain meaning;
probably just a cursing word; "filthy")

Both as the same, or rather ours the elder,°
The breese° upon her, like a cow in June,
Hoists sails, and flies.

Enobarbus.   That I beheld: 15
Mine eyes did sicken at the sight, and could not
Endure a further view.

Scarus.   She once being loofed,°
The noble ruin of her magic, Antony,
Claps on his sea wing, and (like a doting mallard)°
Leaving the fight in height, flies after her.   20
I never saw an action of such shame;
Experience, manhood, honor, ne'er before
Did violate so itself.

Enobarbus.   Alack, alack!

Enter Canidius.

Canidius. Our fortune on the sea is out of breath,
And sinks most lamentably. Had our general   25
Been what he knew himself,° it had gone well.
O, he has given example for our flight
Most grossly by his own.

Enobarbus.   Ay, are you thereabouts?°
Why then, good night indeed.

Canidius. Toward Peloponnesus are they fled.   30

Scarus. 'Tis easy to 't; and there I will attend
What further comes.

Canidius.   To Caesar will I render
My legions and my horse; six kings already
Show me the way of yielding.

13 **elder** greater 14 **breese** gadfly (with pun on "breeze," "wind")
17 **loofed** (1) luffed, i.e., with the head of a ship turned into the wind (2)
aloofed, rapidly departing 19 **mallard** wild duck 26 **Been ... himself** been his true self—and he knew what that was 28 **are you thereabouts** is that where your thoughts are

Enobarbus.   I'll yet follow
35   The wounded chance° of Antony, though my rea-
      son
      Sits in the wind against me.°   [*Exeunt.*]

[Scene 11. *Alexandria. Cleopatra's palace.*]

Enter Antony with Attendants.

Antony. Hark! The land bids me tread no more upon't,
     It is ashamed to bear me. Friends, come hither.
     I am so lated° in the world that I
     Have lost my way forever. I have a ship
5   Laden with gold: take that, divide it; fly,
     And make your peace with Caesar.

Omnes.   Fly? Not we.

Antony. I have fled myself, and have instructed cow-
      ards
     To run and show their shoulders. Friends, be gone.
     I have myself resolved upon a course
10   Which has no need of you. Be gone.
     My treasure's in the harbor. Take it. O,
     I followed that° I blush to look upon.
     My very hairs do mutiny, for the white
     Reprove the brown for rashness,° and they them
15   For fear and doting. Friends, be gone; you shall
     Have letters from me to some friends that will
     Sweep your way for you. Pray you, look not sad,
     Nor make replies of loathness; take the hint°
     Which my despair proclaims. Let that be left

35 **wounded chance** broken fortunes   36 **Sits ... me** is opposed to
me   3.11.3 **lated** belated (as of a traveler, caught by the encroaching
night)   12 **that** what   14 **rashness** foolishness   18 **hint** opportunity

Which leaves itself.° To the seaside straightway!	20
I will possess you of that ship and treasure.
Leave me, I pray, a little: pray you now,
Nay, do so; for indeed I have lost command,°
Therefore I pray you. I'll see you by and by.

Sits down.

Enter Cleopatra led by Charmian,
[Iras,] and Eros.

Eros. Nay, gentle madam, to him, comfort him.	25

Iras. Do, most dear queen.

Charmian. Do: why, what else?

Cleopatra. Let me sit down. O, Juno!

Antony. No, no, no, no, no.

Eros. See you here, sir?	30

Antony. O, fie, fie, fie!

Charmian. Madam!

Iras. Madam, O, good empress!

Eros. Sir, sir!

Antony. Yes, my lord, yes. He° at Philippi kept	35
His sword e'en like a dancer,° while I struck
The lean and wrinkled Cassius; and 'twas I
That the mad Brutus ended; he alone
Dealt on lieutenantry,° and no practice had
In the brave squares° of war: yet now—— No
matter.	40

Cleopatra. Ah, stand by.

Eros. The Queen, my lord, the Queen.

19–20 Let that . . . itself leave the man who has taken leave of his senses
(?); leave the man who has given himself up for lost (?)	**23 I have lost
command** (1) my feelings are becoming uncontrollable (2) I have lost
the right to order you	**35 He** i.e., Octavius	**36 like a dancer,** i.e., for
ornament only	**39 Dealt on lieutenantry** told his subordinates how to
fight	**40 squares** squadrons

Iras. Go to him, madam, speak to him;
    He is unqualitied° with very shame.

45 *Cleopatra.* Well then, sustain me. O!

Eros. Most noble sir, arise. The Queen approaches.
    Her head's declined, and death will seize her, but°
    Your comfort makes the rescue.

Antony. I have offended reputation,°
    A most unnoble swerving.

50 *Eros.*   Sir, the Queen.

Antony. O, whither hast thou led me, Egypt? See
    How I convey my shame out of thine eyes
    By looking back° what I have left behind
    'Stroyed in dishonor.

Cleopatra.   O my lord, my lord,
55   Forgive my fearful sails! I little thought
    You would have followed.

Antony.   Egypt, thou knew'st too well
    My heart was to thy rudder tied by th' strings,
    And thou shouldst tow me after. O'er my spirit
    Thy full supremacy thou knew'st, and that
60   Thy beck might from the bidding of the gods
    Command me.

Cleopatra.   O, my pardon!

Antony.   Now I must
    To the young man send humble treaties, dodge
    And palter in the shifts of lowness,° who
    With half the bulk o' th' world played as I pleased,
65   Making and marring fortunes. You did know
    How much you were my conqueror, and that
    My sword, made weak by my affection,° would
    Obey it on all cause.

---

44 **unqualitied** beside himself   47 **but** unless   49 **reputation** honor
53 **By looking back** i.e., by averting my eyes and by lonely meditation
on   63 **palter ... lowness** employ the tricks of a man brought low
67 **affection** love

Cleopatra.   Pardon, pardon!

Antony. Fall° not a tear, I say; one of them rates°
    All that is won and lost. Give me a kiss;   70
    Even this repays me. We sent our schoolmaster:°
    Is 'a come back? Love, I am full of lead.
    Some wine, within there, and our viands! Fortune
        knows
    We scorn her most when most she offers blows.

                                                        Exeunt.

[Scene 12. *Egypt. Caesar's camp.*]

*Enter Caesar, Agrippa, Dolabella, [Thidias,] with
                    others.*

Caesar. Let him appear that's come from Antony.
    Know you him?

Dolabella.   Caesar, 'tis his schoolmaster:
    An argument that he is plucked, when hither
    He sends so poor a pinion of his wing,
    Which had superfluous kings for messengers   5
    Not many moons gone by.

                Enter Ambassador from Antony.

Caesar.   Approach and speak.

Ambassador. Such as I am, I come from Antony.
    I was of late as petty to his ends
    As is the morn-dew on the myrtle leaf
    To his grand sea.°

69 **Fall** let fall   69 **rates** (1) is worth (2) berates, rebukes as unimportant   71 **our schoolmaster** i.e., the tutor of his and Cleopatra's children.   3.12.10 **To his grand sea** (1) to the great sea that is its source and
end (2) to the great sea that is Antony.

10 *Caesar.*   Be't so. Declare thine office.

    Ambassador. Lord of his fortunes he salutes thee, and
        Requires° to live in Egypt; which not granted,
        He lessons° his requests, and to thee sues
        To let him breathe between the heavens and earth,
15   A private man in Athens: this for him.
        Next, Cleopatra does confess thy greatness,
        Submits her to thy might, and of thee craves
        The circle° of the Ptolemies for her heirs,
        Now hazarded to thy grace.°

    Caesar.   For Antony,
20   I have no ears to his request. The Queen
        Of audience nor desire shall fail, so° she
        From Egypt drive her all-disgracèd friend
        Or take his life there. This if she perform,
        She shall not sue unheard. So to them both.

    Ambassador. Fortune pursue thee!

25 *Caesar.*   Bring him through the bands.
                                      [*Exit Ambassador.*]
        [*To Thidias*] To try thy eloquence now 'tis time.
            Dispatch.
        From Antony win Cleopatra: promise,
        And in our name, what she requires; add more,
        From thine invention, offers.° Women are not
30   In their best fortunes strong, but want will perjure°
        The ne'er-touched vestal.° Try thy cunning,
            Thidias;
        Make thine own edict° for thy pains, which we
        Will answer as a law.

    Thidias.   Caesar, I go.

---

12 **Requires** requests   13 **lessons** disciplines (though perhaps the word
should be emended to "lessens")   18 **circle** crown   19 **Now hazarded
to thy grace** now dependent for its fate on your favor   21 **so** provided
that   27–29 **promise . . . offers** (possibly corrupt; rearranges to the
much more lucid: "promise/What she requires; and in our name add
more/Offers from thine invention")   30 **perjure** make a perjuror
of   31 **ne'er-touched vestal** immaculate virgin   32 **Make thine own
edict** decree what you think the right reward

Caesar. Observe how Antony becomes his flaw,°
　　And what thou think'st his very action speaks   35
　　In every power that moves.

Thidias.　　　　　　　Caesar, I shall.   *Exeunt.*

[Scene 13. *Alexandria. Cleopatra's palace.*]

　Enter Cleopatra, Enobarbus, Charmian, and Iras.

Cleopatra. What shall we do, Enobarbus?

Enobarbus.　　　　　　　Think, and die.

Cleopatra. Is Antony, or we, in fault for this?

Enobarbus. Antony only, that would make his will°
　　Lord of his reason. What though you fled
　　From that great face of war, whose several ranges   5
　　Frighted each other? Why should he follow?
　　The itch of his affection° should not then
　　Have nicked° his captainship, at such a point,
　　When half to half the world opposed, he being
　　The mered question.° 'Twas a shame no less   10
　　Than was his loss, to course° your flying flags
　　And leave his navy gazing.

Cleopatra.　　　　　　　Prithee, peace.

　　　Enter the Ambassador, with Antony.

Antony. Is that his answer?

Ambassador. Ay, my lord.

Antony. The Queen shall then have courtesy, so° she   15

34 **becomes his flaw** takes his fall　3.13.3 **will** desire, lust　7 **affection**
passion　8 **nicked** (1) maimed (2) got the better of　10 **merèd question**
sole ground of dispute　11 **course** pursue　15 **so** if

Will yield us up.

Ambassador.   He says so.

Antony.   Let her know't.
To the boy Caesar send this grizzled head,
And he will fill thy wishes to the brim
With principalities.

Cleopatra.   That head, my lord?

20   *Antony.* To him again! Tell him he wears the rose
        Of youth upon him; from which the world should
            note
        Something particular.° His coin, ships, legions
        May be a coward's, whose ministers would prevail
        Under the service of a child as soon
25   As i' th' command of Caesar. I dare him therefore
        To lay his gay comparisons° apart
        And answer me declined,° sword against sword,
        Ourselves alone. I'll write it: follow me.
                    [*Exeunt Antony and Ambassador.*]

Enobarbus. [*Aside*] Yes, like enough: high-battled°
        Caesar will
30   Unstate his happiness and be staged to th' show
        Against a sworder!° I see men's judgments are
        A parcel° of their fortunes, and things outward
        Do draw the inward quality after them
        To suffer all alike.° That he should dream,
35   Knowing all measures,° the full Caesar will
        Answer his emptiness! Caesar, thou hast subdued
        His judgment too.

                    Enter a Servant.

Servant.   A messenger from Caesar.

22 **Something particular** i.e., a fact concerning Caesar   26 **comparisons** i.e., the ships, etc., which make him Antony's superior by
comparison   27 **declined** i.e., in years and fortunes   29 **high-battled**
elevated high by great armies   30–31 **Unstate ... sworder** strip his
good fortune of all its power, and make a public exhibition of himself
against a gladiator   32 **parcel** part   34 **suffer all alike** deteriorate
together   35 **knowing all measures** having experienced every measure
of fortune.

Cleopatra. What, no more ceremony? See, my women,
   Against the blown rose may they stop their nose
   That kneeled unto the buds. Admit him, sir.   40

                              [*Exit Servant.*]

Enobarbus. [*Aside*] Mine honesty and I begin to
   square.°
   The loyalty well held to fools does make
   Our faith° mere folly: yet he that can endure
   To follow with allegiance a fall'n lord
   Does conquer him that did his master conquer   45
   And earns a place i' th' story.

                    Enter Thidias.

Cleopatra.   Caesar's will?

Thidias. Hear it apart.

Cleopatra.   None but friends: say boldly.

Thidias. So, haply,° are they friends to Antony.

Enobarbus. He needs as many, sir, as Caesar has,
   Or needs not us. If Caesar please, our master   50
   Will leap to be his friend; for us, you know,
   Whose he is we are, and that is Caesar's.

Thidias.   So.
   Thus then, thou most renowned: Caesar entreats
   Not to consider in what case thou stand'st
   Further than he is Caesar.°

Cleopatra.   Go on: right royal.   55

Thidias. He knows that you embraced not Antony
   As you did love, but as you feared him.

Cleopatra.   O!

Thidias. The scars upon your honor therefore he
   Does pity, as constrainèd blemishes,
   Not as deserved.

Cleopatra.   He is a god, and knows   60

41 **square** quarrel   43 **faith** faithfulness   48 **haply** perhaps   55 **Caesar**
i.e., famous for generosity

What is most right. Mine honor was not yielded,
    But conquered merely.°

Enobarbus.   [*Aside*] To be sure of that,
    I will ask Antony. Sir, sir, thou art so leaky
    That we must leave thee to thy sinking, for
    Thy dearest quit thee.   *Exit Enobarbus.*

65 *Thidias.*   Shall I say to Caesar
    What you require° of him? For he partly begs
    To be desired to give. It much would please him
    That of his fortunes you should make a staff
    To lean upon. But it would warm his spirits
70 To hear from me you had left Antony,
    And put yourself under his shroud,°
    The universal landlord.

    Cleopatra.   What's your name?

    Thidias. My name is Thidias.

    Cleopatra.   Most kind messenger,
    Say to great Caesar this: in deputation°
75 I kiss his conqu'ring hand; tell him I am prompt
    To lay my crown at's feet, and there to kneel.
    Tell him, from his all-obeying° breath I hear
    The doom of Egypt.°

    Thidias.   'Tis your noblest course:
    Wisdom and fortune combating together,
80 If that the former dare but what it can,°
    No chance may shake it. Give me grace to lay
    My duty° on your hand.

    Cleopatra. [*Giving her hand*] Your Caesar's father oft,
    When he hath mused of taking kingdoms in,

---

62 **merely** utterly   66 **require** request   71 **shroud** protection   74 **in
deputation** by proxy   77 **all-obeying** which all obey   78 **doom of
Egypt** judgment of the Queen of Egypt   80 **If that ... it can** if a wise
man has the courage merely to go on being wise   82 **duty** i.e., a kiss

Bestowed his lips on that unworthy place,
As° it rained kisses.

Enter Antony and Enobarbus.

Antony.   Favors, by Jove that thunders!   85
What art thou, fellow?

Thidias.   One that but performs
The bidding of the fullest° man, and worthiest
To have command obeyed.

Enobarbus.   [*Aside*] You will be whipped.

Antony. [*Calling for Servants*] Approach there! —Ah,
    you kite!° Now, gods and devils!
Authority melts from me. Of late, when I cried
    "Ho!"   90
Like boys unto a muss° kings would start forth,
And cry "Your will?" Have you no ears? I am
Antony yet.

     Enter a Servant [*followed by others*].

          Take hence this Jack° and whip him.

Enobarbus. [*Aside*] 'Tis better playing with a lion's
    whelp
Than with an old one dying.

Antony.   Moon and stars!   95
Whip him! Were't twenty of the greatest tributaries
That do acknowledge Caesar, should I find them
So saucy with the hand of she here—what's her
    name
Since she was Cleopatra? Whip him, fellows,
Till like a boy you see him cringe his face   100
And whine aloud for mercy. Take him hence.

Thidias. Mark Antony—

Antony.   Tug him away. Being whipped,

---

85 **As** as if   87 **fullest** greatest (in character and fortunes)   89 **kite**
ignoble bird of prey   91 **muss** scramble; fighting heap of bodies
93 **Jack** fellow, knave

Bring him again. The Jack of Caesar's shall
Bear us an errand to him.

>   *Exeunt [Servants] with Thidias.*

105   You were half blasted° ere I knew you. Ha!
Have I my pillow left unpressed in Rome,
Forborne the getting° of a lawful race,
And by a gem of women, to be abused
By one that looks on feeders?°

Cleopatra.   Good my lord—

110 *Antony.* You have been a boggler° ever:
But when we in our viciousness grow hard
(O misery on't!) the wise gods seel° our eyes,
In our own filth drop our clear judgments, make us
Adore our errors, laugh at's while we strut
To our confusion.°

115 *Cleopatra.*   O, is't come to this?

Antony. I found you as a morsel cold upon
Dead Caesar's trencher:° nay, you were a fragment°
Of Gneius Pompey's, besides what hotter hours,
Unregist'red in vulgar fame,° you have
120   Luxuriously picked out.° For I am sure,
Though you can guess what temperance should be,
You know not what it is.

Cleopatra.   Wherefore is this?

Antony. To let a fellow that will take rewards
And say "God quit° you!" be familiar with
125   My playfellow, your hand, this kingly seal
And plighter of high hearts. O, that I were
Upon the hill of Basan to outroar

---

105 **blasted** worn out   107 **getting** begetting   109 **feeders** servants,
parasites   110 **boggler** waverer   112 **seel** blind (in falconry, a hawk's
eyelids are seeled, or sewn up, before it grows used to being hooded)
115 **confusion** destruction   117 **trencher** wooden dish   117 **fragment**
leftover   119 **vulgar fame** common knowledge, popular rumor
120 **Luxuriously picked out** lecherously selected   124 **quit** reward

The hornèd herd!° For I have savage cause,
And to proclaim it civilly were like
A haltered neck which does the hangman thank   130
For being yare° about him.

Enter a Servant with Thidias.

                              Is he whipped?

Servant. Soundly, my lord.

Antony.   Cried he? And begged 'a pardon?

Servant. He did ask favor.

Antony. If that thy father live, let him repent
Thou wast not made his daughter; and be thou sorry   135
To follow Caesar in his triumph, since
Thou hast been whipped for following him. Hence-
    forth
The white hand of a lady fever thee,
Shake thou to look on't. Get thee back to Caesar,
Tell him thy entertainment:° look thou say   140
He makes me angry with him; for he seems
Proud and disdainful, harping on what I am,
Not what he knew I was. He makes me angry,
And at this time most easy 'tis to do't,
When my good stars that were my former guides   145
Have empty left their orbs° and shot their fires
Into th' abysm of hell. If he mislike
My speech and what is done, tell him he has
Hipparchus, my enfranchèd° bondman, whom
He may at pleasure whip, or hang, or torture,   150
As he shall like, to quit me. Urge it thou.
Hence with thy stripes, be gone!   *Exit Thidias.*

Cleopatra. Have you done yet?

Antony.   Alack, our terrene moon°

126–28 O that . . . hornèd herd i.e., Antony is so well provided with the
cuckold's horns that he should be among the "fat bulls of Basan" of
Psalm 22   131 yare deft   140 entertainment reception   146 orbs
spheres   149 enfranchèd freed   153 terrene moon earthly Isis (goddess of the moon)

Is now eclipsed, and it portends alone
The fall of Antony.

155 *Cleopatra.*   I must stay his time.°

Antony. To flatter Caesar, would you mingle eyes
With one that ties his points?°

Cleopatra.   Not know me yet?

Antony. Cold-hearted toward me?

Cleopatra.   Ah, dear, if I be so,
From my cold heart let heaven engender hail,
160 And poison it in the source, and the first stone
Drop in my neck: as it determines,° so
Dissolve my life! The next Caesarion smite,
Till by degrees the memory° of my womb,
Together with my brave Egyptians all,
165 By the discandying° of this pelleted storm,
Lie graveless, till the flies and gnats of Nile
Have buried them for prey!

Antony.   I am satisfied.
Caesar sits down in Alexandria, where
I will oppose his fate.° Our force by land
170 Hath nobly held; our severed navy too
Have knit again, and fleet,° threat'ning most sea-
    like.
Where hast thou been, my heart?° Dost thou hear,
    lady?
If from the field I shall return once more
To kiss these lips, I will appear in blood;°
175 I and my sword will earn our chronicle.°
There's hope in't yet.

Cleopatra. That's my brave lord!

___

155 **stay his time** i.e., wait till his rage ends   157 **one that ties his
points** one who laces up his clothes, i.e., a valet   161 **determines** comes
to an end, melts   163 **memory** memorials, heirs   165 **discandying**
melting   169 **oppose his fate** challenge his destiny   171 **fleet** float
172 **heart** courage   174 **in blood** (1) covered with blood (2) in full
vigor   175 **chronicle** place in history

Antony. I will be treble-sinewed, hearted, breathed,°
　　And fight maliciously; for when mine hours
　　Were nice° and lucky, men did ransom lives   *180*
　　Of me for jests; but now I'll set my teeth
　　And send to darkness all that stop me. Come,
　　Let's have one other gaudy° night: call to me
　　All my sad captains; fill our bowls once more;
　　Let's mock the midnight bell.

Cleopatra.　　　　　　　　　It is my birthday.   *185*
　　I had thought t' have held it poor. But since my lord
　　Is Antony again, I will be Cleopatra.

Antony. We will yet do well.

Cleopatra. Call all his noble captains to my lord.

Antony. Do so, we'll speak to them; and tonight I'll
　　force   *190*
　　The wine peep through their scars. Come on, my
　　　queen,
　　There's sap in't yet! The next time I do fight,
　　I'll make death love me, for I will contend
　　Even with his pestilent scythe.
　　　　　　　　　　Exeunt [all but Enobarbus].

Enobarbus. Now he'll outstare the lightning. To be
　　furious   *195*
　　Is to be frighted out of fear, and in that mood
　　The dove will peck the estridge;° and I see still
　　A diminution in our captain's brain
　　Restores his heart. When valor preys on reason,
　　It eats the sword it fights with. I will seek   *200*
　　Some way to leave him.　　　　　　　*Exit.*

178 **I will ... breathed** I will have the strength, courage, and exper-
tise of three men   180 **nice** delicate, wanton   183 **gaudy** joyful
197 **estridge** goshawk (?) ostrich (?)

[ACT 4

Scene 1. *Before Alexandria. Caesar's camp.*]

*Enter Caesar, Agrippa, and Maecenas, with his
Army, Caesar reading a letter.*

Caesar. He calls me boy, and chides as he had power
To beat me out of Egypt. My messenger
He hath whipped with rods; dares me to personal
   combat.
Caesar to Antony: let the old ruffian know
5   I have many other ways to die; meantime
Laugh at his challenge.

Maecenas.   Caesar must think,
When one so great begins to rage,° he's hunted‾
Even to falling. Give him no breath, but now
Make boot of his distraction:° never anger
Made good guard for itself.

10 *Caesar.*   Let our best heads
Know that tomorrow the last of many battles
We mean to fight. Within our files° there are,
Of those that served Mark Antony but late,
Enough to fetch him in.° See it done,

4.1.7 **rage** grow mad   9 **Make boot of his distraction** profit from his
rage   12 **files** ranks   14 **fetch him in** capture him

98

And feast the army; we have store to do't,   15
And they have earned the waste. Poor Antony!

                                        Exeunt.

[Scene 2. *Alexandria. Cleopatra's palace.*]

Enter Antony, Cleopatra, Enobarbus, Charmian,
Iras, Alexas, with others.

Antony. He will not fight with me, Domitius?

Enobarbus.   No.

Antony. Why should he not?

Enobarbus. He thinks, being twenty times of better
    fortune,
He is twenty men to one.

Antony.   Tomorrow, soldier,
By sea and land I'll fight: or° I will live,   5
Or bathe my dying honor in the blood
Shall make it live again. Woo't° thou fight well?

Enobarbus. I'll strike, and cry "Take all!"°

Antony.   Well said, come on;
Call forth my household servants; let's tonight
Be bounteous at our meal.

            Enter three or four Servitors.

                        Give me thy hand,   10
Thou hast been rightly honest—so hast thou—
Thou—and thou—and thou: you have served me
    well,
And kings have been your fellows.°

Cleopatra.   [*Aside to Enobarbus*] What means this?

4.2.5 **or** either 7 **Woo't** wilt 8 **Take all** all or nothing 13 **kings
have been your fellows** kings have served me too, but no better

Enobarbus. [*Aside to Cleopatra*] 'Tis one of those
        odd tricks which sorrow shoots
    Out of the mind.

15 *Antony.*   And thou art honest too.
    I wish I could be made so many men,
    And all of you clapped up together in
    An Antony, that I might do you service
    So good as you have done.

Omnes.   The gods forbid!

20 *Antony.* Well, my good fellows, wait on me tonight:
    Scant not my cups, and make as much of me
    As when mine empire was your fellow too
    And suffered my command.°

Cleopatra.   [*Aside to Enobarbus*] What does he mean?

Enobarbus. [*Aside to Cleopatra*] To make his fol-
        lowers weep.

Antony.   Tend me tonight;
25 May be it is the period° of your duty.
    Haply° you shall not see me more; or if,
    A mangled shadow. Perchance tomorrow
    You'll serve another master. I look on you
    As one that takes his leave. Mine honest friends,
30 I turn you not away, but like a master
    Married to your good service; stay till death.
    Tend me tonight two hours, I ask no more,
    And the gods yield° you for't!

Enobarbus.   What mean you, sir,
    To give them this discomfort? Look, they weep,
35 And I, an ass, am onion-eyed; for shame,
    Transform us not to women.

Antony.   Ho, ho, ho!
    Now the witch take me° if I meant it thus!

_____

23 **suffered my command** served under my authority   25 **period** end
26 **Haply** perhaps   33 **yield** reward   37 **the witch take me** may I be
bewitched

Grace° grow where those drops fall! My hearty
    friends,
You take me in too dolorous a sense,
For I spake to you for your comfort, did desire you   40
To burn this night with torches. Know, my hearts,
I hope well of tomorrow, and will lead you
Where rather I'll expect victorious life
Than death and honor.° Let's to supper, come,
And drown consideration.   *Exeunt.*   45

[Scene 3. *Alexandria. Before Cleopatra's palace.*]

Enter a Company of Soldiers.

First Soldier. Brother, good night: tomorrow is the
    day.

Second Soldier. It will determine one way: fare you
    well.
Heard you of nothing strange about the streets?

First Soldier. Nothing. What news?

Second Soldier. Belike° 'tis but a rumor. Good night
    to you.   5

First Soldier. Well, sir, good night.
                They meet other Soldiers.

Second Soldier.   Soldiers, have careful watch.

Third Soldier. And you. Good night, good night.

They place themselves in every corner of the stage.

Second Soldier. Here we;° and if tomorrow

38 **Grace** (1) God's grace, favor (2) herb of grace, rue   44 **death and
honor** honorable death   4.3.5 **Belike** probably   8 **Here we** here is our
post

Our navy thrive, I have an absolute hope
Our landmen will stand up.

10 *First Soldier.*   'Tis a brave army,
And full of purpose.
                    Music of the hautboys is under the stage.

Second Soldier.   Peace! What noise?

First Soldier.   List, list!

Second Soldier. Hark!

First Soldier.   Music i' th' air.

Third Soldier.   Under the earth.

Fourth Soldier. It signs° well, does it not?

Third Soldier.   No.

First Soldier.   Peace, I say!
What should this mean?

Second Soldier. 'Tis the god Hercules, whom Antony
15   loved,
Now leaves him.

First Soldier. Walk; let's see if other watchmen
Do hear what we do.

Second Soldier. How now, masters?

20 *Omnes.* (*Speak together*) How now? How now? Do
you hear this?

First Soldier. Ay. Is't not strange?

Third Soldier. Do you hear, masters? Do you hear?

First Soldier. Follow the noise so far as we have
quarter.
25   Let's see how it will give off.°

Omnes. Content. 'Tis strange.   *Exeunt.*

13 **signs** signifies   25 **give off** cease

[Scene 4. *Alexandria. Cleopatra's palace.*]

Enter Antony and Cleopatra, with [Charmian and]
others [attending].

Antony. Eros! Mine armor, Eros!

Cleopatra.   Sleep a little.

Antony. No, my chuck.° Eros! Come, mine armor,
     Eros!

          Enter Eros [with armor].

     Come, good fellow, put thine iron° on.
     If fortune be not ours today, it is
     Because we brave her.° Come.

Cleopatra.   Nay, I'll help too.   5
     What's this for?

Antony.   Ah, let be, let be! Thou art
     The armorer of my heart. False,° false; this, this.

Cleopatra. Sooth, la, I'll help: thus it must be.

Antony.   Well, well,
     We shall thrive now. Seest thou, my good fellow?
     Go put on thy defenses.

Eros.   Briefly,° sir.   10

Cleopatra. Is not this buckled well?

Antony.   Rarely, rarely:
     He that unbuckles this, till we do please
     To daff't° for our repose, shall hear a storm.

4.4.2 **chuck** chick   3 **thine iron** that armor (of mine) you hold
4–5 **If fortune ... brave her** (1) if fortune is not friendly to us today,
it will be because we defy her (2) we shall be fortunate today, or we
shall defy fortune   7 **False** i.e., wrong piece   10 **Briefly** soon   13 **daff't**
put it off

Thou fumblest, Eros, and my queen's a squire
15 More tight° at this than thou. Dispatch. O, love,
That thou couldst see my wars today, and knew'st
The royal occupation:° thou shouldst see
A workman° in't.

Enter an armed Soldier.

           Good morrow to thee; welcome:
Thou look'st like him that knows a warlike charge.°
20 To business that we love we rise betime
And go to't with delight. ·

Soldier.   A thousand, sir,
Early though't be, have on their riveted trim,°
And at the port° expect you.

*Shout. Trumpets flourish. Enter Captains and
Soldiers.*

Captain. The morn is fair. Good morrow, General.

All. Good morrow, General.

25 *Antony.*   'Tis well blown,° lads.
This morning, like the spirit of a youth
That means to be of note, begins betimes.
So, so. Come, give me that: this way; well said.°
Fare thee well, dame; whate'er becomes of me,
30 This is a soldier's kiss. Rebukable
And worthy shameful check° it were to stand
On more mechanic compliment.° I'll leave thee
Now like a man of steel. You that will fight,
Follow me close; I'll bring you to't. Adieu.
          Exeunt [all but Cleopatra and Charmian].

Charmian. Please you retire to your chamber?

35 *Cleopatra.*   Lead me.
He goes forth gallantly. That he and Caesar might

15 **tight** skilled 17 **royal occupation** kingly trade 18 **workman** professional 19 **charge** duty 22 **riveted trim** armor 23 **port** gate 25 **well blown** (1) i.e., on the trumpets (2) in full flower (of the morning) 28 **well said** well done 31 **shameful check** shaming rebuke 31–32 **to stand ... compliment** to make a business of vulgar civilities

Determine this great war in single fight!
Then Antony—but now— Well, on.   *Exeunt.*

[Scene 5. *Alexandria. Antony's camp.*]

*Trumpets sound. Enter Antony and Eros, [a
soldier meeting them].*

Soldier. The gods make this a happy° day to Antony!

Antony. Would thou and those thy scars had once pre-
    vailed
To make me fight at land!

Soldier.   Hadst thou done so,
The kings that have revolted, and the soldier
That has this morning left thee, would have still   *5*
Followèd thy heels.

Antony.   Who's gone this morning?

Soldier.   Who?
One ever near thee: call for Enobarbus,
He shall not hear thee, or from Caesar's camp
Say "I am none of thine."

Antony.   What sayest thou?

Soldier.   Sir,
He is with Caesar.

Eros.   Sir, his chests and treasure   *10*
He has not with him.

Antony.   Is he gone?

Soldier.   Most certain.

Antony. Go, Eros, send his treasure after; do it;
Detain no jot, I charge thee. Write to him

4.5.1 **happy** fortunate

15   (I will subscribe)° gentle adieus and greetings;
     Say that I wish he never find more cause
     To change a master. O, my fortunes have
     Corrupted honest men! Dispatch. Enobarbus!
                         Exit [with Eros and Soldier].

[Scene 6. *Alexandria. Caesar's camp.*]

Flourish. Enter Agrippa, Caesar, with Enobarbus,
                and Dolabella.

Caesar. Go forth, Agrippa, and begin the fight.
     Our will is Antony be took alive:
     Make it so known.

Agrippa. Caesar, I shall.   [*Exit.*]

5   *Caesar.* The time of universal peace is near.
     Prove this a prosp'rous day, the three-nooked°
        world
     Shall bear the olive freely.

                Enter a Messenger.

Messenger.   Antony
     Is come into the field.

Caesar.   Go charge Agrippa
     Plant those that have revolted in the vant,°
10   That Antony may seem to spend his fury
     Upon himself.   *Exeunt [all but Enobarbus].*

Enobarbus. Alexas did revolt and went to Jewry on
     Affairs of Antony; there did dissuade°
     Great Herod to incline himself to Caesar
15   And leave his master Antony. For this pains

14 **subscribe** sign   4.6.6 **three-nooked** three-cornered (Europe, Asia,
Africa)   9 **vant** first lines   13 **dissuade** i.e., persuade to leave Antony

Caesar hath hanged him. Canidius and the rest
That fell away have entertainment, but
No honorable trust. I have done ill,
Of which I do accuse myself so sorely
That I will joy no more.

Enter a Soldier of Caesar's.

Soldier.   Enobarbus, Antony   20
 Hath after thee sent all thy treasure, with
 His bounty overplus. The messenger
 Came on my guard, and at thy tent is now
 Unloading of his mules.

Enobarbus.   I give it you.

Soldier. Mock not, Enobarbus: 25
 I tell you true: best you safed the bringer
 Out of the host;° I must attend mine office
 Or would have done't myself. Your emperor
 Continues still a Jove.   *Exit.*

Enobarbus. I am alone the° villain of the earth,   30
 And feel I am so most.° O, Antony,
 Thou mine of bounty, how wouldst thou have paid
 My better service, when my turpitude
 Thou dost so crown with gold! This blows° my
   heart.
 If swift thought° break it not, a swifter mean   35
 Shall outstrike thought; but thought will do't, I feel.
 I fight against thee! No, I will go seek
 Some ditch wherein to die: the foul'st best fits
 My latter part of life.   *Exit.*

26–27 **best . . . host** you had better see that the man who brought them
has safe-conduct through enemy lines   30 **alone the** the only   31 **And
feel I am so most** and no one could be more bitterly aware of it
34 **blows** swells   35 **thought** sorrow

[Scene 7. *Field of battle between the camps.*]

Alarum. Drums and Trumpets. Enter Agrippa
[and Soldiers].

Agrippa. Retire; we have engaged ourselves too far:
    Caesar himself has work,° and our oppression°
    Exceeds what we expected.   *Exit [with Soldiers].*

Alarums. Enter Antony, and Scarus wounded.

Scarus. O my brave emperor, this is fought indeed!
5   Had we done so at first, we had droven them home
    With clouts° about their heads.

Antony.   Thou bleed'st apace.

Scarus. I had a wound here that was like a *T*,
    But now 'tis made an *H*.°   [*Retreat sounded*] *far off.*

Antony.   They do retire.

Scarus. We'll beat 'em into bench holes.° I have yet
10   Room for six scotches° more.

                    Enter Eros.

Eros. They are beaten, sir, and our advantage serves
    For a fair victory.

Scarus.   Let us score° their backs
    And snatch 'em up, as we take hares, behind:
    'Tis sport to maul a runner.

Antony.   I will reward thee

4.7.2 **has work** is hard-pressed   2 **our oppression** the pressure on
us   6 **clouts** (1) blows (2) bandages   8 **H** (pun on "ache," pronounced
"aitch")   9 **bench holes** holes in a privy   10 **scotches** gashes   12 **score**
slash

Once for thy sprightly° comfort, and tenfold · 15
For thy good valor. Come thee on.

Scarus.   I'll halt° after. *Exeunt.*

[Scene 8. *Before Alexandria.*]

*Alarum. Enter Antony again in a march; Scarus,
with others.*

Antony. We have beat him to his camp. Run one
      before
And let the Queen know of our gests.° Tomorrow,
Before the sun shall see's, we'll spill the blood
That has today escaped. I thank you all,
For doughty-handed are you, and have fought   5
Not as you served the cause, but as't had been
Each man's like mine: you have shown all Hectors.
Enter the city, clip° your wives, your friends,
Tell them your feats, whilst they with joyful tears
Wash the congealment from your wounds, and kiss   10
The honored gashes whole.

                    Enter Cleopatra.

                    [*To Scarus*] Give me thy hand;

To this great fairy° I'll commend thy acts,
Make her thanks bless thee. ——O thou day o' th'
      world,
Chain mine armed neck; leap thou, attire and all,
Through proof of harness° to my heart, and there   15
Ride on the pants triumphing.

15 **sprightly** high-hearted   16 **halt** limp   4.8.2 **gests** deeds   8 **clip**
embrace   12 **fairy** enchantress   15 **proof of harness** impenetrable
armor

Cleopatra.   Lord of lords!
O infinite virtue,° com'st thou smiling from
The world's great snare uncaught?

Antony.   Mine nightingale,
We have beat them to their beds. What, girl! Though
          gray
Do something mingle with our younger brown, yet
20   ha' we
A brain that nourishes our nerves, and can
Get goal for goal of youth.° Behold this man:
Commend unto his lips thy favoring hand.—
Kiss it, my warrior.—He hath fought today
25   As if a god in hate of mankind had
Destroyed in such a shape.

Cleopatra.   I'll give thee, friend,
An armor all of gold; it was a king's.

Antony. He has deserved it, were it carbuncled°
Like holy Phoebus' car.° Give me thy hand.
30   Through Alexandria make a jolly march;
Bear our hacked targets° like the men that owe°
          them.
Had our great palace the capacity
To camp this host, we all would sup together
And drink carouses to the next day's fate,
35   Which promises royal peril. Trumpeters,
With brazen din blast you the city's ear,
Make mingle with our rattling tabourines,°
That heaven and earth may strike their sounds
          together,
Applauding our approach.   *Exeunt.*

17 **virtue** valor   22 **Get goal for goal of youth** keep pace with every
point won by youth   28 **carbuncled** jeweled   29 **Phoebus' car** the sun
god's chariot   31 **targets** shields   31 **owe** own   37 **tabourines** small
drums

[Scene 9. *Caesar's camp.*]

*Enter a Sentry and his Company. Enobarbus
follows.*

Sentry. If we be not relieved within this hour,
We must return to th' court of guard. The night
Is shiny, and they say we shall embattle
By th' second hour i' th' morn.

First Watch.   This last day was
A shrewd° one to's.

Enobarbus.   O, bear me witness, night—   5

Second Watch. What man is this?

First Watch.   Stand close, and list him.

Enobarbus. Be witness to me, O, thou blessèd moon,
When men revolted shall upon record
Bear hateful memory, poor Enobarbus did
Before thy face repent!

Sentry.   Enobarbus?

Second Watch.   Peace: 10
Hark further.

Enobarbus. O sovereign mistress° of true melancholy,
The poisonous damp of night disponge° upon me,
That life, a very rebel to my will,
May hang no longer on me. Throw my heart   15
Against the flint and hardness of my fault,
Which, being dried with grief, will break to powder,
And finish all foul thoughts. O, Antony,
Nobler than my revolt is infamous,

4.9.5 **shrewd** curst, bad   12 **mistress** i.e., the moon   13 **disponge** drip

20   Forgive me in thine own particular,°
    But let the world rank me in register°
    A master-leaver° and a fugitive.
    O, Antony! O, Antony!   [*Dies.*]

First Watch.   Let's speak to him.

Sentry. Let's hear him, for the things he speaks
    May concern Caesar.

25 *Second Watch.*   Let's do so. But he sleeps.

Sentry. Swoons rather, for so bad a prayer as his
    Was never yet for° sleep.

First Watch.   Go we to him.

Second Watch. Awake, sir, awake; speak to us.

First Watch.   Hear you, sir?

Sentry. The hand of death hath raught° him.
                      Drums afar off.
                      Hark! The drums
30   Demurely° wake the sleepers. Let us bear him
    To th' court of guard: he is of note. Our hour
    Is fully out.

Second Watch. Come on then; he may recover yet.
                    Exeunt [*with the body*].

[Scene 10. *Between the two camps.*]

Enter Antony and Scarus, with their Army.

Antony. Their preparation is today by sea;
    We please them not by land.

---

20 **in thine own particular** yourself 21 **in register** in its records
22 **master-leaver** (1) supreme traitor (2) runaway servant 27 **for** a pre-
lude to 29 **raught** reached 30 **Demurely** soberly, with a low sound

Scarus.   For both, my lord.

Antony. I would they'd fight i' th' fire or i' th' air;°
  We'd fight there too. But this it is: our foot
  Upon the hills adjoining to the city   5
  Shall stay with us—order for sea is given;
  They have put forth the haven—
  Where their appointment we may best discover
  And look on their endeavor.   *Exeunt.*

[Scene 11. *Between the two camps.*]

Enter Caesar and his Army.

Caesar. But being charged,° we will be still by land—
  Which, as I take't, we shall, for his best force
  Is forth to man his galleys. To the vales,
  And hold our best advantage.°   *Exeunt.*

[Scene 12. *Before Alexandria.*]

Enter Antony and Scarus.

Antony. Yet there are not joined.° Where yond pine
    does stand
  I shall discover all. I'll bring thee word

4.10.3 **i' th' fire or i' th' air** i.e., as well as the other two elements, earth
and water (land and sea)   4.11.1 **But being charged** unless we are
attacked   4 **hold our best advantage** take up the best position we can
4.12.1 **joined** i.e., in battle

Straight how 'tis like to go.   *Exit.*
          Alarum afar off, as at a sea fight.°

Scarus.   Swallows have built
      In Cleopatra's sails their nests. The augurers
5   Say they know not, they cannot tell, look grimly,
      And dare not speak their knowledge. Antony
      Is valiant, and dejected, and by starts
      His fretted° fortunes give him hope and fear
      Of what he has, and has not.

                    Enter Antony.

Antony.   All is lost!
10   This foul Egyptian hath betrayèd me:
      My fleet hath yielded to the foe, and yonder
      They cast their caps up and carouse together
      Like friends long lost. Triple-turned° whore! 'Tis
          thou
      Hast sold me to this novice, and my heart
15   Makes only wars on thee. Bid them all fly;
      For when I am revenged upon my charm,°
      I have done all. Bid them all fly, be gone.
                              [Exit Scarus.]
      O sun, thy uprise shall I see no more.
      Fortune and Antony part here, even here
20   Do we shake hands. All come to this? The hearts
      That spanieled me at heels, to whom I gave
      Their wishes, do discandy,° melt their sweets
      On blossoming Caesar; and this pine is barked,°
      That overtopped them all. Betrayed I am.
25   O this false soul of Egypt! This grave charm,°
      Whose eye becked forth my wars, and called them
          home,
      Whose bosom was my crownet, my chief end,°

3 s.d. **Alarum ... sea fight** (the Folio prints this direction just before
the entrance of Antony and Scarus; if F's placement is correct, the noise
fills the otherwise empty stage for a moment and makes ironic Antony's
first line, but probably the direction should be placed either in its present
position or in the middle of line 9)   8 **fretted** (1) checkered (2) worn,
decayed   13 **Triple-turned** i.e., from Pompey, from Julius Caesar, from
Antony   16 **charm** witch   22 **discandy** dissolve   23 **barked** stripped
bare   25 **grave charm** deadly witch   27 **crownet, my chief end** crown
and end of all I did

Like a right° gypsy hath at fast and loose°
Beguiled me, to the very heart of loss.
What, Eros, Eros!

                    Enter Cleopatra.

                Ah, thou spell! Avaunt!°   30

Cleopatra. Why is my lord enraged against his love?

Antony. Vanish, or I shall give thee thy deserving
    And blemish Caesar's triumph. Let him take thee
    And hoist thee up to the shouting plebeians;°
    Follow his chariot, like the greatest spot°   35
    Of all thy sex: most monsterlike be shown
    For poor'st diminutives,° for dolts, and let
    Patient Octavia plow thy visage up
    With her preparèd nails.   *Exit Cleopatra.*
                    'Tis well th' art gone,
    If it be well to live; but better 'twere   40
    Thou fell'st into my fury, for one death
    Might have prevented many. Eros, ho!
    The shirt of Nessus is upon me; teach me,
    Alcides, thou mine ancestor, thy rage.
    Let me lodge Lichas on the horns o' th' moon,°   45
    And with those hands that grasped the heaviest club
    Subdue my worthiest self. The witch shall die:
    To the young Roman boy she hath sold me, and
        I fall
    Under this plot: she dies for't. Eros, ho!   *Exit.*

28 **right** true   28 **fast and loose** (a cheating game played by gypsies, in which the dupe inevitably fails to make fast a coiled rope)   30 **Avaunt** begone   34 **plebeians** (accented on first syllable)   35 **spot** blemish   37 **diminutives** little people, i.e., the populace   43–45 **Nessus . . . moon** (the death of Antony's ancestor Hercules—called Alcides in line 44—is here recalled. Hercules killed the centaur Nessus with a poisoned arrow, for trying to rape his wife Deianira; the dying Nessus in revenge gave his robe, soaked in poisoned blood, to Deianira, pretending it would act as a love charm. She sent it to her husband for this purpose; in his dying agonies Hercules hurled the bringer of it, Lichas, high in the air)

[Scene 13. *Alexandria. Cleopatra's palace.*]

Enter Cleopatra, Charmian, Iras, Mardian.

Cleopatra. Help me, my women! O, he's more mad
　　Than Telamon° for his shield; the boar of Thessaly°
　　Was never so embossed.°

Charmian.　　　　　　To th' monument:
　　There lock yourself, and send him word you are
　　　　dead.
5　　The soul and body rive° not more in parting
　　Than greatness going off.

Cleopatra.　　　　　　To th' monument!
　　Mardian, go tell him I have slain myself;
　　Say that the last I spoke was "Antony"
　　And word it, prithee, piteously. Hence, Mardian,
　　And bring me how he takes my death. To th' monu-
10　　ment!　　　　　　　　　　　　　　　　*Exeunt.*

4.13.2 Telamon i.e., Ajax, who went mad and killed himself when he
lost the contest between himself and Odysseus for the arms and shield of
Achilles　**2 the boar of Thessaly** (sent by Artemis to ravage the country
of King Oeneus, and killed by his son Meleager)　**3 embossed** (of a
hunted animal) foaming at the mouth from fury and exhaustion　**5 rive**
rend

[Scene 14. *Alexandria. Cleopatra's palace.*]

Enter Antony and Eros.

Antony. Eros, thou yet behold'st me?

Eros.   Ay, noble lord.

Antony. Sometime we see a cloud that's dragonish,
A vapor sometime like a bear or lion,
A towered citadel, a pendant rock,
A forkèd mountain, or blue promontory   5
With trees upon't that nod unto the world
And mock our eyes with air. Thou hast seen these
    signs:
They are black vesper's pageants.°

Eros.   Ay, my lord.

Antony. That which is now a horse, even with a
    thought
The rack dislimns,° and makes it indistinct   10
As water is in water.

Eros.   It does, my lord.

Antony. My good knave° Eros, now thy captain is
Even such a body: here I am Antony,
Yet cannot hold this visible shape, my knave.
I made these wars for Egypt; and the Queen—   15
Whose heart I thought I had, for she had mine,
Which, whilst it was mine, had annexed unto't
A million moe,° now lost—she, Eros, has

4.14.8 **black vesper's pageants** evening's brightly colored but unreal
scenery (*pageants*=floats of the mystery plays, hence plays, masques,
etc.) 9–10 **even ... dislimns** as swift as thought the cloud formation
(**rack**) obliterates 12 **knave** boy 18 **moe** more

Packed cards with Caesar, and false-played my glory
20   Unto an enemy's triumph.°
Nay, weep not, gentle Eros, there is left us
Ourselves to end ourselves.

Enter Mardian.

                         O, thy vile lady!
She has robbed me of my sword.°

Mardian.   No, Antony;
My mistress loved thee, and her fortunes mingled
With thine entirely.

25   *Antony.*   Hence, saucy eunuch, peace!
She hath betrayed me and shall die the death.

Mardian. Death of one person can be paid but once,
And that she has discharged. What thou wouldst do
Is done unto thy hand.° The last she spake
30   Was "Antony! most noble Antony!"
Then in the midst a tearing groan did break
The name of Antony; it was divided
Between her heart and lips: she rend'red° life,
Thy name so buried in her.

Antony.   Dead, then?

Mardian.   Dead.

35   *Antony.* Unarm, Eros. The long day's task is done,
And we must sleep. [*To Mardian*] That thou depart'st
     hence safe
Does pay thy labor richly: go.   *Exit Mardian.*
                         Off, pluck off:
The sevenfold shield of Ajax° cannot keep
The battery° from my heart. O, cleave, my sides!
40   Heart, once be stronger than thy continent,°

19–20 **Packed cards ... triumph** stacked the cards to favor herself and
Caesar, and so treacherously played her hand as to allow Caesar to trump
my glory   23 **sword** i.e., soldiership, masculinity   29 **unto thy hand**
already for you   33 **rend'red** surrendered   38 **sevenfold shield of
Ajax** (made of brass and lined with seven layers of oxhide)   39 **battery**
bombardment   40 **thy continent** what holds you in

Crack thy frail case! Apace, Eros, apace.
No more a soldier. Bruisèd pieces,° go;
You have been nobly borne. —From me awhile.

Exit Eros.

I will o'ertake thee, Cleopatra, and
Weep for my pardon. So it must be, for now　　45
All length° is torture: since the torch is out,
Lie down, and stray no farther. Now all labor
Mars what it does; yea, very force entangles
Itself with strength.° Seal then,° and all is done.
Eros! —I come, my queen. —Eros! —Stay for me.　　50
Where souls do couch on flowers, we'll hand in hand,
And with our sprightly° port° make the ghosts gaze:
Dido and her Aeneas° shall want troops,°
And all the haunt be ours. —Come, Eros, Eros!

Enter Eros.

Eros. What would my lord?

Antony.　　　　　　　　Since Cleopatra died,　　55
I have lived in such dishonor that the gods
Detest my baseness. I, that with my sword
Quartered° the world and o'er green Neptune's back
With ships made cities, condemn myself to lack°
The courage of a woman; less noble mind　　60
Than she which by her death our Caesar tells
"I am conqueror of myself." Thou art sworn, Eros,
That, when the exigent° should come, which now
Is come indeed, when I should see behind me
Th' inevitable prosecution° of　　65
Disgrace and horror, that on my command
Thou then wouldst kill me. Do't, the time is come.

---

42 pieces armor　**46 length** length of life　**48–49 very force . . . strength** (the image probably is of a creature caught more tightly in a net by the very violence of its struggles)　**49 Seal then** finish then (i.e., the final act of sealing a document, especially a will)　**52 sprightly** (1) high-hearted, gay (2) ghostly　**52 port** bearing　**53 Dido . . . Aeneas** (the legendary lovers are brought together, though in Vergil, Dido repulses forever the faithless Aeneas)　**53 want troops** lack retinue　**58 Quartered** (1) covered with troops (2) carved up　**59 to lack** for lacking　**63 exigent** need　**65 inevitable prosecution** unescapable pursuit

Thou strik'st not me, 'tis Caesar thou defeat'st.
Put color in thy cheek.

Eros.   The gods withhold me!
70   Shall I do that which all the Parthian darts,
Though enemy, lost aim and could not?

Antony.   Eros,
Wouldst thou be windowed in great Rome and see
Thy master thus: with pleached° arms, bending down
His corrigible° neck, his face subdued
75   To penetrative shame,° whilst the wheeled seat
Of fortunate Caesar, drawn before him, branded
His baseness that ensued?°

Eros.   I would not see't.

Antony. Come then; for with a wound I must be cured.
Draw that thy honest sword, which thou hast worn
Most useful for thy country.

80   *Eros.*   O, sir, pardon me.

Antony. When I did make thee free, swor'st thou not
then
To do this when I bade thee? Do it at once,
Or thy precedent° services are all
But accidents unpurposed. Draw, and come.

85   *Eros.* Turn from me then that noble countenance
Wherein the worship of the whole world lies.

Antony. Lo thee!°   [*Turns from him.*]

Eros. My sword is drawn.

Antony.   Then let it do at once
The thing why thou hast drawn it.

Eros.   My dear master,

---

73 **pleached** folded (twisted behind?)   74 **corrigible** submissive
74–75 **subdued/To penetrative shame** filled with the humiliation of
deepest shame   76–77 **branded . . . ensued** made as hideously clear as
the mark branded on a criminal or animal the abject nature of the man
who followed   83 **precedent** former   87 **Lo thee** there you are, then

My captain, and my emperor, let me say,   *90*
Before I strike this bloody stroke, farewell.

Antony. 'Tis said, man, and farewell.

Eros. Farewell, great chief. Shall I strike now?

Antony.   Now, Eros.

Eros. Why, there then! Thus I do escape the sorrow
Of Antony's death.   *Kills himself.*

Antony.   Thrice-nobler than myself,   *95*
Thou teachest me, O valiant Eros, what
I should, and thou couldst not. My queen and Eros
Have by their brave instruction got upon me
A nobleness in record.° But I will be
A bridegroom in my death, and run into't   *100*
As to a lover's bed. Come then; and, Eros,
Thy master dies thy scholar. To do thus
                              [*Falls on his sword.*]
I learned of thee. How? Not dead? Not dead?
The guard, ho! O, dispatch me!

    Enter [*Decretas and*] *a* [*Company of the*] *Guard.*

First Guard.   What's the noise?

Antony. I have done my work ill, friends. O, make an
     end   *105*
Of what I have begun.

Second Guard.   The star is fall'n.

First Guard. And time is at his period.°

All.   Alas, and woe!

Antony. Let him that loves me strike me dead.

First Guard.   Not I.

Second Guard. Nor I.

Third Guard. Nor anyone.   *Exeunt* [*Guard*].   *110*

Decretas. Thy death and fortunes bid thy followers fly.

98–99 **got ... record** beaten me in achieving a noble place in the
story   107 **period** end

This sword but shown to Caesar, with this tidings,
Shall enter° me with him.

Enter Diomedes.

Diomedes. Where's Antony?

Decretas.   There, Diomed, there.

Diomedes.   Lives he?
115   Wilt thou not answer, man?   [*Exit Decretas.*]

Antony. Art thou there, Diomed? Draw thy sword, and
       give me
   Sufficing strokes for death.

Diomedes.   Most absolute lord,
   My mistress Cleopatra sent me to thee.

Antony. When did she send thee?

Diomedes.   Now, my lord.

Antony.   Where is she?

Diomedes. Locked in her monument. She had a
120   prophesying fear
   Of what hath come to pass; for when she saw
   (Which never shall be found) you did suspect
   She had disposed° with Caesar, and that your rage
   Would not be purged,° she sent you word she was
       dead;
125   But, fearing since how it might work, hath sent
   Me to proclaim the truth, and I am come,
   I dread, too late.

Antony. Too late, good Diomed. Call my guard, I
       prithee.

Diomedes. What ho! The Emperor's guard! The guard,
       what ho!
130   Come, your lord calls!

       Enter four or five of the Guard of Antony.

Antony. Bear me, good friends, where Cleopatra bides;

113 **enter** recommend   123 **disposed** settled things   124 **purged** cured

'Tis the last service that I shall command you.

First Guard. Woe, woe are we, sir, you may not live
    to wear
All your true followers out.°

All.   Most heavy day!

Antony. Nay, good my fellows, do not please sharp
    fate   135
To grace it with your sorrows. Bid that welcome
Which comes to punish us, and we punish it,
Seeming to bear it lightly. Take me up:
I have led you oft; carry me now, good friends,
And have my thanks for all.   140
                Exit [the Guard,] bearing Antony.

[Scene 15. *Alexandria. The monument.*]

*Enter Cleopatra and her Maids aloft,° with
Charmian and Iras.*

Cleopatra. O, Charmian, I will never go from hence.

Charmian. Be comforted, dear madam.

Cleopatra.   No, I will not.
All strange and terrible events are welcome,
But comforts we despise. Our size of sorrow,
Proportioned to our cause, must be as great   5
As that which makes it.

           Enter Diomed [below].

               How now? Is he dead?

Diomedes. His death's upon him, but not dead.

133–34 **live ... out** outlive all your faithful men   4.15.s.d. **aloft** (presumably on the upper stage at the back of the main stage)

Look out o' th' other side your monument;
His guard have brought him thither.

*Enter, [below,] Antony, and the Guard [bearing
          him].*

Cleopatra.   O sun,
      Burn the great sphere thou mov'st in: darkling°
10   stand
      The varying shore o' th' world! O Antony,
      Antony, Antony! Help, Charmian, help, Iras, help:
      Help, friends below, let's draw him hither.°

Antony.   Peace!
      Not Caesar's valor hath o'erthrown Antony,
15   But Antony's hath triumphed on itself.

Cleopatra. So it should be, that none but Antony
      Should conquer Antony, but woe 'tis so!

Antony. I am dying, Egypt, dying; only
      I here importune° death awhile, until
20   Of many thousand kisses the poor last
      I lay upon thy lips.

Cleopatra.   I dare not,° dear;
      Dear my lord, pardon: I dare not,
      Lest I be taken. Not th' imperious show
      Of the full-fortuned Caesar ever shall
25   Be brooched with me,° if knife, drugs, serpents have
      Edge, sting, or operation. I am safe:
      Your wife Octavia, with her modest eyes
      And still conclusion,° shall acquire no honor
      Demuring° upon me. But come, come, Antony—
30   Help me, my women—we must draw thee up:
      Assist, good friends.

Antony.   O, quick, or I am gone.

10 **darkling** in darkness   12–13 **help … hither** (Shakespeare appears
to have made a false start, afterwards left uncanceled, in lines 12–13, or
even to line 29; Cleopatra's plan for getting Antony in is passed over,
then repeated, in a curious way; and Antony's "I am dying" is also
repeated)   19 **importune** beg   21 **dare not** i.e., dare not descend, or
open the gates   25 **Be brooched with me** have me as its ornament
28 **still conclusion** (1) silent judgment (2) impassive finality
29 **Demuring** looking soberly

Cleopatra. Here's sport indeed! How heavy weighs my
        lord!
    Our strength is all gone into heaviness,°
    That makes the weight. Had I great Juno's power,
    The strong-winged Mercury should fetch thee up   35
    And set thee by Jove's side. Yet come a little,
    Wishers were ever fools. O, come, come, come.
                They heave Antony aloft to Cleopatra.
    And welcome, welcome! Die when thou hast lived,
    Quicken° with kissing. Had my lips that power,
    Thus would I wear them out.

All.   A heavy sight!   40

Antony. I am dying, Egypt, dying.
    Give me some wine, and let me speak a little.

Cleopatra. No, let me speak, and let me rail so high
    That the false housewife° Fortune break her wheel,°
    Provoked by my offense.°

Antony.   One word, sweet queen.   45
    Of Caesar seek your honor, with your safety. O!

Cleopatra. They do not go together.

Antony.   Gentle, hear me:
    None about Caesar trust but Proculeius.

Cleopatra. My resolution and my hands I'll trust,
    None about Caesar.   50

Antony. The miserable change now at my end
    Lament nor sorrow at, but please your thoughts
    In feeding them with those my former fortunes,
    Wherein I lived; the greatest prince o' th' world,
    The noblest; and do now not basely die,   55
    Not cowardly put off my helmet to
    My countryman; a Roman, by a Roman

---

33 **heaviness** (1) weight (2) sorrow   39 **Quicken** come to life   44 **false
housewife** treacherous hussy, strumpet   44 **wheel** (1) spinning wheel
(the especial property of a "housewife") (2) wheel of Fortune, whose
turns govern the affairs of men   45 **offense** insults

Valiantly vanquished. Now my spirit is going,
I can no more.

Cleopatra.   Noblest of men, woo't die?
60   Hast thou no care of me? Shall I abide
In this dull world, which in thy absence is
No better than a sty? O, see, my women,

                    [*Antony dies.*]

The crown o' th' earth doth melt. My lord!
O, withered is the garland° of the war,
65   The soldier's pole° is fall'n: young boys and girls
Are level now with men. The odds° is gone,
And there is nothing left remarkable°
Beneath the visiting moon.   [*Faints.*]

Charmian.   O, quietness, lady!

Iras. She's dead too, our sovereign.

Charmian.   Lady!

Iras.   Madam!

70   *Charmian.* O madam, madam, madam!

Iras. Royal Egypt! Empress!

Charmian.   Peace, peace, Iras!

Cleopatra. No more but e'en a woman, and commanded
By such poor passion as the maid that milks
And does the meanest chares.° It were for me
75   To throw my scepter at the injurious gods,
To tell them that this world did equal theirs
Till they had stol'n our jewel. All's but naught.
Patience is sottish,° and impatience does
Become a dog that's mad: then is it sin
80   To rush into the secret house of death
Ere death dare come to us? How do you, women?
What, what, good cheer! Why, how now, Charmian?
My noble girls! Ah, women, women, look,

---

64 **garland** flower, crown   65 **pole** (1) standard (2) polestar (3) May-
pole (suggested by "garland")   66 **odds** measure, distinctive value
67 **remarkable** wonderful   74 **chares** chores   78 **sottish** dully stupid

Our lamp is spent, it's out. Good sirs,° take heart:
We'll bury him; and then, what's brave, what's noble,　85
Let's do't after the high Roman fashion,
And make death proud to take us. Come, away.
This case of that huge spirit now is cold.
Ah, women, women! Come; we have no friend
But resolution, and the briefest° end.　90

　　　　　　Exeunt, bearing off Antony's body.

84 **sirs** (used of women, as of men)　90 **briefest** swiftest

[ACT 5

Scene 1. *Alexandria. Caesar's camp.*]

Enter Caesar, Agrippa, Dolabella, Maecenas,
[Gallus, Proculeius,] with his Council of War.

Caesar. Go to him, Dolabella, bid him yield:
Being so frustrate, tell him, he mocks
The pauses that he makes.°

Dolabella.   Caesar, I shall.   [*Exit.*]

Enter Decretas, with the sword of Antony.

Caesar. Wherefore is that? And what art thou that
    dar'st
Appear thus° to us?

5 *Decretas.*   I am called Decretas.
Mark Antony I served, who best was worthy
Best to be served. Whilst he stood up and spoke,
He was my master, and I wore my life
To spend upon his haters. If thou please
10 To take me to thee, as I was to him
I'll be to Caesar; if thou pleasest not,
I yield thee up my life.

Caesar.   What is't thou say'st?

5.1.2–3 **Being so . . . he makes** tell him that, since he is truly defeated,
these delays are a mere mockery   5 **thus** i.e., holding a naked sword

128

Decretas. I say, O Caesar, Antony is dead.

Caesar. The breaking° of so great a thing should make
　A greater crack.° The round world　　　　　　　　　15
　Should have shook lions into civil° streets
　And citizens to their dens. The death of Antony
　Is not a single doom; in the name lay
　A moiety° of the world.

Decretas.　　　　　　　　He is dead, Caesar,
　Not by a public minister of justice　　　　　　　　20
　Nor by a hirèd knife; but that self° hand
　Which writ his honor in the acts it did
　Hath, with the courage which the heart did lend it,
　Splitted the heart. This is his sword,
　I robbed his wound of it: behold it stained　　　　　25
　With his most noble blood.

Caesar.　　　　　[*Weeping*] Look you, sad friends.
　The gods rebuke me, but it is tidings
　To wash the eyes of kings.

Agrippa.　　　　　　　　And strange it is
　That nature must compel us to lament
　Our most persisted° deeds.

Maecenas.　　　　　　　His taints and honors　　　30
　Waged equal with° him.

Agrippa.　　　　　　　A rarer spirit never
　Did steer humanity; but you gods will give us
　Some faults to make us men. Caesar is touched.

Maecenas. When such a spacious mirror's set before
　　him,
　He needs must see himself.

---

14 **breaking** (1) destruction (2) disclosure, report　15 **crack** (1) breach
(2) explosive sound　16 **civil** city　19 **moiety** half　21 **self** selfsame
30 **persisted** persisted in　31 **Waged equal with** were equally matched in

35   *Caesar.*   O Antony,
        I have followed° thee to this. But we do launch°
        Diseases in our bodies. I must perforce
        Have shown to thee such a declining day
        Or look on thine: we could not stall° together
40   In the whole world. But yet let me lament
        With tears as sovereign° as the blood of hearts
        That thou, my brother, my competitor
        In top of all design,° my mate in empire,
        Friend and companion in the front of war,
45   The arm of mine own body, and the heart
        Where mine his° thoughts did kindle—that our
           stars,
        Unreconciliable, should divide
        Our equalness to this. Hear me, good friends—

                         Enter an Egyptian.

        But I will tell you at some meeter season.
50   The business of this man looks out of him;
        We'll hear him what he says. Whence are you?

     Egyptian. A poor Egyptian yet.° The Queen my
           mistress,
        Confined in all she has, her monument,
        Of thy intents desires instruction,
55   That she preparèdly may frame herself
        To th' way she's forced to.

     Caesar.   Bid her have good heart:
        She soon shall know us, by some of ours,
        How honorable and how kindly we
        Determine for her. For Caesar cannot live
        To be ungentle.

60   *Egyptian.*   So the gods preserve thee!   *Exit.*

     Caesar. Come hither, Proculeius. Go and say
        We purpose her no shame: give her what comforts
        The quality of her passion° shall require,

36 **followed** pursued   36 **launch** lance   39 **stall** dwell   41 **sovereign**
potent   42–43 **my competitor . . . design** my partner in noblest enter-
prise   46 **his** its   52 **yet** still (though Egypt will soon be Roman)
63 **passion** strong emotion (here, grief)

   Lest, in her greatness, by some mortal stroke
   She do defeat us. For her life in Rome   65
   Would be eternal in our triumph.° Go,
   And with your speediest bring us what she says
   And how you find of her.

Proculeius.   Caesar, I shall.
                                        Exit Proculeius.

Caesar. Gallus, go you along. [*Exit Gallus.*] Where's
      Dolabella,
   To second Proculeius?

All.   Dolabella!   70

Caesar. Let him alone, for I remember now
   How he's employed. He shall in time be ready.
   Go with me to my tent, where you shall see
   How hardly° I was drawn into this war,
   How calm and gentle I proceeded still   75
   In all my writings. Go with me, and see
   What I can show in this.   *Exeunt.*

[Scene 2. *Alexandria. The monument.*]

   Enter Cleopatra, Charmian, Iras, and Mardian.

Cleopatra. My desolation does begin to make
   A better life. 'Tis paltry to be Caesar:
   Not being Fortune, he's but Fortune's knave,°
   A minister of her will. And it is great
   To do that thing that ends all other deeds,   5
   Which shackles accidents and bolts up change;

65–66 **For her ... our triumph** alive, in Rome, walking in my triumphal procession, she would manifest my power to the end of time
74 **hardly** reluctantly   5.2.3 **knave** servant

Which sleeps, and never palates° more the dung,
The beggar's nurse and Caesar's.°

Enter, [to the gates of the monument,] Proculeius,
[Gallus, and Soldiers].

Proculeius. Caesar sends greeting to the Queen of
    Egypt,
10 And bids thee study on what fair demands
    Thou mean'st to have him grant thee.

Cleopatra.   What's thy name?

Proculeius. My name is Proculeius.

Cleopatra.   Antony
    Did tell me of you, bade me trust you, but
    I do not greatly care to be deceived,°
15 That have no use for trusting. If your master
    Would have a queen his beggar, you must tell him
    That majesty, to keep decorum, must
    No less beg than a kingdom: if he please
    To give me conquered Egypt for my son,
20 He gives me so much of mine own as I
    Will kneel to him with thanks.

Proculeius.   Be of good cheer:
    Y' are fall'n into a princely hand, fear nothing.
    Make your full reference freely° to my lord,
    Who is so full of grace that it flows over
25 On all that need. Let me report to him
    Your sweet dependency, and you shall find
    A conqueror that will pray in aid for kindness,°
    Where he for grace is kneeled to.

Cleopatra.   Pray you, tell him
    I am his fortune's vassal, and I send him
30 The greatness he has got. I hourly learn
    A doctrine of obedience, and would gladly
    Look him i' th' face.

---

7 **palates** tastes   7–8 **the dung ... Caesar's** the dungy earth, whose fruits
are the source of life to beggar and to emperor   14 **to be deceived** whether
or not I am deceived   23 **Make ... freely** hand your affairs
fully   27 **pray in aid for kindness** beg you to assist him to be kind to you

Proculeius.   This I'll report, dear lady.
  Have comfort, for I know your plight is pitied
  Of him that caused it.

    [*Enter Gallus and Soldiers behind.*]°

  You see how easily she may be surprised.   35
              [*They seize Cleopatra.*]
  Guard her till Caesar come.

Iras. Royal Queen!

Charmian. O, Cleopatra! Thou art taken, Queen.

Cleopatra. Quick, quick, good hands!
             [*Draws a dagger.*]

Proculeius.   Hold, worthy lady, hold!
             [*Disarms her.*]
  Do not yourself such wrong, who are in this   40
  Relieved,° but not betrayed.

Cleopatra.   What, of death too,
  That rids our dogs of languish?°

Proculeius.   Cleopatra,
  Do not abuse my master's bounty by
  Th' undoing of yourself: let the world see
  His nobleness well acted, which your death   45
  Will never let come forth.°

Cleopatra.   Where art thou, death?
  Come hither, come! Come, come, and take a queen
  Worth many babes and beggars!

Proculeius.   O, temperance, lady!

Cleopatra. Sir, I will eat no meat, I'll not drink, sir—
  If idle talk will once be necessary—   50
  I'll not sleep neither. This mortal house I'll ruin,
  Do Caesar what he can. Know, sir, that I
  Will not wait pinioned° at your master's court.

34 s.d. (the Folio gives no stage direction here; it was presumably left to
the stage performance to decide on the procedure by which the Romans
capture the tomb) 41 **Relieved** rescued 42 **languish** lingering illness
46 **let come forth** allow to be revealed 53 **pinioned** with clipped wings

Nor once be chastised with the sober eye
55   Of dull Octavia. Shall they hoist me up
And show me to the shouting varletry°
Of censuring Rome? Rather a ditch in Egypt
Be gentle grave unto me! Rather on Nilus' mud
Lay me stark nak'd and let the waterflies
60   Blow° me into abhorring! Rather make
My country's high pyramides° my gibbet
And hang me up in chains!

Proculeius.   You do extend
These thoughts of horror further than you shall
Find cause in Caesar.

Enter Dolabella.

Dolabella.   Proculeius,
65   What thou hast done, thy master Caesar knows,
And he hath sent for thee. For the Queen,
I'll take her to my guard.

Proculeius.   So, Dolabella,
It shall content me best: be gentle to her.
[*To Cleopatra*] To Caesar I will speak what you
    shall please,
If you'll employ me to him.

70 Cleopatra.   Say, I would die.
                  Exit Proculeius [with Soldiers].

Dolabella. Most noble Empress, you have heard of me.

Cleopatra. I cannot tell.

Dolabella.   Assuredly you know me.

Cleopatra. No matter, sir, what I have heard or known.
You laugh when boys or women tell their dreams;
Is't not your trick?°

75 Dolabella.   I understand not, madam.

Cleopatra. I dreamt there was an Emperor Antony.

56 **varletry** mob   60 **Blow** swell   61 **pyramides** (four syllables,
accented on second)   75 **trick** way

O, such another sleep, that I might see
But such another man.

Dolabella.   If it might please ye—

Cleopatra. His face was as the heav'ns, and therein
    stuck
A sun and moon, which kept their course and lighted   80
The little *O, th*' earth.

Dolabella.   Most sovereign creature—

Cleopatra. His legs bestrid the ocean: his reared arm
Crested the world: his voice was propertied
As all the tunèd spheres,° and that to friends;
But when he meant to quail° and shake the orb,   85
He was as rattling thunder. For his bounty,
There was no winter in't: an autumn 'twas
That grew the more by reaping. His delights
Were dolphinlike, they showed his back above
The element they lived in. In his livery°   90
Walked crowns and crownets:° realms and islands
    were
As plates° dropped from his pocket.

Dolabella.   Cleopatra—

Cleopatra. Think you there was or might be such a man
As this I dreamt of?

Dolabella.   Gentle madam, no.

Cleopatra. You lie, up to the hearing of the gods.   95
But if there be nor ever were one such,
It's past the size of dreaming;° nature wants stuff
To vie strange forms with fancy, yet t' imagine

83–84 **propertied . . . spheres** musical as the spheres (referring to the belief in the music of the spheres, made by the harmonious blend of each planet's "note" and normally too fine for human ears to catch)   85 **quail** make quail   90 **livery** (1) service (2) possession, guardianship (legal term)   91 **crowns and crownets** i.e., kings and princes   92 **plates** silver coins   96–97 **But if . . . dreaming** but suppose you were right, and no such man exists, and never did exist, how can I have imagined such a man, for no mere dreaming fantasy could make something so great

An Antony were nature's piece 'gainst fancy,
Condemning shadows quite.°

100 *Dolabella.*   Hear me, good madam.
Your loss is as yourself, great; and you bear it
As answering to the weight. Would I might never
O'ertake pursued success, but I do° feel,
By the rebound of yours, a grief that smites
My very heart at root.

105 *Cleopatra.*   I thank you, sir.
Know you what Caesar means to do with me?

Dolabella. I am loath to tell you what I would you
knew.

Cleopatra. Nay, pray you, sir.

Dolabella.   Though he be honorable——

Cleopatra. He'll lead me, then, in triumph?

110 *Dolabella.* Madam, he will. I know't.

> *Flourish. Enter Proculeius, Caesar, Gallus,
> Maecenas, and others of his Train.*

All. Make way there! Caesar!

Caesar. Which is the Queen of Egypt?

Dolabella. It is the Emperor, madam.

> *Cleopatra kneels.*

Caesar. Arise! You shall not kneel:
I pray you rise; rise, Egypt.

115 *Cleopatra.*   Sir, the gods
Will have it thus. My master and my lord
I must obey.

Caesar.   Take to you no hard thoughts.
The record of what injuries you did us,

97–100 **nature ... quite** reality lacks the material to compete with
imagination in the creation of strange forms, yet the creation of an
Antony would be a masterpiece of conception on the part of reality, surpassing and discrediting all the illusions of imagination   103 **but I do** if
I do not

Though written in our flesh, we shall remember
As things but done by chance.

Cleopatra.   Sole sir o' th' world,   *120*
I cannot project° mine own cause so well
To make it clear,° but do confess I have
Been laden with like frailties which before
Have often shamed our sex.

Caesar.   Cleopatra, know,
We will extenuate rather than enforce.°   *125*
If you apply° yourself to our intents,
Which towards you are most gentle, you shall find
A benefit in this change; but if you seek
To lay on me a cruelty by taking
Antony's course, you shall bereave yourself   *130*
Of my good purposes, and put your children
To that destruction which I'll guard them from
If thereon you rely. I'll take my leave.

Cleopatra. And may, through all the world: 'tis yours,
   and we,
Your scutcheons° and your signs of conquest, shall   *135*
Hang in what place you please. Here, my good lord.
                              [*Hands him a paper.*]

Caesar. You shall advise me in all for Cleopatra.

Cleopatra. This is the brief° of money, plate, and
   jewels
I am possessed of. 'Tis exactly valued,
Not petty things admitted. [*Calling*] Where's
   Seleucus?   *140*

                    [*Enter Seleucus.*]

Seleucus. Here, madam.

Cleopatra. This is my treasurer; let him speak, my lord,
   Upon his peril, that I have reserved
   To myself nothing. Speak the truth, Seleucus.

121 **project** set forth (accented on first syllable)   122 **clear** innocent
125 **enforce** emphasize   126 **apply** conform   135 **scutcheons** armorial
bearings (alluding to the captured shields displayed by a conqueror)
138 **brief** summary

145 *Seleucus.* Madam,
　　I had rather seel° my lips than to my peril
　　Speak that which is not.

　　Cleopatra.　　　　　　What have I kept back?

　　Seleucus. Enough to purchase what you have made
　　known.

　　Caesar. Nay, blush not, Cleopatra, I approve
　　Your wisdom in the deed.

150 *Cleopatra.*　　　　　　See, Caesar: O, behold,
　　How pomp is followed! Mine° will now be yours,
　　And should we shift estates, yours would be mine.
　　The ingratitude of this Seleucus does
　　Even make me wild. O slave, of no more trust
155　Than love that's hired! What, goest thou back? Thou
　　　shalt
　　Go back, I warrant thee; but I'll catch thine eyes,
　　Though they had wings. Slave, soulless villain, dog!
　　O rarely° base!

　　Caesar.　　　Good Queen, let us entreat you.

　　Cleopatra. O Caesar, what a wounding shame is this,
160　That thou vouchsafing here to visit me,
　　Doing the honor of they lordliness
　　To one so meek, that mine own servant should
　　Parcel° the sum of my disgraces by
　　Addition to his envy.° Say, good Caesar,
165　That I some lady° trifles have reserved,
　　Immoment° toys, things of such dignity
　　As we greet modern° friends withal; and say
　　Some nobler token I have kept apart
　　For Livia° and Octavia, to induce
170　Their mediation—must I be unfolded
　　With° one that I have bred? The gods! it smites me

146 **seel** sew up 151 **Mine** i.e., my followers 158 **rarely** exceptionally 163 **Parcel** piece out 164 **envy** malice 165 **lady** lady's 166 **Immoment** unimportant 167 **modern** ordinary 169 **Livia** Caesar's wife 170–71 **unfolded/With** exposed by

Beneath the fall I have. [*To Seleucus*] Prithee go
   hence,
Or I shall show the cinders° of my spirits
Through th' ashes of my chance.° Wert thou a man,
Thou wouldst have mercy on me.

Caesar.   Forbear, Seleucus. 175
                    [*Exit Seleucus.*]

Cleopatra. Be it known that we, the greatest, are mis-
   thought°
For things that others do, and when we fall,
We answer others' merits in our name,°
Are therefore to be pitied.

Caesar.   Cleopatra,
Not what you have reserved, nor what acknowledged, 180
Put we i' th' roll of conquest: still be't yours,
Bestow it at your pleasure, and believe
Caesar's no merchant, to make prize° with you
Of things that merchants sold. Therefore be cheered,
Make not your thoughts your prisons: no, dear
   Queen,   185
For we intend so to dispose you as
Yourself shall give us counsel. Feed and sleep:
Our care and pity is so much upon you
That we remain your friend; and so adieu.

Cleopatra. My master, and my lord!

Caesar.   Not so. Adieu. 190
          Flourish. Exeunt Caesar and his Train.

Cleopatra. He words me, girls, he words me, that I
   should not
Be noble to myself! But hark thee, Charmian.
                    [*Whispers to Charmian.*]

Iras. Finish, good lady, the bright day is done,
And we are for the dark.

---

173 **cinders** burning coals   174 **chance** fortune   176 **misthought** mis-
judged   178 **We … name** (1) we have to be responsible for faults committed in our name (*merits*=deserts, acts deserving punishment) (2) our
name is used to validate the actions of others   183 **make prize** haggle

Cleopatra.   Hie thee again:
195 I have spoke already, and it is provided;
     Go put it to the haste.

Charmian.   Madam, I will.

                    Enter Dolabella.

Dolabella. Where is the Queen?

Charmian.   Behold, sir.   [*Exit.*]

Cleopatra.   Dolabella!

Dolabella. Madam, as thereto sworn, by your command
     (Which my love makes religion to obey)
200 I tell you this: Caesar through Syria
     Intends his journey, and within three days
     You with your children will he send before.
     Make your best use of this. I have performed
     Your pleasure, and my promise.

Cleopatra.   Dolabella,
     I shall remain your debtor.

205 *Dolabella.*   I, your servant.
     Adieu, good Queen; I must attend on Caesar.

Cleopatra. Farewell, and thanks.   *Exit* [*Dolabella*].
                    Now, Iras, what think'st thou?
     Thou, an Egyptian puppet,° shall be shown
     In Rome as well as I: mechanic slaves°
210 With greasy aprons, rules, and hammers shall
     Uplift us to the view. In their thick breaths,
     Rank of gross diet,° shall we be enclouded,
     And forced to drink their vapor.

Iras.   The gods forbid!

Cleopatra. Nay, 'tis most certain, Iras. Saucy lictors°
215 Will catch at us like strumpets, and scald° rhymers
     Ballad us out o' tune. The quick comedians

208 **puppet** (she envisages Iras as a doll manipulated by the puppeteer, Octavius—i.e., a figure posed on a float following Caesar in the triumphal procession)   209 **mechanic slaves** vulgar workmen   212 **Rank of gross diet** stinking of bad food   214 **Saucy lictors** insolent officers   215 **scald** scurvy

Extemporally will stage us, and present
Our Alexandrian revels: Antony
Shall be brought drunken forth, and I shall see
Some squeaking Cleopatra boy my greatness°   220
I' th' posture of a whore.

Iras.   O, the good gods!

Cleopatra. Nay, that's certain.

Iras. I'll never see't! For I am sure mine nails
Are stronger than mine eyes.

Cleopatra.   Why, that's the way
To fool their preparation, and to conquer   225
Their most absurd intents.

                    Enter Charmian.

                    Now, Charmian!
Show me, my women, like a queen: go fetch
My best attires. I am again for Cydnus,
To meet Mark Antony. Sirrah° Iras, go.
Now, noble Charmian, we'll dispatch indeed,   230
And when thou hast done this chare,° I'll give thee
    leave
To play till doomsday. —Bring our crown and all.
                    [*Exit Iras.*] *A noise within.*
Wherefore's this noise?

                    Enter a Guardsman.

Guardsman.   Here is a rural fellow
That will not be denied your Highness' presence:
He brings you figs.   235

Cleopatra. Let him come in.   *Exit Guardsman.*
                    What poor an° instrument
May do a noble deed! He brings me liberty.
My resolution's placed,° and I have nothing

220 **boy my greatness** reduce my greatness to the crude imitation that
a boy can manage (in England women's parts were acted by boys or
young men)   229 **Sirrah** (an address to inferiors, used equally of men
or women)   231 **chare** chore   236 **What poor an** what a poor
238 **placed** fixed

Of woman in me: now from head to foot
240   I am marble-constant: now the fleeting moon°
No planet is of mine.

Enter Guardsman and Clown° [*with basket*].

Guardsman.   This is the man.

Cleopatra. Avoid,° and leave him.   *Exit Guardsman.*
Hast thou the pretty worm of Nilus° there,
That kills and pains not?

245   *Clown.* Truly I have him; but I would not be the party
that should desire you to touch him, for his biting is
immortal:° those that do die of it do seldom or never
recover.

Cleopatra. Remember'st thou any that have died on't?

250   *Clown.* Very many, men and women too. I heard of°
one of them no longer than yesterday; a very honest°
woman, but something given to lie, as a woman
should not do but in the way of honesty; how she
died of the biting of it, what pain she felt; truly, she
255   makes a very good report o' th' worm; but he that
will believe all that they say shall never be saved
by half that they do; but this is most falliable, the
worm's an odd worm.

Cleopatra. Get thee hence, farewell.

260   *Clown.* I wish you all joy of the worm.
                    [*Sets down his basket.*]

Cleopatra. Farewell.

Clown. You must think this, look you, that the worm
will do his kind.°

Cleopatra. Ay, ay, farewell.

240 **fleeting moon** (a symbol of fickleness, especially in women;
and Cleopatra's special symbol, as being Isis or moon goddess)
241 s.d. **Clown** rustic   242 **Avoid** depart   243 **worm of Nilus** serpent
of Nile, i.e., asp or small viper   247 **immortal** (his blunder for "mortal")
250 **heard of** heard from   251 **honest** (1) chaste (2) truthful (similar
innuendoes fill the speech, with puns on "lie" and "die")   263 **do his
kind** act according to his nature

Clown. Look you, the worm is not to be trusted but in   265
the keeping of wise people: for indeed there is no
goodness in the worm.

Cleopatra. Take thou no care; it shall be heeded.

Clown. Very good. Give it nothing, I pray you, for it
is not worth the feeding.   270

Cleopatra. Will it eat me?

Clown. You must not think I am so simple but I know
the devil himself will not eat a woman. I know that
a woman is a dish for the gods, if the devil dress°
her not. But truly, these same whoreson devils do   275
the gods great harm in their women; for in every
ten that they make, the devils mar five.

Cleopatra. Well, get thee gone, farewell.

Clown. Yes, forsooth. I wish you joy o' th' worm. *Exit.*

[*Enter Iras with a robe, crown, etc.*]

Cleopatra. Give me my robe, put on my crown, I have   280
Immortal longings° in me. Now no more
The juice of Egypt's grape shall moist this lip.
Yare,° yare, good Iras; quick: methinks I hear
Antony call: I see him rouse himself
To praise my noble act. I hear him mock   285
The luck of Caesar, which the gods give men
To excuse their after wrath.° Husband, I come:
Now to that name my courage prove my title!
I am fire, and air; my other elements
I give to baser life.° So, have you done?   290
Come then, and take the last warmth of my lips.
Farewell, kind Charmian, Iras, long farewell.
[*Kisses them. Iras falls and dies.*]

---

274 **dress** (1) prepare (i.e., of food) (2) clothe, equip   281 **Immortal
longings** (1) the desires of a goddess (2) longings for immor-
tality   283 **Yare** quickly   287 **their after wrath** the retributive punish-
ments heaped by the gods on those who have been too proud of their
good fortune   289–90 **I am fire ... life** (man was believed to be made
up of four elements, two higher—fire and air—and two lower or baser—
earth and water)

Have I the aspic° in my lips? Dost fall?
If thou and nature can so gently part,
295   The stroke of death is a lover's pinch,
Which hurts, and is desired. Dost thou lie still?
If thus thou vanishest, thou tell'st the world
It is not worth leave-taking.

Charmian. Dissolve, thick cloud, and rain, that I may say
The gods themselves do weep.

300   *Cleopatra.*   This proves me base:
If she first meet the curlèd° Antony,
He'll make demand of her, and spend that kiss
Which is my heaven to have. Come, thou mortal wretch,°

[*To an asp, which she applies to her breast.*]
With thy sharp teeth this knot intrinsicate°
305   Of life at once untie. Poor venomous fool,
Be angry, and dispatch.° O, couldst thou speak,
That I might hear thee call great Caesar ass
Unpolicied!°

Charmian.   O eastern star!°

Cleopatra.   Peace, peace!
Dost thou not see my baby at my breast,
That sucks the nurse asleep?

310   *Charmian.*   O, break! O, break!

Cleopatra. As sweet as balm, as soft as air, as gentle—
O, Antony! Nay, I will take thee too:

[*Applies another asp to her arm.*]
What° should I stay—   *Dies.*°

---

293 **aspic** asp   301 **curlèd** freshly barbered   303 **thou mortal wretch**
you deadly little object (**wretch,** like **fool** in line 305, is often an affec-
tionate term, used especially of children)   304 **intrinsicate** intricate
306 **dispatch** quickly end it   308 **Unpolicied** lacking statecraft
308 **eastern star** morning star, Venus   313 **What** why   313 s.d. **Dies**
(modern actresses prefer to die upright, seated regally, but Caesar's
penultimate and final speeches suggest that Cleopatra dies—as in
Plutarch—"upon a bed")

Charmian. In this wild world? So, fare thee well.
Now boast thee, death, in thy possession lies   *315*
A lass unparalleled. Downy windows, close;
And golden Phoebus° never be beheld
Of eyes again so royal! Your crown's awry;
I'll mend it, and then play—

   Enter the Guard, rustling in.

First Guard. Where's the Queen?

Charmian.   Speak softly, wake her not.   *320*

First Guard. Caesar hath sent—

Charmian.   Too slow a messenger.
           [Applies an asp.]
O, come apace, dispatch; I partly feel thee.

First Guard. Approach, ho! All's not well: Caesar's
beguiled.

Second Guard. There's Dolabella sent from Caesar;
call him.

First Guard. What work is here! Charmian, is this well
done?   *325*

Charmian. It is well done, and fitting for a princess
Descended of so many royal kings.
Ah, soldier!   *Charmian dies.*

    Enter Dolabella.

Dolabella. How goes it here?   *330*

Second Guard.   All dead.

Dolabella.   Caesar, thy thoughts
Touch their effects° in this: thyself art coming
To see performed the dreaded act which thou
So sought'st to hinder.

   Enter Caesar and all his Train, marching.

All.   A way there, a way for Caesar!

317 **Phoebus** sun god 330 **Touch their effects** meet with realization

Dolabella. O, sir, you are too sure an augurer:
That you did fear is done.

Caesar. Bravest at the last,
335 She leveled at° our purposes, and being royal,
Took her own way. The manner of their deaths?
I do not see them bleed.

Dolabella. Who was last with them?

First Guard. A simple countryman, that brought her figs.
This was his basket.

Caesar. Poisoned, then.

First Guard. O, Caesar,
340 This Charmian lived but now, she stood and spake;
I found her trimming up the diadem
On her dead mistress; tremblingly she stood,
And on the sudden dropped.

Caesar. O, noble weakness!
If they had swallowed poison, 'twould appear
345 By external swelling; but she looks like sleep,
As she would catch another Antony
In her strong toil° of grace.

Dolabella. Here, on her breast,
There is a vent° of blood, and something blown;°
The like is on her arm.

350 *First Guard.* This is an aspic's trail; and these fig leaves
Have slime upon them, such as th' aspic leaves
Upon the caves of Nile.

Caesar. Most probable
That so she died: for her physician tells me
She hath pursued conclusions° infinite
355 Of easy ways to die. Take up her bed,
And bear her women from the monument.
She shall be buried by her Antony.

335 **leveled at** (1) guessed (2) fought against   347 **toil** snare   348 **vent**
discharge   348 **blown** swollen   354 **conclusions** experiments

No grave upon the earth shall clip° in it
A pair so famous. High events as these
Strike° those that make them; and their story is　　360
No less in pity, than his glory which
Brought them to be lamented. Our army shall
In solemn show attend this funeral,
And then to Rome. Come, Dolabella, see
High order in this great solemnity.　　*Exeunt omnes.*　365

FINIS

358 **clip** clasp　　360 **Strike** touch

Textual Note

Antony and Cleopatra was entered in the Stationers' Register in May, 1608. Though this procedure normally suggested that publication would follow shortly, the play remained, in fact, unprinted until 1623, when it appeared in the "Tragedies" section of the First Folio. This First Folio text of the play is therefore the single authoritative one, and all succeeding editions—including of course the present one—derive from it.

It is widely agreed that the Folio text of *Antony and Cleopatra* was almost certainly printed direct from Shakespeare's own manuscript, and not from a transcript or prompter's copy. The features of the Folio text that suggest a source in Shakespearean manuscript may be briefly summarized as follows. First, it contains unusual spellings and word usages, some of which seem to be peculiar to Shakespeare, and some of which were, at any rate, archaic by the time the Folio was printed. Secondly, many of the Folio misprints are of the kind (occurring also in other texts of the plays) that would seem to arise from the individual character of Shakespeare's own handwriting. Thirdly, it lacks all act and scene divisions, except for the opening "Actus Primus, Scoena Prima"; a lack which indicates copy prepared primarily for the theater. Fourthly, its stage directions are unusually full and detailed, and are often of the nature of an author's "notes on the text"; for example, "Alarum afar off, as at a sea fight." And lastly, the Folio text contains a passage in the first Monument scene (4.15.12–29) that suggests the direct carrying over of the author's deletions and rewritings. (See relevant footnote to text.) None of this is absolutely conclusive, but taken together the evidence leaves little doubt that the Folio text was printed direct from Shakespeare's manuscript.

As a text, it is relatively good: it contains many slips but few real difficulties. Its major flaw is the occurrence of very frequent mislineation. This has been silently adjusted in the present edition, as the "correct" lineation is either clear, or, where doubtful, immaterial. The present edition also adds a list of dramatis personae, which is lacking in the Folio; and it adds act and scene divisions, and indications of locality, except for the Folio's opening "Actus Primus, Scoena Prima" which is here translated. It also supplements the existing stage directions. All such additions and supplementations are indicated by square brackets. The positions of a few stage directions have been slightly altered; speech prefixes and other abbreviations are expanded, punctuation and spelling are modernized. The spelling of proper names is regularized: for example, "Cleopatra" is given, though in F "Cleopater" also appears; again, "Decretas" is given though in F "Decretus" also appears; "Canidius" is given for F's "Camidius," "Camidias," and "Camindius"; and so forth. (In a few instances, where the change is more marked, the reading is listed below.) All other departures from the Folio text are listed below, and utilize earlier editorial emendations; the adopted reading is given in italics, and then the original reading in roman. As in the footnotes to the text, a line number followed by "s.d." indicates the stage direction which follows the given line, or which interrupts it.

1.1.39 *On* One   50 *whose* who

1.2.4 *charge* change   40 *fertile* foretell   63 *Alexas* [F treats "Alexas" as a speech prefix and gives him the rest of the speech here given to Charmian]   81 *Saw* Saue   113 [F adds s.d.: Enter another Messenger]   114 *ho, the news!* how the newes?   115 *First Attendant* 1 Mes   116 *Second Attendant* 2 Mes   119 *Messenger* 3 Mes   131 *Ho now, Enobarbus!* How now Enobarbus.   138 *occasion* an occasion   181 *leave* loue   186 *Hath* Haue   195 *hair* heire

1.3.25 *first* fitst   43 *services* Seruicles   82 *by my sword* by Sword

1.4.3 *Our* One   8 *Vouchsafed* vouchsafe   9 *abstract* abstracts
44 *deared* fear'd   46 *lackeying* lacking   56 *wassails* Vassailes
58 *Pansa* Pausa   75 *we* me

1.5.34 s.d. *Antony* Caesar   50 *dumbed* dumbe   61 *man* mans

2.1.16,18,38 [F's speech prefix here, as for all speeches in the scene
other than those of Pompey and Varrius, is *"Mene."* But the context
clearly indicates that Menas as well as Menecrates speaks in the
scene]   21 *waned* wand   41 *warred* wan'd

2.2.125 *not so* not, say   126 *reproof* proofe   176 s.d. *Exit* Exit omnes.
Manet   210 *glow* gloue   212 *gentlewomen* Gentlewoman   229 *heard*
hard   238 *pow'r breathe* powr breath

2.3.23 *afeard* a feare   31 *away* alway

2.5.12 *Tawny-finned* Tawny fine   43 *is* 'tis

2.6.s.d. *Agrippa, with* Agrippa, Menas with   19 *is* his   52 *jailer*
Iaylor   58 *composition* composion   66 *meanings* meaning   69 *more
of* more

2.7.1 *their* th' their   4 *high-colored* high Conlord   12 *lief* liue
36 *pyramises* Pyramisis   94 *then* then he   102 *grows* grow   113 *bear*
beate   126 *Splits* Spleet's   130 *father's* Father   131–35 *Take heed
. . . sound out* [F gives all to Enobarbus, mistaking (?) speech prefix
"Menas" for vocative]

3.1.5 *Silius* Romaine [so throughout scene]   8 *whither* whether

3.2.10 *Agrippa* Ant   16 *figures* Figure   59 *wept* weepe

3.4.9 *took't* look't   24 *yours* your   30 *Your* You   38 *has* he's

3.5.14 *world, thou hast* would thou hadst   16 *the one the other* the
other

3.6.13 *he there* hither   13 *kings of kings* King of Kings   74 *Comagene* Comageat

3.7.4 *it is* it it   5 *Is't* If   23 *Toryne* Troine   35 *muleters* Militers
51 *Actium* Action   69 *led* leade   72 *Canidius* Ven

3.10.s.d. *Enobarbus* Enobarbus and Scarus   14 *June* Inne   27 *he* his

3.11.19 *that* them   44 *He is* Hee's   47 *seize* cease   51 *whither*
whether   58 *tow* stowe   59 *Thy* The

3.13.10 *merèd* meered   55 *Caesar* Caesars   56 *embraced* embrace
74 *deputation* disputation   104 *errand* arrant   162 *smite* smile
165 *discandying* discandering   168 *sits* sets   199 *preys on* prayes
in 201 *s.d. Exit* Exeunt

4.2.1 *Domitius* Domitian

4.3.7 *Third Soldier* 1

4.4.5–8 *Nay, I'll help . . . must be* [F gives all to Cleopatra, mistaking
(?) speech prefix "Anthony" for vocative, and misplacing (?) it after
"help too"]   8 *Sooth, la* Sooth-law   13 *daff't* daft   24 *Captain* Alex

4.5.1,3,6 *Soldier* Eros

4.8.2 *gests* guests   23 *favoring* sauoring

4.12.4 *augurers* Auguries   21 *spanieled* pannelled

4.14.4 *towered* toward   10 *dislimns* dislimes   19 *Caesar* Caesars
104 *ho!* how?

4.15.72 *e'en* in   90 *s.d. off* of

5.1.s.d. *Maecenas* Menas   28,31 *Agrippa* Dol   59 *live* leaue

5.2.56 *varletry* Varlotarie   81 *little O, th' earth* little o' th' earth
87 *autumn 'twas* Anthony it was   104 *smites* suites   216 *Ballad*
Ballads   216 *o'tune* a Tune   228 *Cydnus* Cidrus   318 *awry* away
319 *s.d. rustling in* rustling in and Dolabella

The Source of *Antony and Cleopatra*

The principal source of *Antony and Cleopatra* is the "Life of Marcus Antonius," in Sir Thomas North's translation of Plutarch's *Lives of the Noble Grecians and Romans* (published 1579). Shakespeare seems to have known parts, at least, of North's Plutarch for some ten years before he wrote *Antony and Cleopatra*; and he had already used the early part of the "Life of Marcus Antonius" when gathering materials for *Julius Caesar*, seven or so years before. The use Shakespeare makes of this "Life" for *Antony and Cleopatra*, however, is far more thorough, more extensive, and more interesting. Considerable insight into Shakespeare's artistry and method of working may be gained from a comparison of the source with the play: so much does Shakespeare take from Plutarch, and so radically does he transform it. From Plutarch's whole conception of Antony, down to the last few words of his Charmion, Shakespeare borrows heavily and directly, humanizing and deepening all that he borrows; and the process is illuminating. For this reason, all the space available here will be given to the selections from Plutarch. A reader interested in the other works which contributed to the play (to a much smaller degree, but still interestingly) will find a discussion of them in Professor Kenneth Muir's valuable study, *Shakespeare's Sources* (London, 1957), Vol. I, "Comedies and Tragedies," pp. 201–19.

Shakespeare's handling of his main source may be briefly outlined as follows. Plutarch's life of Antony is full, leisurely, and detailed: the excerpts given here represent only about a quarter of the whole. Shakespeare takes from Plutarch all the major events of Antony's later life, with one exception: the long and unsuccessful campaign against the Parthians; he also makes use of events that take place before the opening of the play, such as Antony's first meeting with Cleopatra and what ensues from it. In addition, he borrows—sometimes to an exceptional degree—from Plutarch's vivid, pithy, and dignified narration of speeches and events. In each case, the rehandling is instructive.

Two examples of the first kind of borrowing must suffice here. First, the situation at the opening of the play. Plutarch recounts how Antony, while with Cleopatra in Alexandria, hears news both of Fulvia's and Lucius' wars against Caesar, their defeat and expulsion from Italy, and of Labienus' victories in Asia; Antony prepares to meet the Parthians but is recalled to Italy by letters from his wife, and on the journey hears of her death. At a later point, after his marriage to Octavia, the threat from Sextus Pompeius arises. All this Shakespeare compacts into the news brought, with an effect of rapidly mounting disaster, to Antony in Cleopatra's court, violently challenging his former mood of serene and triumphant exhilaration and necessitating his immediate departure. Thus, in the first two scenes of the play, Shakespeare uses Plutarch's materials cogently and with strong effect, establishing thereby the major conflict of the play. For a second example: his handling of the events succeeding Actium. Shakespeare abbreviates and rearranges, so that the defeat's importance and finality (and Cleopatra's blame in it) are accentuated; the desertion of Domitius (a minor character in Plutarch, whom Shakespeare converts into the far more important Enobarbus) is moved from before Actium to after it, accentuating Antony's isolation in defeat, and the deserter dies not of illness but of a broken heart; and the one successful sally against Caesar, Shakespeare places after, instead of before, Antony's farewell to his servants and the departure of Hercules—thus making the isolated Antony's last exhilaration of victory the more ironic and pathetic, and yet paradoxically heroic. In each of these examples, Shakespeare is not merely compacting and rearranging for dramatic purposes; he is making great tragedy out of good history.

The same may be said of some of the passages where the verbal echoes and reminiscences are strongest. For example, Enobarbus' famous "The barge she sat in, like a burnished throne . . ." is extremely close to Plutarch's beautiful description of Cleopatra at Cydnus. But where Plutarch is describing a rich and exquisite scene, Shakespeare is creating—by small additions and alterations—the extraordinary power of Cleopatra that draws the people, the winds, and the water longingly after her. By giving the speech of reminiscence to the tough and common-sense Enobarbus, and touching it with his humor and "Roman" sanity, Shakespeare heightens, by contrast, the hyperbolical praise of Cleopatra; and, more, he brings alive the conflicting values of the play. Antony is about to marry Octavia; Enobarbus' speech revives the full and fatal power of Cleopatra, at her first meeting with Antony. Both the recreation of the speech and its placing in the play throw the greatest light on Shakespeare's artistic intentions.

The selections that follow offer a wealth of such comparisons, revealing both Shakespeare's large-scale handling of his materials and his transformation of work that is, in its own right, not without excellence and interest.

PLUTARCH

From "Life of Marcus Antonius," in
The Lives of the Noble Grecians and Romans

He had a noble presence, and showed a countenance of
one of a noble house: he had a goodly thick beard, a broad
forehead, crook-nosed, and there appeared such a manly
look in his countenance as is commonly seen in Hercules'
pictures, stamped or graven in metal. Now it had been a
speech of old time that the family of the Antonii were
descended from one Anton, the son of Hercules, whereof
the family took name. This opinion did Antonius seek to
confirm in all his doings, not only resembling him in the
likeness of his body, as we have said before, but also in the
wearing of his garments. For when he would openly show
himself abroad before many people, he would always wear
his cassock girt down low upon his hips, with a great sword
hanging by his side, and upon that some ill-favored cloak.
Furthermore, things that seem intolerable in other men, as
to boast commonly, to jest with one or other, to drink like a
good fellow with everybody, to sit with the soldiers when

Spelling and punctuation have been modernized. Large excisions are
made from Plutarch's account of Antony's life before the meeting with
Cleopatra; after this point, omissions are briefly summarized between
square brackets. The reader who wishes to read Plutarch's words (in North's
translation) rather than the editor's occasional summaries, can find them
conveniently in *Shakespeare's Plutarch*, ed. Walter W. Skeat (London,
1875), and in *Shakespeare's Plutarch*, ed. C. F. Tucker Brooke (London,
1909).

they dine, and to eat and drink with them soldierlike, it is incredible what wonderful love it won him amongst them.

And furthermore, being given to love, that made him the more desired, and by that means he brought many to love him. For he would further every man's love, and also would not be angry that men should merrily tell him of those he loved. But besides all this, that which most procured his rising and advancement was his liberality, who gave all to the soldiers and kept nothing for himself; and when he was grown to great credit, then was his authority and power also very great, the which notwithstanding himself did over-throw by a thousand other faults he had.

. . . Antonius being thus inclined, the last and extremist mischief of all other (to wit, the love of Cleopatra) lighted on him, who did waken and stir up many vices yet hidden in him, and were never seen to any; and if any spark of good-ness or hope of rising were left him, Cleopatra quenched it straight and made it worse than before. The manner how he fell in love with her was this. Antonius, going to make war with the Parthians, sent to command Cleopatra to appear personally before him, when he came into Cilicia, to answer unto such accusations as were laid against her, being this: that she had aided Cassius and Brutus in their war against him. The messenger sent unto Cleopatra to make this summons unto her was called Dellius, who when he had thoroughly considered her beauty, the excellent grace and sweetness of her tongue, he nothing mistrusted that Antonius would do any hurt to so noble a lady, but rather assured himself that within few days she should be in great favor with him. Thereupon he did her great honor and persuaded her to come into Cilicia as honorably furnished as she could possible, and bade her not to be afraid at all of Antonius, for he was a more courteous lord than any that she had ever seen. Cleopatra, on the other side, believing Dellius' words, and guessing by the former access and credit she had with Julius Caesar and Cneius Pompey (the son of Pompey the Great) only for her beauty, she began to have good hope that she might more easily win Antonius. For Caesar and Pompey knew her when she was but a young thing, and knew not then what the world meant; but now she went to Antonius at the age when a woman's beauty is at the prime, and she also of best judgment. So, she furnished herself with a world of gifts, store of gold and silver, and of riches and other sumptuous ornaments as is credible enough she might bring from so great a house, and from so wealthy and rich a realm as Egypt was. But yet she carried nothing with her wherein she trusted more than in herself, and in the charms and enchantment of her passing beauty and grace. Therefore when she was sent unto by divers letters, both from Antonius himself and also from his friends, she made so light of it and mocked Antonius so much that she disdained to set forward otherwise, but to take her barge in the river of Cydnus, the poop whereof was of gold, the sails of purple, and the oars of silver, which kept stroke in rowing after the sound of the music of flutes, hautboys, citherns, viols, and such other instruments as they played upon in the barge. And now for the person of herself: she was laid under a pavilion of cloth of gold of tissue, appareled and attired like the goddess Venus commonly drawn in picture; and hard by her, on either hand of her, pretty fair boys appareled as painters do set forth god Cupid, with little fans in their hands, with the which they fanned wind upon her. Her ladies and gentlewomen also, the fairest of them were appareled like the nymphs Nereides (which are the mermaids of the waters) and like the Graces, some steering the helm, others tending the tackle and ropes of the barge, out of the which there came a wonderful passing sweet savor of perfumes that perfumed the wharf's side, pestered with innumerable multitudes of people. Some of them followed the barge all alongst the river's side; others also ran out of the city to see her coming in. So that in the end, there ran such multitudes of people one after another to see her that Antonius was left post alone in the market place in his imperial seat to give audience, and there went a rumor in the people's mouths that the goddess Venus was come to play with the god Bacchus for the general good of all Asia. When Cleopatra landed, Antonius sent to invite her to supper to him. But she sent him word again, he should do better rather to come and sup with her. Antonius, therefore, to show himself courteous unto her at her arrival, was contented to obey her, and went to supper to her, where he found such passing sumptuous fare that no tongue can express it. But amongst all other things, he most wondered at the infinite number of lights and torches hanged on the top of the house, giving light in every place, so artificially set and ordered by devices, some round, some square, that it was the rarest thing to behold that eye could discern, or that ever books could mention. The next night, Antonius feasting her contended to pass her in magnificence and fineness, but she overcame him in both. So that he himself began to scorn the gross service of his house, in respect of Cleopatra's sumptuousness and fineness. And, when Cleopatra found Antonius' jests and slents to be but gross and soldierlike in plain manner, she gave it him finely and without fear taunted him thoroughly. Now her beauty (as it is reported) was not so passing, as unmatchable of other women, nor yet such as upon present view did enamor men with her; but so sweet was her company and conversation that a man could not possibly but be taken. And besides her beauty, the good grace she had to talk and discourse, her courteous nature that tempered her words and deeds, was a spur that pricked to the quick. Furthermore, besides all these, her voice and words were marvelous pleasant, for her tongue was an instrument of music to divers sports and pastimes, the which she easily turned to any language that pleased her. She spake unto few barbarous people by interpreter, but made them answer herself, or at least the most part of them: as the Ethiopians, the Arabians, the Troglodytes, the Hebrews, the Syrians, the Medes, and the Parthians, and to many others also, whose languages she had learned. Whereas divers of her progenitors, the kings of Egypt, could scarce learn the Egyptian tongue only, and many of them forgot to speak the Macedonian. Now Antonius was so ravished with the love of Cleopatra that though his wife Fulvia had great wars, and much ado with Caesar for his affairs, and that the army of the Parthians (the which the king's lieutenants had given to the only leading of Labienus) was now assembled in Mesopotamia ready to invade Syria, yet, as though all this had nothing touched him, he yielded himself to go with

Cleopatra into Alexandria, where he spent and lost in childish sports (as a man might say) and idle pastimes the most precious thing a man can spend, as Antiphon saith, and that is, time.

. . . For she, were it in sport or in matter of earnest, still devised new delights to have Antonius at commandment, never leaving him night nor day, nor once letting him go out of her sight. For she would play at dice with him, drink with him, and hunt commonly with him, and also be with him when he went to any exercise or activity of body. And sometime also, when he would go up and down the city disguised like a slave in the night, and would peer into poor men's windows and their shops, and scold and brawl with them within the house, Cleopatra would be also in a chambermaid's array, and amble up and down the streets with him, so that ofttimes Antonius bear away both mocks and blows. Now, though most men misliked this manner, yet the Alexandrians were commonly glad of this jollity, and liked it well, saying very gallantly and wisely that Antonius showed them a comical face, to wit, a merry countenance; and the Romans a tragical face, to say, a grim look. But to reckon up all the foolish sports they made, reveling in this sort, it were too fond a part of me, and therefore I will only tell you one among the rest. On a time he went to angle for fish, and when he could take none he was as angry as could be, because Cleopatra stood by. Wherefore he secretly commanded the fishermen that when he cast in his line they should straight dive under the water and put a fish on his hook which they had taken before; and so snatched up his angling rod and brought up fish twice or thrice. Cleopatra found it straight, yet she seemed not to see it, but wondered at his excellent fishing; but, when she was alone by herself among her own people, she told them how it was and bade them the next morning to be on the water to see the fishing. A number of people came to the haven and got into the fisher boats to see this fishing. Antonius then threw in his line, and Cleopatra straight commanded one of her men to dive underwater before Antonius' men, and to put some old salt fish upon his bait, like unto those that are brought out of the country of Pont. When he had hung the fish on his hook, Antonius, thinking he had taken a fish indeed, snatched up his line presently. Then they all fell a-laughing. Cleopatra laughing also, said unto him: "Leave us (my lord) Egyptians (which dwell in the country of Pharus and Canobus) your angling rod: this is not thy profession; thou must hunt after conquering of realms and countries." Now Antonius, delighting in these fond and childish pastimes, very ill news were brought him from two places. The first from Rome, that his brother Lucius and Fulvia his wife fell out first between themselves and afterwards fell to open war with Caesar, and had brought all to nought that they were both driven to fly out of Italy. The second news, as bad as the first: that Labienus conquered all Asia with the army of the Parthians, from the river of Euphrates and from Syria, unto the countries of Lydia and Ionia. Then began Antonius with much ado a little to rouse himself, as if he had been wakened out of a deep sleep, and as a man may say, coming out of a great drunkenness. So, first of all he bent himself against the Parthians and went as far as the country of Phoenicia; but there he received lamentable letters from his wife Fulvia. Whereupon he straight returned towards Italy with two hundred sail; and as he went, took up his friends by the way that fled out of Italy to come to him. By them he was informed that his wife Fulvia was the only cause of this war, who, being of a peevish, crooked, and troublesome nature, had purposely raised this uproar in Italy, in hope thereby to withdraw him from Cleopatra. But by good fortune his wife Fulvia, going to meet with Antonius, sickened by the way and died in the city of Sicyon; and therefore Octavius Caesar and he were the easilier made friends together. For when Antonius landed in Italy, and that men saw Caesar asked nothing of him, and that Antonius on the other side laid all the fault and burden on his wife Fulvia, the friends of both parties would not suffer them to unrip any old matters and to prove or defend who had the wrong or right and was who the first procurer of this war, fearing to make matters worse between them; but they made them friends together and divided the Empire of Rome between them, making the sea Ionium the bounds of their division. For they gave all the

provinces eastward unto Antonius, and the countries west-
ward unto Caesar: and left Africk unto Lepidus, and make a
law that they three one after another should make their
friends consuls, when they would not be themselves. This
seemed to be a sound counsel, but yet it was to be confirmed with a straiter bond, which fortune offered thus.
There was Octavia, the eldest sister of Caesar, not by one
mother, for she came of Ancharia, and Caesar himself
afterwards of Accia. It is reported that he dearly loved his
sister Octavia, for indeed she was a noble lady and left the
widow of her first husband Caius Marcellus, who died not
long before; and it seemed also that Antonius had been widower ever since the death of his wife Fulvia. For he denied
not that he kept Cleopatra, but so did he not confess that he
had her as his wife; and so with reason he did defend the
love he bare unto this Egyptian Cleopatra. Thereupon every
man did set forward this marriage, hoping thereby that this
Lady Octavia, having an excellent grace, wisdom, and honesty, joined unto so rare a beauty, that when she were with
Antonius (he loving her as so worthy a lady deserveth) she
should be a good mean to keep good love and amity betwixt
her brother and him. So, when Caesar and he had made the
match between them, they both went to Rome about this
marriage, although it was against the law that a widow
should be married within ten months after her husband's
death. Howbeit the Senate dispensed with the law, and so
the marriage proceeded accordingly. Sextus Pompeius at
that time kept in Sicilia and so made many an inroad into
Italy with a great number of pinnaces and other pirates'
ships, of the which were captains two notable pirates,
Menas and Menecrates, who so scoured all the sea thereabouts that none durst peep out with a sail. Furthermore,
Sextus Pompeius had dealt very friendly with Antonius, for
he had courteously received his mother, when she fled out
of Italy with Fulvia; and therefore they thought good to
make peace with him. So they met all three together by the
mount of Misenum, upon a hill that runneth far into the sea,
Pompey having his ships riding hard by at anchor, and
Antonius and Caesar their armies upon the shore side,
directly over against him. Now, after they had agreed that

Sextus Pompeius should have Sicile and Sardinia, with this condition, that he should rid the sea of all thieves and pirates and make it safe for passengers and withal that he should send a certain [amount] of wheat to Rome, one of them did feast another and drew cuts who should begin. It was Pompeius' chance to invite them first. Whereupon Antonius asked him: "And where shall we sup?" "There," said Pompey and showed him his admiral galley which had six banks of oars: "That," said he, "is my father's house they have left me." He spake it to taunt Antonius, because he had his father's house, that was Pompey the Great. So he cast anchors enow into the sea to make his galley fast, and then built a bridge of wood to convey them to his galley from the head of Mount Misenum, and there he welcomed them and made them great cheer. Now in the midst of the feast, when they fell to be merry with Antonius' love unto Cleopatra, Menas the pirate came to Pompey and, whispering in his ear, said unto him: "Shall I cut the cables of the anchors and make thee lord not only of Sicile and Sardinia, but of the whole Empire of Rome besides?" Pompey, having paused awhile upon it, at length answered him: "Thou shouldst have done it, and never have told it me, but now we must content us with that we have. As for myself, I was never taught to break my faith nor to be counted a traitor." The other two also did likewise feast him in their camp, and then he returned into Sicile. Antonius, after this agreement made, sent Ventidius before into Asia to stay the Parthians and to keep them they should come no further; and he himself in the meantime, to gratify Caesar, was contented to be chosen Julius Caesar's priest and sacrificer, and so they jointly together dispatched all great matters concerning the state of the Empire. But in all other manner of sports and exercises, wherein they passed the time away the one with the other, Antonius was ever inferior unto Caesar and always lost, which grieved him much. With Antonius there was a soothsayer or astronomer of Egypt that could cast a figure and judge of men's nativities, to tell them what should happen to them. He, either to please Cleopatra or else for that he found it so by his art, told Antonius plainly that his fortune (which of itself was excellent good and very great) was altogether blemished and obscured by Caesar's fortune; and therefore he counseled him utterly to leave his company and to get him as far from him as he could. "For thy Demon," said he, "that is to say, the good angel and spirit that keepeth thee, is afraid of his, and being courageous and high when he is alone, becometh fearful and timorous when he cometh near unto the other." Howsoever it was, the events ensuing proved the Egyptian's words true. For it is said that as often as they two drew cuts for pastime, who should have anything, or whether they played at dice, Antonius always lost. Oftentimes, when they were disposed to see cockfight, or quails that were taught to fight one with another, Caesar's cocks or quails did ever overcome. The which spited Antonius in his mind, although he made no outward show of it, and therefore he believed the Egyptian the better. In fine, he recommended the affairs of his house unto Caesar and went out of Italy with Octavia his wife, whom he carried into Greece after he had had a daughter by her. So Antonius lying all the winter at Athens, news came unto him of the victories of Ventidius, who had overcome the Parthians in battle, in the which also were slain Labienus and Pharnabates, the chiefest captain King Orodes had. For these good news he feasted all Athens and kept open house for all the Grecians, and many games of price were played at Athens, of the which he himself would be judge. . . .

In the meantime, Ventidius once again overcame Pacorus (Orodes' son, King of Parthia) in a battle fought in the country of Cyrrestica, he being come again with a great army to invade Syria, at which battle was slain a great number of the Parthians and among them Pacorus the King's own son slain. This noble exploit, as famous as ever any was, was a full revenge to the Romans of the shame and loss they had received before by the death of Marcus Crassus, and he made the Parthians fly and glad to keep themselves within the confines and territories of Mesopotamia and Media, after they had thrice together been overcome in several battles. Howbeit Ventidius durst not undertake to follow them any further, fearing lest he should have gotten Antonius' displeasure by it. . . . Ventidius was the only man that ever triumphed of the Parthians until this present day, a mean man born and of no noble house nor family, who only came to that he attained unto through Antonius' friendship, the which delivered him happy occasion to achieve to great matters. And yet, to say truly, he did so well quit himself in all his enterprises that he confirmed that which was spoken of Antonius and Caesar, to wit, that they were always more fortunate when they made war by their lieutenants, than by themselves. For Sossius, one of Antonius' lieutenants in Syria, did notable good service, and Canidius, whom he had also left his lieutenant in the borders of Armenia, did conquer it all.

[Hostility develops again between Antony and Octavius, but Octavia makes peace between them. After a brief interval Antony rejoins Cleopatra and heaps honors on her and their children. His long unsuccessful campaign against the Parthians follows. Octavia prepares to rejoin Antony, encouraged by Octavius, who hopes to find grounds for war if she is rebuffed by her husband; and she is rebuffed. The patience and charity of her behavior on her return angers all Rome against Antony, an anger increased by his gifts of lands to Cleopatra's children. Octavius declares war against Cleopatra. Antony and Octavius prepare for war; Cleopatra persuades Antony to let her accompany him.]

Now Antonius was made so subject to a woman's will that though he was a great deal the stronger by land, yet for Cleopatra's sake he would needs have this battle tried by sea, though he saw before his eyes, that, for lack of watermen, his captains did press by force all sorts of men out of Greece that they could take up in the field, as travelers, muleteers, reapers, harvest men, and young boys, and yet could they not sufficiently furnish his galleys so that the most part of them were empty, and could scant row, because they lacked watermen enow. But on the contrary side Caesar's ships were not built for pomp, high and great, only for a sight and bravery, but they were light of yarage, armed and furnished with watermen as many as they needed, and had them all in readiness in the havens of Tarentum and Brundusium. So Octavius Caesar sent unto

Antonius, to will him to delay no more time, but to come on with his army into Italy, and that for his own part he would give him safe harbor, to land without any trouble, and that he would withdraw his army from the sea as far as one horse could run, until he had put his army ashore and had lodged his men. Antonius on the other side bravely sent him word again and challenged the combat of him man to man, though he were the elder, and that if he refused him so, he would then fight a battle with him in the fields of Pharsalia, as Julius Caesar and Pompey had done before. Now whilst Antonius rode at anchor, lying idly in the harbor at the head of Actium, in the place where the city of Nicopolis standeth at this present, Caesar had quickly passed the sea Ionium and taken a place called Toryne, before Antonius understood that he had taken ship. Then began his men to be afraid, because his army by land was left behind. But Cleopatra making light of it, "And what danger, I pray you," said she, "if Caesar keep at Toryne?" The next morning by break of day, his enemies coming with full force of oars in battle against him, Antonius was afraid that if they came to join they would take and carry away his ships, that had no men of war in them. So he armed all his watermen and set them in order of battle upon the forecastle of their ships, and then lift up all his ranks of oars toward the elements, as well of the one side as the other, with the prows against the enemies, at the entry and mouth of the gulf which beginneth at the point of Actium, and so kept them in order of battle, as if they had been armed and furnished with watermen and soldiers. Thus Octavius Caesar, being finely deceived by this stratagem, retired presently, and therewithal Antonius very wisely and suddenly did cut him off from fresh water. For, understanding that the places where Octavius Caesar landed had very little store of water, and yet very bad, he shut them in with strong ditches and trenches he cast, to keep them from sallying out at their pleasure, and so to go seek water further off. Furthermore, he dealt very friendly and courteously with Domitius, and against Cleopatra's mind. For, he being sick of an ague when he went and took a little boat to go to Caesar's camp, Antonius was very sorry for it, but yet he sent after him all his carriage, train, and men; and the same Domitius, as though he gave him to understand that he repented his open treason, he died immediately after. There were certain kings also that forsook him, and turned on Caesar's side: as Amyntas and Deïotarus. Furthermore his fleet and navy that was unfortunate in all things, and unready for service, compelled him to change his mind and to hazard battle by land. And Canidius also, who had charge of his army by land, when time came to follow Antonius' determination, he turned him clean contrary and counseled him to send Cleopatra back again, and himself to retire into Macedon, to fight there on the mainland. And furthermore told him, that Dicomes King of the Getae promised him to aid him with a great power, and that it should be no shame nor dishonor to him to let Caesar have the sea (because himself and his men both had been well practiced and exercised in battles by sea, in the war of Sicilia against Sextus Pompeius), but rather than he should do against all reason, he having so great skill and experience of battles by land as he had, if he should not employ the force and valiantness of so many lusty armed footmen as he had ready, but would weaken his army by dividing them into ships. But now, notwithstanding all these good persuasions, Cleopatra forced him to put all to the hazard of battle by sea, considering with herself how she might fly and provide for her safety, not to help him to win the victory, but to fly more easily after the battle lost. Betwixt Antonius' camp and his fleet of ships there was a great high point of firm land that ran a good way into the sea, the which Antonius often used for a walk, without mistrust of fear or danger. One of Caesar's men perceived it, and told his master that he would laugh an [i.e., if] they could take up Antonius in the midst of his walk. Thereupon Caesar sent some of his men to lie in ambush for him, and they missed not much of taking of him, for they took him that came before him, because they discovered too soon, and so Antonius scaped very hardly. So, when Antonius had determined to fight by sea, he set all the other ships afire but threescore ships of Egypt, and reserved only but the best and the greatest galleys, from three banks unto ten banks of oars. In them he put two-and-twenty thousand fighting men, with two thousand darters and slingers. Now, as he was setting his men in order of battle, there was a captain and a valiant man that had served Antonius in many battles and conflicts and had all his body hacked and cut, who, as Antonius passed by him, cried out unto him and said: "O noble Emperor, how cometh it to pass that you trust to these vile brittle ships? What, do you mistrust these wounds of mine and this sword? Let the Egyptians and Phoenicians fight by sea, and set us on the mainland, where we use to conquer or to be slain on our feet." Antonius passed by him and said never a word, but only beckoned to him with his hand and head, as though he willed him to be of good courage, although indeed he had no great courage himself.

[An account of the battle follows.]

. . . Howbeit the battle was yet of even hand, and the victory doubtful, being indifferent to both, when suddenly they saw the threescore ships of Cleopatra busy about their yard masts and hoisting sail to fly. So they fled through the midst of them that were in fight, for they had been placed behind the great ships, and did marvelously disorder the other ships. For the enemies themselves wondered much to see them sail in that sort, with full sail towards Peloponnesus. There Antonius showed plainly that he had not only lost the courage and heart of an emperor, but also of a valiant man, and that he was not his own man (proving that true which an old man spake in mirth, that the soul of a lover lived in another body, and not in his own); he was so carried away with the vain love of this woman, as if he had been glued unto her and that she could not have removed without moving of him also. For when he saw Cleopatra's ship under sail, he forgot, forsook, and betrayed them that fought for him and embarked upon a galley with five banks of oars, to follow her that had already begun to overthrow him and would in the end be his utter destruction. When she knew this galley afar off, she lift up a sign in the poop of her ship, and so Antonius coming to it was plucked up where Cleopatra was; howbeit he saw her not at his first coming, nor she him, but went and sate down alone in the prow of his ship, and said never a word, clapping his head between both his hands. . . .

Now for himself, he determined to cross over into Africk and took one of his carracks or hulks loaden with gold and silver and other rich carriage and gave it unto his friends, commanding them to depart and to seek to save themselves. They answered him weeping, that they would neither do it nor yet forsake him. Then Antonius very courteously and lovingly did comfort them and prayed them to depart; and wrote unto Theophilus, Governor of Corinth, that he would see them safe, and help to hide them in some secret place, until they had made their way and peace with Caesar. . . .

Many plainly saw Antonius fly, and yet could hardly believe it that he, that had nineteen legions whole by land and twelve thousand horsemen upon the seaside, would so have forsaken them and have fled so cowardly, as if he had not oftentimes proved both the one and the other fortune, and that he had not been thoroughly acquainted with the diverse changes and fortunes of battles. And yet his soldiers still wished for him and ever hoped that he would come by some means or other unto them. Furthermore, they showed themselves so valiant and faithful unto him that after they certainly knew he was fled, they kept themselves whole together seven days. In the end Canidius, Antonius' lieutenant, flying by night and forsaking his camp, when they saw themselves thus destitute of their heads and leaders, they yielded themselves unto the stronger.

[Antony retires hopeless to the isle of Pharos; but on hearing that his army is totally lost and the last of his allies have deserted to Caesar, he at length takes up again his life of revelry with Cleopatra, who begins to experiment to find a painless method of suicide.]

This notwithstanding, they sent ambassadors unto Octavius Caesar in Asia, Cleopatra requesting the realm of Egypt for her children, and Antonius praying that he might be suffered to live at Athens like a private man if Caesar would not let him remain in Egypt. And, because they had no other men of estimation about them, for that some were fled and those that remained, they did not greatly trust them, they were enforced to send Euphronius, the schoolmaster of their children. For Alexas Laodicean, who was brought into Antonius' house and favor by means of Timagenes, and afterwards was in greater credit with him than any other Grecian (for that he had always been one of Cleopatra's ministers to win Antonius and to overthrow all his good determinations to use his wife Octavia well) him Antonius had sent unto Herodes King of Jewry, hoping still to keep him his friend, that he should not revolt from him. But he remained there and betrayed Antonius. For where he should have kept Herodes from revolting from him, he persuaded him to turn to Caesar; and trusting King Herodes, he presumed to come in Caesar's presence. Howbeit Herodes did him no pleasure, for he was presently taken prisoner and sent in chains to his own country and there by Caesar's commandment put to death. Thus was Alexas in Antonius' lifetime put to death for betraying of him. Furthermore, Caesar would not grant unto Antonius' requests; but for Cleopatra, he made her answer that he would deny her nothing reasonable, so that she would either put Antonius to death or drive him out of her country. Therewithal he sent Thyreus one of his men unto her, a very wise and discreet man, who, bringing letters of credit from a young lord unto a noble lady, and that besides greatly liked her beauty, might easily by his eloquence have persuaded her. He was longer in talk with her than any man else was, and the Queen herself also did him great honor, insomuch as he made Antonius jealous of him. Whereupon Antonius caused him to be taken and well-favoredly whipped, and so sent him unto Caesar, and bade him tell him that he made him angry with him, because he showed himself proud and disdainful towards him, and now specially when he was easy to be angered, by reason of his present misery. "To be short, if this mislike thee," said he, "thou hast Hipparchus one of my enfranchised bondmen with thee; hang him if thou wilt, or whip him at thy pleasure, that we may cry quittance." From thenceforth Cleopatra, to clear herself of the suspicion he had of her, she made more of him than ever she did. For first of all, where she did solemnize the day of her birth very meanly and sparingly, fit for her present misfortune, she now in contrary manner did keep it with such solemnity that she exceeded all measure of sumptuousness and magnificence, so that the guests that were bidden to the feasts, and came poor, went away rich.

[After the winter, Caesar advances upon Antony and Cleopatra; she withdraws her treasures into her tombs and monuments.]

So Caesar came, and pitched his camp hard by the city, in the place where they run and manage their horses. Antonius made a sally upon him and fought very valiantly, so that he drave Caesar's horsemen back, fighting with his men even into their camp. Then he came again to the palace, greatly boasting of this victory, and sweetly kissed Cleopatra, armed as he was when he came from the fight, recommending one of his men of arms unto her, that had valiantly fought on this skirmish. Cleopatra to reward his manliness gave him an armor and headpiece of clean gold; howbeit the man-at-arms, when he received this rich gift, stale away by night and went to Caesar. Antonius sent again to challenge Caesar to fight with him hand to hand. Caesar answered him that he had many other ways to die than so. Then Antonius, seeing there was no way more honorable for him to die than fighting valiantly, he determined to set up his rest, both by sea and land. So, being at supper (as it is reported), he commanded his officers and household servants that waited on him at his board, that they should fill his cups full and make as much of him as they could: "For," said he, "you know not whether you shall do so much for me tomorrow or not, whether you shall serve another master, and it may be you shall see me no more, but a dead body." This notwithstanding, perceiving that his friends and men fell a-weeping to hear him say so, to salve that he had spoken, he added this more unto it, that he would not lead them to battle, where he thought not rather safely to return with victory than valiantly to die with honor. Furthermore, the selfsame night within little of midnight, when all the city was quiet, full of fear and sorrow, thinking what would be the issue and end of this war, it is said that suddenly they heard a marvelous sweet harmony of sundry sorts of instruments of music, with the cry of a multitude of people, as they had been dancing and had sung

as they use in Bacchus' feasts, with movings and turnings
after the manner of the satyrs; and it seemed that this dance
went through the city unto the gate that opened to the enemies, and that all the troop that made this noise they heard
went out of the city at that gate. Now, such as in reason
sought the depth of the interpretation of this wonder,
thought that it was the god unto whom Antonius bare singular devotion to counterfeit and resemble him, that did
forsake them. The next morning by break of day, he went to
set those few footmen he had in order upon the hills
adjoining unto the city; and there he stood to behold his galleys which departed from the haven and rowed against the
galleys of his enemies, and so stood still, looking what
exploits his soldiers in them would do. But when by force
of rowing they were come near unto them, they first saluted
Caesar's men, and then Caesar's men resaluted them also,
and of two armies made but one, and then did all together
row toward the city. When Antonius saw that his men did
forsake him and yielded unto Caesar, and that his footmen
were broken and overthrown, he then fled into the city,
crying out that Cleopatra had betrayed him unto them, with
whom he had made war for her sake. Then she, being afraid
of his fury, fled into the tomb which she had caused to be
made, and there locked the doors unto her and shut all the
springs of the locks with great bolts, and in the meantime
sent unto Antonius to tell him that she was dead. Antonius,
believing it, said unto himself: "What dost thou look for
further, Antonius, sith spiteful fortune hath taken from thee
the only joy thou hadst, for whom thou yet reservedst thy
life?" When he had said these words, he went into a
chamber and unarmed himself, and being naked said thus:
"O Cleopatra, it grieveth me not that I have lost thy company, for I will not be long from thee; but I am sorry that,
having been so great a captain and emperor, I am indeed
condemned to be judged of less courage and noble mind
than a woman." Now he had a man of his called Eros,
whom he loved and trusted much, and whom he had long
before caused to swear unto him that he should kill him
when he did command him; and then he willed him to keep
his promise. His man drawing his sword lift it up as though

he had meant to have stricken his master, but turning his head at one side he thrust his sword into himself and fell down dead at his master's foot. Then said Antonius, "O noble Eros, I thank thee for this, and it is valiantly done of thee, to show me what I should do to myself, which thou couldst not do for me." Therewithal he took his sword and thrust it into his belly and so fell down upon a little bed. The wound he had killed him not presently, for the blood stinted a little when he was laid; and when he came somewhat to himself again, he prayed them that were about him to dispatch him. But they all fled out of the chamber and left him crying out and tormenting himself, until at last there came a secretary unto him called Diomedes, who was commanded to bring him into the tomb or monument where Cleopatra was. When he heard that she was alive, he very earnestly prayed his men to carry his body thither, and so he was carried in his men's arms into the empty of the monument. Notwithstanding, Cleopatra would not open the gates, but came to the high windows and cast out certain chains and ropes, in the which Antonius was trussed; and Cleopatra her own self, with two women only, which she had suffered to come with her into these monuments, triced Antonius up. They that were present to behold it said they saw so pitiful a sight. For they plucked up poor Antonius all bloody as he was, and drawing on with pangs of death, who holding up his hand to Cleopatra raised up himself as well as he could. It was a hard thing for these women to do, to lift him up; but Cleopatra stooping down with her head, putting to all her strength to her uttermost power, did lift him up with much ado and never let go her hold, with the help of the women beneath that bade her be of good courage and were as sorry to see her labor so as she herself. So when she had gotten him in after that sort and laid him on a bed, she rent her garments upon him, clasping her breast and scratching her face and stomach. Then she dried up his blood that had betrayed his face and called him her lord, her husband, and emperor, forgetting her own misery and calamity for the pity and compassion she took of him. Antonius made her ease her lamenting and called for wine, either because he was athirst or else for that he thought thereby to hasten his death. When he had drunk, he earnestly prayed her and persuaded her that she would seek to save her life, if she could possible, without reproach and dishonor, and that chiefly she should trust Proculeius above any man else about Caesar. And, as for himself, that she should not lament nor sorrow for the miserable change of his fortune at the end of his days, but rather that she should think him the more fortunate for the former triumphs and honors he had received, considering that while he lived he was the noblest and greatest prince of the world, and that now he was overcome not cowardly, but valiantly, a Roman by another Roman. As Antonius gave the last gasp, Proculeius came that was sent from Caesar. For after Antonius had thrust his sword in himself, as they carried him into the tombs and monuments of Cleopatra, one of his guard called Dercetaeus took his sword with the which he had stricken himself, and hid it; then he secretly stale away and brought Octavius Caesar the first news of his death and showed him his sword that was bloodied. Caesar hearing these news straight withdrew himself into a secret place of his tent and there burst out with tears, lamenting his hard and miserable fortune that had been his friend and brother-in-law, his equal in the Empire and companion with him in sundry great exploits and battles. Then he called for all his friends and showed them the letters Antonius had written to him and his answers also sent him again during their quarrel and strife, and how fiercely and proudly the other answered him to all just and reasonable matters he wrote unto him. After this, he sent Proculeius and commanded him to do what he could possible to get Cleopatra alive, fearing lest otherwise all the treasure would be lost; and furthermore, he thought that if he could take Cleopatra and bring her alive to Rome, she would marvelously beautify and set out his triumph. But Cleopatra would never put herself into Proculeius' hands, although they spake together. For Proculeius came to the gates that were very thick and strong and surely barred, but yet there were some cranews through the which her voice might be heard, and so they without understood that Cleopatra demanded the kingdom of Egypt for her sons, and that Proculeius answered her that she should be of good cheer and not be afraid to refer all unto Caesar. After he had viewed the place very well, he came and reported her answer unto Caesar, who immediately sent Gallus to speak once again with her and bade him purposely hold her with talk whilst Proculeius did set up a ladder against that high window by the which Antonius was triced up, and came down into the monument with two of his men, hard by the gate where Cleopatra stood to hear what Gallus said unto her. One of her women which was shut in her monuments with her saw Proculeius by chance as he came down and shrieked out: "O poor Cleopatra, thou art taken." Then, when she saw Proculeius behind her as she came from the gate, she thought to have stabbed herself in with a short dagger she ware of purpose by her side. But Proculeius came suddenly upon her, and taking her by both the hands said unto her: "Cleopatra, first thou shalt do thyself great wrong, and secondly unto Caesar, to deprive him of the occasion and opportunity openly to show his bounty and mercy, and to give his enemies cause to accuse the most courteous and noble prince that ever was, and to appeach him as though he were a cruel and merciless man that were not to be trusted." So even as he spake the word, he took her dagger from her and shook her clothes for fear of any poison hidden about her. Afterwards Caesar sent one of his enfranchised men called Epaphroditus, whom he straightly charged to look well unto her and to beware in any case that she made not herself away, and, for the rest, to use her with all the courtesy possible.

[Cleopatra, after burying Antony royally, gives way to intense grief.]

Shortly after, Caesar came himself in person to see her and to comfort her. Cleopatra being laid upon a little low bed in poor estate, when she saw Caesar come into her chamber she suddenly rose up, naked in her smock, and fell down at his feet marvelously disfigured, both for that she had plucked her hair from her head, as also for that she had martyred all her face with her nails, and besides, her voice was small and trembling, her eyes sunk into her head with continual blubbering, and moreover they might see the most part of her stomach torn in sunder. To be short, her body was not much better than her mind; yet her good grace and comeliness and the force of her beauty was not altogether defaced. But notwithstanding this ugly and pitiful state of hers, yet she showed herself within by her outward looks and countenance. When Caesar had made her lie down again and sat by her bed's side, Cleopatra began to clear and excuse herself for that she had done, laying all to the fear she had of Antonius; Caesar, in contrary manner, reproved her in every point. Then she suddenly altered her speech and prayed him to pardon her, as though she were afraid to die and desirous to live. At length, she gave him a brief and memorial of all the ready money and treasure she had. But by chance there stood Seleucus by, one of her treasurers, who to seem a good servant came straight to Caesar to disprove Cleopatra that she had not set in all, but kept many things back of purpose. Cleopatra was in such a rage with him that she flew upon him and took him by the hair of the head and boxed him well-favoredly. Caesar fell a-laughing and parted the fray. "Alas," said she, "O Caesar, is not this a great shame and reproach, that thou having vouchsafed to take the pains to come unto me, and hast done me this honor, poor wretch and caitiff creature, brought into this pitiful and miserable estate, and that mine own servants should come now to accuse me, though it may be that I have reserved some jewels and trifles meet for women, but not for me (poor soul) to set out myself withal, but meaning to give some pretty present and gifts unto Octavia and Livia, that they making means and intercession for me to thee, thou mightest yet extend thy favor and mercy upon me?" Caesar was glad to hear her say so, persuading himself thereby that she had yet a desire to save her life. So he made her answer that he did not only give her that to dispose of at her pleasure which she had kept back, but further promised to use her more honorably and bountifully than she would think fit; and so he took his leave of her, supposing he had deceived her, but indeed he was deceived himself. There was a young gentleman Cornelius Dolabella that was one of Caesar's very great familiars, and besides did bear no evil will unto Cleopatra. He sent her word secretly as she had requested him, that Caesar determined to take his journey through Syria, and that within three days he would send her away before with her children. When this was told Cleopatra, she requested Caesar that it would please him to suffer her to offer the last oblations of the dead unto the soul of Antonius. This being granted her, she was carried to the place where his tomb was, and there falling down on her knees, embracing the tomb with her women, the tears running down her cheeks, she began to speak in this sort: "O my dear Lord Antonius, not long sithence I buried thee here, being a freewoman; and now I offer unto thee the funeral sprinklings and oblations, being a captive and prisoner, and yet I am forbidden and kept from tearing and murdering this captive body of mine with blows, which they carefully guard and keep, only to triumph of thee; look therefore henceforth for no other honors, offerings, nor sacrifices from me, for these are the last which Cleopatra can give thee, sith now they carry her away. Whilst we lived together, nothing could sever our companies; but now at our death I fear me they will make us change our countries. For as thou, being a Roman, hast been buried in Egypt, even so wretched creature I, an Egyptian, shall be buried in Italy, which shall be all the good that I have received by thy country. If therefore the gods where thou art now have any power and authority, sith our gods here have forsaken us, suffer not thy true friend and lover to be carried away alive, that in me they triumph of thee, but receive me with thee, and let me be buried in one self tomb with thee. For though my griefs and miseries be infinite, yet none hath grieved me more, nor that I could less bear withal than this small time which I have been driven to live alone without thee." Then, having ended these doleful plaints and crowned the tomb with garlands and sundry nosegays and marvelous lovingly embraced the same, she commanded they should prepare her bath, and when she had bathed and washed herself she fell to her meat and was sumptuously served. Now whilst she was at dinner, there came a countryman and brought her a basket. The soldiers that warded at the gates asked him straight what he had in his basket. He opened the basket and took out the leaves that covered the figs and showed them that they were figs he brought. They all of them marveled to see so goodly figs. The countryman laughed to hear them and bade them take some if they would. They believed he told them truly, and so bade him carry them in. After Cleopatra had dined, she sent a certain table written and sealed unto Caesar and commanded them all to go out of the tombs where she was, but the two women; then she shut the doors to her. Caesar, when he received this table and began to read her lamentation and petition, requesting him that he would let her be buried with Antonius, found straight what she meant and thought to have gone thither himself; howbeit he sent one before in all haste that might be, to see what it was. Her death was very sudden. For those whom Caesar sent unto her ran thither in all haste possible and found the soldiers standing at the gate, mistrusting nothing nor understanding of her death. But when they had opened the doors, they found Cleopatra stark dead, laid upon a bed of gold, attired and arrayed in her royal robes, and one of her two women, which was called Iras, dead at her feet, and her other woman called Charmion half dead and trembling, trimming the diadem which Cleopatra were upon her dead. One of the soldiers, seeing her, angrily said unto her: "Is that well done, Charmion?" "Very well," said she again, "and meet for a princess descended from the race of so many noble kings." She said no more, but fell down dead hard by the bed. Some report that this aspic was brought unto her in the basket with the figs, and that she had commanded them to hide it under the fig leaves, that when she should think to take out the figs, the aspic should bite her before she should see her; howbeit that, when she would have taken away the leaves for the figs, she perceived it and said, "Art thou here then?" And so, her arm being naked, she put it to the aspic to be bitten. Other say again, she kept it in a box, and that she did prick and thrust it with a spindle of gold, so that the aspic being angered withal, leapt out with great fury and bit her in the arm. Howbeit few can tell the truth. For they report also that she had hidden poison in a hollow razor which she carried in the hair of her head: and yet there was no mark seen of her body, or any sign discerned that she was poisoned, neither also did they find this serpent in her tomb. But it was reported only that there were seen certain fresh steps or tracks where it had gone, on the tomb side toward the sea and specially by the door's side. Some say also that they found two little pretty bitings in her arm, scant to be discerned, the which it seemeth Caesar himself gave credit unto, because in his triumph he carried Cleopatra's image, with an aspic biting of her arm. And thus goeth the report of her death. Now Caesar, though he was marvelous sorry for the death of Cleopatra, yet he wondered at her noble mind and courage and therefore commanded she should be nobly buried and laid by Antonius, and willed also that her two women should have honorable burial.

Commentaries

SAMUEL JOHNSON

From The Plays of William Shakespeare

This play keeps curiosity always busy, and the passions always interested. The continual hurry of the action, the variety of incidents, and the quick succession of one personage to another, call the mind forward without intermission from the first act to the last. But the power of delighting is derived principally from the frequent changes of the scene; for, except the feminine arts, some of which are too low, which distinguish *Cleopatra*, no character is very strongly discriminated. *Upton*, who did not easily miss what he desired to find, has discovered that the language of *Antony* is, with great skill and learning, made pompous and superb, according to his real practice. But I think his diction not distinguishable from that of others: the most tumid speech in the play is that which *Caesar* makes to *Octavia*.

The events, of which the principal are described according to history, are produced without any art of connection or care of disposition. [1765]

A. C. BRADLEY

Shakespeare's *Antony and Cleopatra*

Coleridge's one page of general criticism on *Antony and Cleopatra* contains some notable remarks. "Of all Shakespeare's historical plays," he writes, *"Antony and Cleopatra* is by far the most wonderful. There is not one in which he has followed history so minutely, and yet there are few in which he impresses the notion of angelic strength so much—perhaps none in which he impresses it more strongly. This is greatly owing to the manner in which the fiery force is sustained throughout." In a later sentence he refers to the play as "this astonishing drama." In another he describes the style: *"feliciter audax* is the motto for its style comparatively with that of Shakespeare's other works." And he translates this motto in the phrase "happy valiancy of style."

Coleridge's assertion that in *Antony and Cleopatra* Shakespeare followed history more minutely than in any other play might well be disputed; and his statement about the style of this drama requires some qualification in view of the results of later criticism as to the order of Shakespeare's works. The style is less individual than he imagined. On the whole it is common to the six or seven dramas

From *Oxford Lectures on Poetry* by A. C. Bradley (London: Macmillan and Co., Ltd., 1909). Reprinted by permission of Macmillan and Co., Ltd., and St. Martin's Press, Inc.

[1]As this lecture was composed after the publication of my *Shakespearean Tragedy*, I ignored in it, as far as possible, such aspects of the play as were noticed in that book, to the Index of which I may refer the reader.

subsequent to *Macbeth,* though in *Antony and Cleopatra,* probably the earliest of them, its development is not yet complete. And we must add that this style has certain special defects, unmentioned by Coleridge, as well as the quality which he points out in it. But it is true that here that quality is almost continuously present; and in the phrase by which he describes it, as in his other phrases, he has signalized once for all some of the most salient features of the drama.

It is curious to notice, for example, alike in books and in conversation, how often the first epithets used in reference to *Antony and Cleopatra* are "wonderful" and "astonishing." And the main source of the feeling thus expressed seems to be the "angelic strength" or "fiery force" of which Coleridge wrote. The first of these two phrases is, I think, the more entirely happy. Except perhaps towards the close, one is not so conscious of fiery force as in certain other tragedies; but one is astonished at the apparent ease with which extraordinary effects are produced, the ease, if I may paraphrase Coleridge, of an angel moving with a wave of the hand that heavy matter which men find so intractable. We feel this sovereign ease in contemplating Shakespeare's picture of the world—a vast canvas, crowded with figures, glowing with color and a superb animation, reminding one spectator of Paul Veronese and another of Rubens. We feel it again when we observe (as we can even without consulting Plutarch) the nature of the material; how bulky it was, and, in some respects, how undramatic; and how the artist, though he could not treat history like legend or fiction, seems to push whole masses aside, and to shift and refashion the remainder, almost with the air of an architect playing (at times rather carelessly) with a child's bricks.

Something similar is felt even in the portrait of Cleopatra. Marvelous as it is, the drawing of it suggests not so much the passionate concentration or fiery force of *Macbeth,* as that sense of effortless and exultant mastery which we feel in the portraits of Mercutio and Falstaff. And surely it is a total mistake to find in this portrait any trace of the distempered mood which disturbs our pleasure in *Troilus and Cressida.* If the sonnets about the dark lady were, as need not be doubted, in some degree autobiographical, Shakespeare may well have used his personal experience both when he drew Cressida and when he drew Cleopatra. And, if he did, the story in the later play was the nearer to his own; for Antony might well have said what Troilus could never say,

> When my love swears that she is made of truth,
> I do believe her, though I know she lies.

But in the later play, not only is the poet's vision unclouded, but his whole nature, emotional as well as intellectual, is free. The subject no more embitters or seduces him than the ambition of Macbeth. So that here too we feel the angelic strength of which Coleridge speaks. If we quarreled with the phrase at all, it would be because we fancied we could trace in Shakespeare's attitude something of the irony of superiority; and this may not altogether suit our conception of an angel.

I have still another sentence to quote from Coleridge: "The highest praise, or rather form of praise, of this play which I can offer in my own mind, is the doubt which the perusal always occasions in me, whether the *Antony and Cleopatra* is not, in all exhibitions of a giant power in its strength and vigor of maturity, a formidable rival of *Macbeth*, *Lear*, *Hamlet*, and *Othello*." Now, unless the clause here about the "giant power" may be taken to restrict the rivalry to the quality of angelic strength, Coleridge's doubt seems to show a lapse in critical judgment. To regard this tragedy as a rival of the famous four, whether on the stage or in the study, is surely an error. The world certainly has not so regarded it; and, though the world's reasons for its verdicts on works of art may be worth little, its mere verdict is worth much. Here, it seems to me, that verdict must be accepted. One may notice that, in calling *Antony and Cleopatra* wonderful or astonishing, we appear to be thinking first of the artist and his activity, while in the case of the four famous tragedies it is the product of this activity, the thing presented, that first engrosses us. I know that I am stating this difference too sharply, but I believe that it is often felt; and, if this is so, the fact is significant. It implies that, although *Antony and Cleopatra* may be for us as wonderful an achievement as the greatest of Shakespeare's plays, it has not an equal value. Besides, in the attempt to rank it with them there is involved something more, and more important, than an error in valuation. There is a failure to discriminate the peculiar marks of *Antony and Cleopatra* itself, marks which, whether or no it be the equal of the earlier tragedies, make it decidedly different. If I speak first of some of these differences it is because they thus contribute to the individuality of the play, and because they seem often not to be distinctly apprehended in criticism.

I

Why, let us begin by asking, is *Antony and Cleopatra*, though so wonderful an achievement, a play rarely acted? For a tragedy, it is not painful. Though unfit for children, it cannot be called indecent; some slight omissions, and such a flattening of the heroine's part as might confidently be expected, would leave it perfectly presentable. It is, no doubt, in the third and fourth acts, very defective in construction. Even on the Elizabethan stage, where scene followed scene without a pause, this must have been felt; and in our theaters it would be felt much more. There, in fact, these two and forty scenes could not possibly be acted as they stand. But defective construction would not distress the bulk of an audience, if the matter presented were that of *Hamlet* or *Othello*, of *Lear* or *Macbeth*. The matter, then, must lack something which is present in those tragedies; and it is mainly owing to this difference in substance that *Antony and Cleopatra* has never attained their popularity either on the stage or off it.

Most of Shakespeare's tragedies are dramatic, in a special sense of the word as well as in its general sense, from beginning to end. The story is not merely exciting and impressive from the movement of conflicting forces towards a terrible issue, but from time to time there come situations and events which, even apart from their bearing on this issue, appeal most powerfully to the dramatic feelings— scenes of action or passion which agitate the audience with alarm, horror, painful expectation, or absorbing sympathies and antipathies. Think of the street fights in *Romeo and Juliet*, the killing of Mercutio and Tybalt, the rapture of the lovers, and their despair when Romeo is banished. Think of the ghost scenes in the first act of *Hamlet*, the passion of the early soliloquies, the scene between Hamlet and Ophelia, the play scene, the sparing of the King at prayer, the killing of Polonius. Is not *Hamlet*, if you choose so to regard it, the best melodrama in the world? Think at your leisure of *Othello*, *Lear*, and *Macbeth* from the same point of view; but consider here and now even the two tragedies which, as dealing with Roman history, are companions of *Antony and Cleopatra*. Recall in *Julius Caesar* the first suggestion of the murder, the preparation for it in a "tempest dropping fire," the murder itself, the speech of Antony over the corpse, and the tumult of the furious crowd; in *Coriolanus* the bloody battles on the stage, the scene in which the hero attains the consulship, the scene of rage in which he is banished. And remember that in each of these seven tragedies the matter referred to is contained in the first three acts.

In the first three acts of our play what is there resembling this? Almost nothing. People converse, discuss, accuse one another, excuse themselves, mock, describe, drink together, arrange a marriage, meet and part; but they do not kill, do not even tremble or weep. We see hardly one violent movement; until the battle of Actium is over we witness scarcely any vehement passion; and that battle, as it is a naval action, we do not see. Even later, Enobarbus, when he dies, simply dies; he does not kill himself.[2] We hear wonderful talk; but it is not talk, like that of Macbeth and Lady Macbeth, or that of Othello and Iago, at which we hold our breath. The scenes that we remember first are those that portray Cleopatra; Cleopatra coquetting, tormenting,

[2]See Note A.

beguiling her lover to stay; Cleopatra left with her women and longing for him; Cleopatra receiving the news of his marriage; Cleopatra questioning the messenger about Octavia's personal appearance. But this is to say that the scenes we remember first are the least indispensable to the plot. One at least is not essential to it at all. And this, the astonishing scene where she storms at the messenger, strikes him, and draws her dagger on him, is the one passage in the first half of the drama that contains either an explosion of passion or an exciting bodily action. Nor is this all. The first half of the play, though it forebodes tragedy, is not decisively tragic in tone. Certainly the Cleopatra scenes are not so. We read them, and we should witness them, in delighted wonder and even with amusement. The only scene that can vie with them, that of the revel on Pompey's ship, though full of menace, is in great part humorous. Enobarbus, in this part of the play, is always humorous. Even later, when the tragic tone is deepening, the whipping of Thyreus [i.e., Thidias], in spite of Antony's rage, moves mirth. A play of which all this can truly be said may well be as masterly as *Othello* or *Macbeth*, and more delightful; but, in the greater part of its course, it cannot possibly excite the same emotions. It makes no attempt to do so; and to regard it as though it made this attempt is to miss its specific character and the intention of its author.

That character depends only in part on Shakespeare's fidelity to his historical authority, a fidelity which, I may remark, is often greatly exaggerated. For Shakespeare did not merely present the story of ten years as though it occupied perhaps one-fifth of that time, nor did he merely invent freely, but in critical places he effected startling changes in the order and combination of events. Still it may be said that, dealing with a history so famous, he could not well make the first half of his play very exciting, moving, or tragic. And this is true so far as mere situations and events are concerned. But, if he had chosen, he might easily have heightened the tone and tension in another way. He might have made the story of Antony's attempt to break his bondage, and the story of his relapse, extremely exciting, by portraying with all his force the severity of the struggle and the magnitude of the fatal step.

And the structure of the play might seem at first to suggest this intention. At the opening, Antony is shown almost in the beginning of his infatuation; for Cleopatra is not sure of her power over him, exerts all her fascination to detain him, and plays the part of the innocent victim who has yielded to passion and must now expect to be deserted by her seducer. Alarmed and ashamed at the news of the results of his inaction, he rouses himself, tears himself away, and speeds to Italy. His very coming is enough to frighten Pompey into peace. He reconciles himself with Octavius, and, by his marriage with the good and beautiful Octavia, seems to have knit a bond of lasting amity with her brother, and to have guarded himself against the passion that threatened him with ruin. At this point his power, the world's peace, and his own peace, appear to be secured; his fortune has mounted to its apex. But soon (very much sooner than in Plutarch's story) comes the downward turn or counterstroke. New causes of offense arise between the brothers-in-law. To remove them Octavia leaves her husband in Athens and hurries to Rome. Immediately Antony returns to Cleopatra and, surrendering himself at once and wholly to her enchantment, is quickly driven to his doom.

Now Shakespeare, I say, with his matchless power of depicting an inward struggle, might have made this story, even where it could not furnish him with thrilling incidents, the source of powerful tragic emotions; and, in doing so, he would have departed from his authority merely in his conception of the hero's character. But he does no such thing till the catastrophe is near. Antony breaks away from Cleopatra without any strenuous conflict. No serious doubt of his return is permitted to agitate us. We are almost assured of it through the impression made on us by Octavius, through occasional glimpses into Antony's mind, through the absence of any doubt in Enobarbus, through scenes in Alexandria which display Cleopatra and display her irresistible. And, finally, the downward turn itself, the fatal step of Antony's return, is shown without the slightest emphasis. Nay, it is not shown, it is only reported; and not a line portrays any inward struggle preceding it. On this side also, then, the drama makes no attempt to rival the other tragedies; and it was essential to its own peculiar character and its most transcendent effects that this attempt should not be made, but that Antony's passion should be represented as a force which he could hardly even desire to resist. By the very scheme of the work, therefore, tragic impressions of any great volume or depth were reserved for the last stage of the conflict; while the main interest, down to the battle of Actium, was directed to matters exceedingly interesting and even, in the wider sense, dramatic, but not overtly either terrible or piteous: on the one hand, to the political aspect of the story; on the other, to the personal causes which helped to make the issue inevitable.

II

The political situation and its development are simple. The story is taken up almost where it was left, years before, in *Julius Caesar*. There Brutus and Cassius, to prevent the rule of one man, assassinate Caesar. Their purpose is condemned to failure, not merely because they make mistakes, but because that political necessity which Napoleon identified with destiny requires the rule of one man. They spill Caesar's blood, but his spirit walks abroad and turns their swords against their own breasts; and the world is left divided among three men, his friends and his heir. Here *Antony and Cleopatra* takes up the tale; and its business, from this point of view, is to show the reduction of these three to one. That Lepidus will not be this one was clear already in *Julius Caesar*; it must be Octavius or Antony. Both ambitious, they are also men of such opposite tempers that they would scarcely long agree even if they wished to, and even if destiny were not stronger than they. As it is, one of them has fixed his eyes on the end, sacrifices everything for it, uses everything as a means to it. The other, though far the greater soldier and worshiped by his followers, has no such singleness of aim; nor yet is power, however desirable to him, the most desirable thing in the world. At the beginning he is risking it for love; at the end he has lost his half of the world, and lost his life, and Octavius rules alone. Whether Shakespeare had this clearly in his mind is a question neither answerable nor important; this is what came out of his mind.

Shakespeare, I think, took little interest in the character of Octavius, and he has not made it wholly clear. It is not distinct in Plutarch's "Life of Antony"; and I have not found traces that the poet studied closely the "Life of Octavius" included in North's volume. To Shakespeare he is one of those men, like Bolingbroke and Ulysses, who have plenty of "judgment" and not much "blood." Victory in the world, according to the poet, almost always goes to such men; and he makes us respect, fear, and dislike them. His Octavius is very formidable. His cold determination half paralyzes Antony; it is so even in *Julius Caesar*. In *Antony and Cleopatra* Octavius is more than once in the wrong; but he never admits it; he silently pushes his rival a step backward; and, when he ceases to fear, he shows contempt. He neither enjoys war nor is great in it; at first, therefore, he is anxious about the power of Pompey and stands in need of Antony. As soon as Antony's presence has served his turn, and he has patched up a union with him and seen him safely off to Athens, he destroys first Pompey and next Lepidus. Then, dexterously using Antony's faithlessness to Octavia and excesses in the East in order to put himself in the right, he makes for his victim with admirable celerity while he is still drunk with the joy of reunion with Cleopatra. For his ends Octavius is perfectly efficient, but he is so partly from his limitations. One phrase of his is exceedingly characteristic. When Antony in rage and desperation challenges him to single combat, Octavius calls him "the old ruffian." There is a horrid aptness in the phrase, but it disgusts us. It is shameful in this boy, as hard and smooth as polished steel, to feel at such a time nothing of the greatness of his victim and the tragedy of his victim's fall. Though the challenge of Antony is absurd, we would give much to see them sword to sword. And when Cleopatra by her death cheats the conqueror of his prize, we feel unmixed delight.

The doubtful point in the character is this. Plutarch

says that Octavius was reported to love his sister dearly; and Shakespeare's Octavius several times expresses such love. When, then, he proposed the marriage with Antony (for of course it was he who spoke through Agrippa), was he honest, or was he laying a trap and, in doing so, sacrificing his sister? Did he hope the marriage would really unite him with his brother-in-law; or did he merely mean it to be a source of future differences; or did he calculate that, whether it secured peace or dissension, it would in either case bring him great advantage? Shakespeare, who was quite as intelligent as his readers, must have asked himself some such question; but he may not have cared to answer it even to himself; and, in any case, he has left the actor (at least the actor in days later than his own) to choose an answer. If I were forced to choose, I should take the view that Octavius was, at any rate, not wholly honest; partly because I think it best suits Shakespeare's usual way of conceiving a character of the kind; partly because Plutarch construed in this manner Octavius's behavior in regard to his sister at a later time, and this hint might naturally influence the poet's way of imagining his earlier action.[3]

Though the character of Octavius is neither attractive nor wholly clear, his figure is invested with a certain tragic dignity, because he is felt to be the Man of Destiny, the agent of forces against which the intentions of an individual would avail nothing. He is represented as having himself some feeling of this sort. His lament over Antony, his grief that their stars were irreconcilable, may well be genuine, though we should be surer if it were uttered in soliloquy. His austere words to Octavia again probably speak his true mind:

---

[3] "Now whilest Antonius was busie in this preparation, Octavia his wife, whom he had left at Rome, would needs take sea to come unto him. Her brother Octauius Cæsar willing vnto it, not for his respect at all (as most authors do report) as for that he might haue an honest colour to make warre with Antonius if he did misuse her, and not esteeme of her as she ought to be."—*Life of Antony* (North's Translation), sect. 29. The view I take does not, of course, imply that Octavius had no love for his sister.

> Be you not troubled with the time, which drives
> O'er your content these strong necessities;
> But let determined things to destiny
> Hold unbewailed their way.

In any case the feeling of fate comes through to us. It is aided by slight touches of supernatural effect; first in the Soothsayer's warning to Antony that his genius or angel is overpowered whenever he is near Octavius; then in the strangely effective scene where Antony's soldiers, in the night before his last battle, hear music in the air or under the earth:

> 'Tis the god Hercules, whom Antony loved,
> Now leaves him.

And to the influence of this feeling in giving impressiveness to the story is added that of the immense scale and world-wide issue of the conflict. Even the distances traversed by fleets and armies enhance this effect.

And yet there seems to be something halfhearted in Shakespeare's appeal here, something even ironical in his presentation of this conflict. Its external magnitude, like Antony's magnificence in lavishing realms and gathering the kings of the East in his support, fails to uplift or dilate the imagination. The struggle in Lear's little island seems to us to have an infinitely wider scope. It is here that we are sometimes reminded of *Troilus and Cressida* and the cold and disenchanting light that is there cast on the Trojan War. The spectacle which he portrays leaves Shakespeare quite undazzled; he even makes it appear inwardly small. The lordship of the world, we ask ourselves, what is it worth, and in what spirit do these "world-sharers" contend for it? They are no champions of their country like Henry V. The conqueror knows not even the glory of battle. Their aims, for all we see, are as personal as if they were captains of banditti; and they are followed merely from self-interest or private attachment. The scene on Pompey's galley is full of this irony. One "third part of the world" is carried drunk to bed. In the midst of this mock boon companionship the pirate whispers to his leader to cut first the cable of his ship and then the throats of the two other emperors; and at the moment we should not greatly care if Pompey took the advice. Later, a short scene, totally useless to the plot and purely satiric in its purport, is slipped in to show how Ventidius fears to pursue his Parthian conquests because it is not safe for Antony's lieutenant to outdo his master.[4] A painful sense of hollowness oppresses us. We know too well what must happen in a world so splendid, so false, and so petty. We turn for relief from the political game to those who are sure to lose it; to those who love some human being better than a prize, to Eros and Charmian and Iras; to Enobarbus, whom the world corrupts, but who has a heart that can break with shame; to the lovers, who seem to us to find in death something better than their victor's life.

This presentation of the outward conflict has two results. First, it blunts our feeling of the greatness of Antony's fall from prosperity. Indeed this feeling, which we might expect to be unusually acute, is hardly so; it is less acute, for example, than the like feeling in the case of Richard II, who loses so much smaller a realm. Our deeper sympathies are focused rather on Antony's heart, on the inward fall to which the enchantment of passion leads him, and the inward recovery which succeeds it. And the second result is this. The greatness of Antony and Cleopatra in their fall is so much heightened by contrast with the world they lose and the conqueror who wins it that the positive element in the final tragic impression, the element of reconciliation, is strongly emphasized. The peculiar effect of the drama depends partly, as we have seen, on the absence of decidedly tragic scenes and events in its first half; but it depends quite as much on this emphasis. In any Shakespearean tragedy we watch some elect spirit colliding, partly through its error and defect, with a superhuman power which bears it down; and yet we feel that this spirit, even in the error and defect, rises by its greatness into ideal union with the power that overwhelms it. In some tragedies this latter feeling is relatively weak. In *Antony and Cleopatra* it is unusually

[4] See Note B.

strong; stronger, with some readers at least, than the fear and grief and pity with which they contemplate the tragic error and the advance of doom.

III

The two aspects of the tragedy are presented together in the opening scene. Here is the first. In Cleopatra's palace one friend of Antony is describing to another, just arrived from Rome, the dotage of their great general; and, as the lovers enter, he exclaims:

> Look, where they come:
> Take but good note, and you shall see in him
> The triple pillar of the world transformed
> Into a strumpet's fool. Behold and see.

With the next words the other aspect appears:

Cleopatra. If it be love indeed, tell me how much.

Antony. There's beggary in the love that can be reckoned.

Cleopatra. I'll set a bourne how far to be beloved.

Antony. Then must thou needs find out new heaven, new earth.

And directly after, when he is provoked by reminders of the news from Rome:

> Let Rome in Tiber melt, and the wide arch
> Of the ranged empire fall! Here is my space.
> Kingdoms are clay: our dungy earth alike
> Feeds beast as man. The nobleness of life
> Is to do thus.

Here is the tragic excess, but with it the tragic greatness, the capacity of finding in something the infinite, and of pursuing it into the jaws of death.

The two aspects are shown here with the exaggeration

proper in dramatic characters. Neither the phrase "a strumpet's fool," nor the assertion "the nobleness of life is to do thus," answers to the total effect of the play. But the truths they exaggerate are equally essential; and the commoner mistake in criticism is to understate the second. It is plain that the love of Antony and Cleopatra is destructive; that in some way it clashes with the nature of things; that, while they are sitting in their paradise like gods, its walls move inward and crush them at last to death. This is no invention of moralizing critics; it is in the play; and anyone familiar with Shakespeare would expect beforehand to find it there. But then to forget because of it the other side, to deny the name of love to this ruinous passion, to speak as though the lovers had utterly missed the good of life, is to mutilate the tragedy and to ignore a great part of its effect upon us. For we sympathize with them in their passion; we feel in it the infinity there is in man; even while we acquiesce in their defeat we are exulting in their victory; and when they have vanished we say,

> The odds is gone,
> And there is nothing left remarkable
> Beneath the visiting moon.

Though we hear nothing from Shakespeare of the cruelty of Plutarch's Antony, or of the misery caused by his boundless profusion, we do not feel the hero of the tragedy to be a man of the noblest type, like Brutus, Hamlet, or Othello. He seeks power merely for himself, and uses it for his own pleasure. He is in some respects unscrupulous; and, while it would be unjust to regard his marriage exactly as if it were one in private life, we resent his treatment of Octavia, whose character Shakespeare was obliged to leave a mere sketch, lest our feeling for the hero and heroine should be too much chilled. Yet, for all this, we sympathize warmly with Antony, are greatly drawn to him, and are inclined to regard him as a noble nature half spoiled by his time.

It is a large, open, generous, expansive nature, quite free from envy, capable of great magnanimity, even of entire devotion. Antony is unreserved, naturally straightforward, we may almost say simple. He can admit faults, accept advice and even reproof, take a jest against himself with good humor. He is courteous (to Lepidus, for example, whom Octavius treats with cold contempt); and, though he can be exceedingly dignified, he seems to prefer a blunt though sympathetic plainness, which is one cause of the attachment of his soldiers. He has none of the faults of the brooder, the sentimentalist, or the man of principle; his nature tends to splendid action and lusty enjoyment. But he is neither a mere soldier nor a mere sensualist. He has imagination, the temper of an artist who revels in abundant and rejoicing appetites, feasts his senses on the glow and richness of life, flings himself into its mirth and revelry, yet feels the poetry in all this, and is able also to put it by and be more than content with the hardships of adventure. Such a man could never have sought a crown by a murder like Macbeth's, or, like Brutus, have killed on principle the man who loved him, or have lost the world for a Cressida.

Beside this strain of poetry he has a keen intellect, a swift perception of the lie of things, and much quickness in shaping a course to suit them. In *Julius Caesar* he shows this after the assassination, when he appears as a dexterous politician as well as a warmhearted friend. He admires what is fine and can fully appreciate the nobility of Brutus; but he is sure that Brutus's ideas are moonshine, that (as he says in our play) Brutus is mad; and, since his mighty friend, who was incomparably the finest thing in the world, has perished, he sees no reason why the inheritance should not be his own. Full of sorrow, he yet uses his sorrow like an artist to work on others and greets his success with the glee of a successful adventurer. In the earlier play he proves himself a master of eloquence, and especially of pathos; and he does so again in the later. With a few words about his fall he draws tears from his followers and even from the caustic humorist Enobarbus. Like Richard II, he sees his own fall with the eyes of a poet, but a poet much greater than the young Shakespeare, who could never have written Antony's marvelous speech about the sunset clouds. But we listen to Antony, as we do not to Richard, with entire sympathy, partly because he is never unmanly, partly because he himself is sympathetic and longs for sympathy.

The first of living soldiers, an able politician, a most persuasive orator, Antony nevertheless was not born to rule the world. He enjoys being a great man, but he has not the love of rule for rule's sake. Power for him is chiefly a means to pleasure. The pleasure he wants is so huge that he needs a huge power; but half the world, even a third of it, would suffice. He will not pocket wrongs, but he shows not the slightest wish to get rid of his fellow triumvirs and reign alone. He never minded being subordinate to Julius Caesar. By women he is not only attracted but governed; from the effect of Cleopatra's taunts we can see that he had been governed by Fulvia. Nor has he either the patience or the steadfastness of a born ruler. He contends fitfully and is prone to take the step that is easiest at the moment. This is the reason why he consents to marry Octavia. It seems the shortest way out of an awkward situation. He does not intend even to try to be true to her. He will not think of the distant consequences.

A man who loved power as much as thousands of insignificant people love it, would have made a sterner struggle than Antony's against his enchantment. He can hardly be said to struggle at all. He brings himself to leave Cleopatra only because he knows he will return. In every moment of his absence, whether he wake or sleep, a siren music in his blood is singing him back to her; and to this music, however he may be occupied, the soul within his soul leans and listens. The joy of life had always culminated for him in the love of women: he could say "no" to none of them: of Octavia herself he speaks like a poet. When he meets Cleopatra he finds his Absolute. She satisfies, nay glorifies, his whole being. She intoxicates his senses. Her wiles, her taunts, her furies and meltings, her laughter and tears, bewitch him all alike. She loves what he loves, and she surpasses him. She can drink him to his bed, outjest his practical jokes, outact the best actress who ever amused him, outdazzle his own magnificence. She is his playfellow, and yet a great queen. Angling in the river, playing billiards, flourishing the sword he used at Philippi,

hopping forty paces in a public street, she remains an
enchantress. Her spirit is made of wind and flame, and the
poet in him worships her no less than the man. He is under
no illusion about her, knows all her faults, sees through her
wiles, believes her capable of betraying him. It makes no
difference. She is his heart's desire made perfect. To love
her is what he was born for. What have the gods in heaven
to say against it? To imagine heaven is to imagine her; to
die is to rejoin her. To deny that this is love is the madness
of morality. He gives her every atom of his heart.

She destroys him. Shakespeare, availing himself of the
historic fact, portrays, on Antony's return to her, the sud-
denness and the depth of his descent. In spite of his own
knowledge, the protests of his captains, the entreaties even
of a private soldier, he fights by sea simply and solely
because she wishes it. Then in mid-battle, when she flies,
he deserts navy and army and his faithful thousands and
follows her. "I never saw an action of such shame," cries
Scarus; and we feel the dishonor of the hero keenly. Then
Shakespeare begins to raise him again. First, his own overwhelming sense of shame redeems him. Next, we watch the
rage of the dying lion. Then the mere sally before the final
defeat—a sally dismissed by Plutarch in three lines—is
magnified into a battle, in which Antony displays to us, and
himself feels for the last time, the glory of his soldiership.
And, throughout, the magnanimity and gentleness which
shine through his desperation endear him to us. How beautiful is his affection for his followers and even for his servants, and the devotion they return! How noble his
reception of the news that Enobarbus has deserted him!
How touchingly significant the refusal of Eros either to kill
him or survive him! How pathetic and even sublime the
completeness of his love for Cleopatra! His anger is born
and dies in an hour. One tear, one kiss, outweighs his ruin.
He believes she has sold him to his enemy, yet he kills himself because he hears that she is dead. When, dying, he
learns that she has deceived him once more, no thought of
reproach crosses his mind: he simply asks to be carried to
her. He knows well that she is not capable of dying because
he dies, but that does not sting him; when, in his last agony,

he calls for wine that he may gain a moment's strength to speak, it is to advise her for the days to come. Shakespeare borrowed from Plutarch the final speech of Antony. It is fine, but it is not miraculous. The miraculous speeches belong only to his own hero:

> I am dying, Egypt, dying; only
> I here importune death awhile, until
> Of many thousand kisses the poor last
> I lay upon thy lips;

or the first words he utters when he hears of Cleopatra's death:

> Unarm, Eros. The long day's task is done,
> And we must sleep.

If he meant the task of statesman and warrior, that is not what his words mean to us. They remind us of words more familiar and less great—

> No rest but the grave for the pilgrim of love.

And he is more than love's pilgrim; he is love's martyr.

IV

To reserve a fragment of an hour for Cleopatra, if it were not palpably absurd, would seem an insult. If only one could hear her own remarks upon it! But I had to choose between this absurdity and the plan of giving her the whole hour; and to that plan there was one fatal objection. She has been described (by Ten Brink) as a courtesan of genius. So brief a description must needs be incomplete, and Cleopatra never forgets, nor, if we read aright, do we forget, that she is a great queen. Still the phrase is excellent; only a public lecture is no occasion for the full analysis and illustration of the character it describes.

Shakespeare has paid Cleopatra a unique compliment.

The hero dies in the fourth act, and the whole of the fifth is devoted to the heroine.[5] In that act she becomes unquestionably a tragic character, but, it appears to me, not till then. This, no doubt, is a heresy; but as I cannot help holding it, and as it is connected with the remarks already made on the first half of the play, I will state it more fully. Cleopatra stands in a group with Hamlet and Falstaff. We might join with them Iago if he were not decidedly their inferior in one particular quality. They are inexhaustible. You feel that, if they were alive and you spent your whole life with them, their infinite variety could never be staled by custom; they would continue every day to surprise, perplex, and delight you. Shakespeare has bestowed on each of them, though they differ so much, his own originality, his genius. He has given it most fully to Hamlet, to whom none of the chambers of experience is shut, and perhaps more of it to Cleopatra than to Falstaff. Nevertheless, if we ask whether Cleopatra, in the first four acts, is a tragic figure like Hamlet, we surely cannot answer "yes." Naturally it does not follow that she is a comic figure like Falstaff. This would be absurd; for, even if she were ridiculous like Falstaff, she is not ridiculous to herself; she is no humorist. And yet there is a certain likeness. She shares a weakness with Falstaff—vanity; and when she displays it, as she does quite naïvely (for instance, in the second interview with the Messenger), she does become comic. Again, though like Falstaff she is irresistible and carries us away no less than the people around her, we are secretly aware, in the midst of our delight, that her empire is built on sand. And finally, as his love for the Prince gives dignity and pathos to Falstaff in his overthrow, so what raises Cleopatra at last into pure tragedy is, in part, that which some critics have denied her, her love for Antony.

Many unpleasant things can be said of Cleopatra; and the more that are said, the more wonderful she appears. The exercise of sexual attraction is the element of her life; and she has developed nature into a consummate art. When she

---

[5] The point of this remark is unaffected by the fact that the play is not divided into acts and scenes in the folios.

cannot exert it on the present lover, she imagines its effects on him in absence. Longing for the living, she remembers with pride and joy the dead; and the past which the furious Antony holds up to her as a picture of shame is, for her, glory. She cannot see an ambassador, scarcely even a messenger, without desiring to bewitch him. Her mind is saturated with this element. If she is dark, it is because the sun himself has been amorous of her. Even when death is close at hand she imagines his touch as a lover's. She embraces him that she may overtake Iras and gain Antony's first kiss in the other world.

She lives for feeling. Her feelings are, so to speak, sacred, and pain must not come near her. She has tried numberless experiments to discover the easiest way to die. Her body is exquisitely sensitive, and her emotions marvelously swift. They are really so; but she exaggerates them so much, and exhibits them so continually for effect, that some readers fancy them merely feigned. They are all-important, and everybody must attend to them. She announces to her women that she is pale, or sick or sullen; they must lead her to her chamber but must not speak to her. She is as strong and supple as a leopard, can drink down a master of revelry, can raise her lover's helpless heavy body from the ground into her tower with the aid only of two women; yet, when he is sitting apart sunk in shame, she must be supported into his presence, she cannot stand, her head droops, she will die (it is the opinion of Eros) unless he comforts her. When she hears of his marriage and has discharged her rage, she bids her women bear her away; she faints; at least she would faint, but that she remembers various questions she wants put to the Messenger about Octavia. Enobarbus has seen her die twenty times upon far poorer moment than the news that Antony is going to Rome.

Some of her feelings are violent, and, unless for a purpose, she does not dream of restraining them; her sighs and tears are winds and waters, storms and tempests. At times, as when she threatens to give Charmian bloody teeth, or hales the luckless Messenger up and down by the hair, strikes him, and draws her knife on him, she resembles (if I

dare say it) Doll Tearsheet sublimated. She is a mother; but
the threat of Octavius to destroy her children if she takes
her own life passes by her like the wind (a point where
Shakespeare contradicts Plutarch). She ruins a great man,
but shows no sense of the tragedy of his ruin. The anguish
of spirit that appears in his language to his servants is
beyond her; she has to ask Enobarbus what he means. Can
we feel sure that she would not have sacrificed him if she
could have saved herself by doing so? It is not even certain
that she did not attempt it. Antony himself believes that she
did—that the fleet went over to Octavius by her orders.
That she and her people deny the charge proves nothing.
The best we can say is that, if it were true, Shakespeare
would have made that clear. She is willing also to survive
her lover. Her first thought, to follow him after the high
Roman fashion, is too great for her. She would live on if
she could, and would cheat her victor too of the best part of
her fortune. The thing that drives her to die is the certainty
that she will be carried to Rome to grace his triumph. That
alone decides her.[6]

   The marvelous thing is that the knowledge of all this
makes hardly more difference to us than it did to Antony. It
seems to us perfectly natural, nay, in a sense perfectly right,
that her lover should be her slave; that her women should
adore her and die with her; that Enobarbus, who foresaw
what must happen, and who opposes her wishes and braves
her anger, should talk of her with rapture and feel no bitter-
ness against her; that Dolabella, after a minute's conversation, should betray to her his master's intention and enable
her to frustrate it. And when Octavius shows himself proof
against her fascination, instead of admiring him we turn
from him with disgust and think him a disgrace to his
species. Why? It is not that we consider him bound to fall in
love with her. Enobarbus did not; Dolabella did not; we
ourselves do not. The feeling she inspires was felt then, and
is felt now, by women no less than men, and would have
been shared by Octavia herself. Doubtless she wrought
magic on the senses, but she had not extraordinary beauty,

[6] See Note C.

like Helen's, such beauty as seems divine.[7] Plutarch says
so. The man who wrote the sonnets to the dark lady would
have known it for himself. He goes out of his way to add to
her age, and tells us of her wrinkles and the waning of her
lip. But Enobarbus, in his very mockery, calls her a wonderful piece of work. Dolabella interrupts her with the cry,
"Most sovereign creature," and we echo it. And yet
Octavius, face to face with her and listening to her voice,
can think only how best to trap her and drag her to public
dishonor in the streets of Rome. We forgive him only for
his words when he sees her dead:

> She looks like sleep,
> As she would catch another Antony
> In her strong toil of grace.

And the words, I confess, sound to me more like Shakespeare's than his.

That which makes her wonderful and sovereign laughs at
definition, but she herself came nearest naming it when, in
the final speech (a passage surpassed in poetry, if at all,
only by the final speech of Othello), she cries,

> I am fire and air; my other elements
> I give to baser life.

The fire and air which at death break from union with those
other elements, transfigured them during her life, and still
convert into engines of enchantment the very things for
which she is condemned. I can refer only to one. She loves
Antony. We should marvel at her less and love her more if
she loved him more—loved him well enough to follow him
at once to death; but it is to blunder strangely to doubt that
she loved him, or that her glorious description of him
(though it was also meant to work on Dolabella) came from
her heart. Only the spirit of fire and air within her refuses to
be trammeled or extinguished; burns its way through the
obstacles of fortune and even through the resistance of her

---

[7] See Note D.

love and grief; and would lead her undaunted to fresh life and the conquest of new worlds. It is this which makes her "strong toil of grace" unbreakable; speaks in her brows' bent and every tone and movement; glorifies the arts and the rages which in another would merely disgust or amuse us; and, in the final scenes of her life, flames into such brilliance that we watch her entranced as she struggles for freedom, and thrilled with triumph as, conquered, she puts her conqueror to scorn and goes to meet her lover in the splendor that crowned and robed her long ago, when her barge burnt on the water like a burnished throne, and she floated to Cydnus on the enamoured stream to take him captive forever.[8]

Why is it that, although we close the book in a triumph which is more than reconciliation, this is mingled, as we look back on the story, with a sadness so peculiar, almost the sadness of disenchantment? Is it that, when the glow has faded, Cleopatra's ecstasy comes to appear, I would not say factitious, but an effort strained and prodigious as well as glorious, not, like Othello's last speech, the final expression of character, of thoughts and emotions which have dominated a whole life? Perhaps this is so, but there is something more, something that sounds paradoxical: we are saddened by the very fact that the catastrophe saddens us so little; it pains us that we should feel so much triumph and pleasure. In *Romeo and Juliet*, *Hamlet*, *Othello*, though in a sense we accept the deaths of hero and heroine, we feel a keen sorrow. We look back, think how noble or beautiful they were, wish that fate had opposed to them a weaker enemy, dream possibly of the life they might then have led. Here we can hardly do this. With all our admiration and sympathy for the lovers we do not wish them to gain the world. It is better for the world's sake, and not less for their own, that they should fail and die. At the very first they came before us, unlike those others, unlike Coriolanus and even Macbeth, in a glory already tarnished, half-ruined by

---

[8] Of the "good" heroines, Imogen is the one who has most of this spirit of fire and air; and this (in union, of course, with other qualities) is perhaps the ultimate reason why for so many readers she is, what Mr. Swinburne calls her, "the woman above all Shakespeare's women."

their past. Indeed one source of strange and most unusual effect in their story is that this marvelous passion comes to adepts in the experience and art of passion, who might be expected to have worn its charm away. Its splendor dazzles us; but, when the splendor vanishes, we do not mourn, as we mourn for the love of Romeo and Othello, that a thing so bright and good should die. And the fact that we mourn so little saddens us.

A comparison of Shakespearean tragedies seems to prove that the tragic emotions are stirred in the fullest possible measure only when such beauty or nobility of character is displayed as commands unreserved admiration or love; or when, in default of this, the forces which move the agents, and the conflict which results from these forces, attain a terrifying and overwhelming power. The four most famous tragedies satisfy one or both of these conditions; *Antony and Cleopatra*, though a great tragedy, satisfies neither of them completely. But to say this is not to criticize it. It does not attempt to satisfy these conditions and then fail in the attempt. It attempts something different and succeeds as triumphantly as *Othello* itself. In doing so it gives us what no other tragedy can give, and it leaves us, no less than any other, lost in astonishment at the powers which created it.

(1905)

NOTE A

We are to understand, surely, that Enobarbus dies of "thought" (melancholy or grief), and has no need to seek a "swifter mean." Cf. 4.6.34 *seq.*, with the death scene and his address there to the moon as the "sovereign mistress of true melancholy" (4.9.11). Cf. also 3.13.1, where, to Cleopatra's question after Actium, "What shall we do, Enobarbus?" he answers, "Think, and die."

The character of Enobarbus is practically an invention of Shakespeare's. The death scene, I may add, is one of the many passages which prove that he often wrote what pleased his imagination but would lose half its effect in the theater. The darkness and moonlight could not be represented on a public stage in his time.

NOTE B

The scene is the first of the third act. Here Ventidius says:

> Caesar and Antony have ever won
> More in their officer than person : Sossius,
> One of my place in Syria, his lieutenant,
> For quick accumulation of renown,
> Which he achieved by the minute, lost his favor.

Plutarch (North, sec. 19) says that "Sossius, one of Antonius' lieutenants in Syria, did notable good service," but I cannot find in him the further statement that Sossius lost Antony's favor. I presume it is Shakespeare's invention, but I call attention to it on the bare chance that it may be found elsewhere than in Plutarch, when it would point to Shakespeare's use of a second authority.

NOTE C

Since this lecture was published (*Quarterly Review,* April, 1906) two notable editions of *Antony and Cleopatra* have been produced. Nothing recently written on Shakespeare, I venture to say, shows more thorough scholarship or better judgment than Mr. Case's edition in the Arden series; and Dr. Furness has added to the immense debt which students of Shakespeare owe to him, and (if that is possible) to the admiration and respect with which they regard him, by the appearance of *Antony and Cleopatra* in his New Variorum edition.

On one question about Cleopatra both editors, Mr. Case more tentatively and Dr. Furness very decidedly, dissent from the interpretation given in the last pages of my lecture. The question is how we are to understand the fact that, although on Antony's death Cleopatra expresses her intention of following him, she does not carry out this intention until she has satisfied herself that Octavius means to carry her to Rome to grace his triumph. Though I do not profess to feel certain that my interpretation is right, it still seems to me a good deal the most probable, and therefore I have not altered what I wrote. But my object here is not to defend my view or to criticize other views, but merely to call attention to the discussion of the subject in Mr. Case's Introduction and Dr. Furness's Preface.

NOTE D

Shakespeare, it seems clear, imagined Cleopatra as a gypsy. And this, I would suggest, may be the explanation of a word which has caused much difficulty. Antony, when "all is lost," exclaims (4.12.25–29):

> O this false soul of Egypt! this grave charm—
> Whose eye beck'd forth my wars, and call'd them home,
> Whose bosom was my crownet, my chief end—
> Like a right gypsy, hath, at fast and loose,
> Beguil'd me to the very heart of loss.

Pope changed "grave" in the first line into "gay." Others conjecture "great" and "grand." Steevens says that "grave" means "deadly," and that the word "is often used by Chapman" thus; and one of his two quotations supports this statement; but certainly in Shakespeare the word does not elsewhere bear this sense. It could mean "majestic," as Johnson takes it here. But why should it not have its usual meaning? Cleopatra, we know, was a being of "infinite variety," and her eyes may sometimes have had, like those of some gypsies, a mysterious gravity or solemnity which would exert a spell more potent than her gaiety. Their color, presumably, was what is called "black"; but surely they were not, like those of Tennyson's Cleopatra, "*bold* black eyes." Readers interested in seeing what criticism is capable of may like to know that it has been proposed to read, for the first line of the quotation above, "O this false fowl of Egypt! haggard charmer." [Though I have not canceled this note I have modified some phrases in it, as I have not much confidence in my suggestion, and am inclined to think that Steevens was right.]

JOHN F. DANBY

Antony and Cleopatra:

A Shakespearian Adjustment

At each stage in his development Shakespeare displays a surprising capacity for renewal. Let us assume that *Antony and Cleopatra* comes after *King Lear*, that it goes with *Coriolanus*, and that both it and *Coriolanus* immediately precede the so-called "last period." Between *Antony and Cleopatra* and the plays that have gone before there is no obvious connection in theme or technique. At the same time, only Plutarch links it with *Coriolanus*. Nothing in it would normally prepare us for *Cymbeline* or *The Winter's Tale* to follow. This apparent isolation is one of the main obstacles to a correct focus on the play. There seems to be a break in the internal continuity of the Shakespearian series—a continuity of series which stretches, I think, from *Henry VI* to *King Lear* at least, and which could possibly be extended to include *Timon*: though here again there is something of a lesion, and special factors, external to the "inner biography" of Shakespeare as a playwright, might have to be invoked to explain all that is happening. *Timon*, however, it might be granted, is the aftermath of *King Lear*. Can the same be said about *Antony and Cleopatra*?

From *Poets on Fortune's Hill* by John F. Danby (London: Faber and Faber, Ltd., 1952). Reprinted by permission of Faber and Faber, Ltd.

I

To describe the swiftness of *Antony and Cleopatra* we need to draw on the imagery of the cinema. There is more cinematic movement, more panning, tracking, and playing with the camera, more mixing of shots than in any other of Shakespeare's tragedies. At the same time the technique is always under deliberate, almost cool, control. *Antony and Cleopatra* has none of the haphazardies of *Pericles* nor any of the plot-imposed vagaries of the last period. The technique is inwardly related to the meaning Shakespeare has to express. What is indicated is not enervation or indifference, but rather what Coleridge recognized as "giant power," an "angelic strength."

The swift traverse of time and space has often been commented upon. There is also the mixing. Egypt is called up vividly in Rome by Enobarbus's descriptions. Rome is always felt as a real presence in Egypt. On the frontiers of Empire Ventidius discusses what repercussions his victories will have on the people at staff headquarters. Equally the present is interpenetrated by the past. Antony's past, particularly, is always powerfully put before us:

>   Antony,
> Leave thy lascivious wassails. When thou once
> Was beaten from Modena, where thou slew'st
> Hirtius and Pansa, consuls, at thy heels
> Did famine follow, whom thou fought'st against
> (Though daintily brought up) with patience more
> Than savages could suffer. Thou didst drink
> The stale of horses, and the gilded puddle
> Which beasts would cough at. Thy palate then did deign
> The roughest berry on the rudest hedge.
> Yea, like the stag, when snow the pasture sheets,
> The barks of trees thou browsed. On the Alps
> It is reported thou didst eat strange flesh,
> Which some did die to look on.　　　　　(1.4.55–68)

So, too, is Cleopatra's:

> I found you as a morsel cold upon
> Dead Caesar's trenchar: nay, you were a fragment
> Of Cneius Pompey's, besides what hotter hours,
> Unregister'd in vulgar fame, you have
> Luxuriously picked out.
> (3.13.116–20)

The hinterland of the quarrels that alternately divide and bring together again the triumvirate is constantly being suggested, troubles, truces, and maneuvers that go back (like Cleopatra's love affairs) to Julius Caesar's days. In no other of his plays is Shakespeare at such pains to suggest the stream of time past and its steady course through the present. In the public world of Roman affairs this is especially so. In the other world of Cleopatra the same suggestion of perspective always frames what is said and done. Is Antony merely the last of a long succession of such lovers? Or is this affair singular and unique as all love affairs claim to be? Not enough weight has been given in recent assessments of the play to the ambiguity which invests everything in Egypt equally with all things in Rome. Yet this ambiguity is central to Shakespeare's experience in the play. If it is wrong to see the "mutual pair" as a strumpet and her fool, it is also wrong to see them as a Phoenix and a Turtle.

In addition to the swiftness and the variety of the impacts, and the interpenetration of the parts of time and space as they mix in the speech of the people immediately before us, there is also the added burden which Shakespeare's "giant power" of compelling presentation imposes. The effects are at once those of a rapid impressionism and a careful lapidary enrichment. Each figure, however minor, has its moment when it comes up into the brilliant foreground light—the Soothsayer with his "infinite book of secrecy" (1.2.9), the Old Man wishing "much joy o' the worm" (5.2.260), Enobarbus describing the barge on the Nile, Lepidus asking "What manner o' thing is your crocodile?" (2.7.42) Ventidius giving once for all the field officer's view of the higher-ups, the Eunuch and the game of billiards, Dolabella,

Octavia, even Fulvia whom we never see: The canvas seems covered with Constable's snow.

Another feature of Shakespeare's technique which makes for the impression of uniqueness might be pointed to here. Shakespeare seems to be innovating also in methods of character portrayal. Some of the stage conventions, as described by Miss Bradbrook, do not seem to apply. Which, for example, are we to believe—what Caesar says about Antony after he is dead, or what he says about him, and his conduct towards him, while he is alive? What was Fulvia's "character," about whom we have such conflicting reports? Throughout the play we are forced by Shakespeare himself not to take comment at its face value. Judgments are more personal here than elsewhere. Goneril and Regan discussing their father's condition are reliable judges. Caesar, Antony, Enobarbus, the soldiers Demetrius and Philo, are not—or not to the same extent. Judgment knits itself back into character as it might do in Ibsen, and character issues from a mutable and ambiguous flux of things. Antony's momentary *anagnorisis* can be generalized to cover the whole play:

> Sometimes we see a cloud that's dragonish,
> A vapor sometimes like a bear or lion,
> A towered citadel, a pendant rock,
> A forked mountain, or blue promontory,
> With trees upon't that nod unto the world
> And mock our eyes with air. Thou hast seen these signs:
> They are black vespers pageants. . . .
> That which is now a horse, even with a thought
> The rack dislimns, and makes it indistinct
> As water is in water. . . .
> My good knave Eros, now thy captain is
> Even such a body: here I am Antony,
> Yet cannot hold this visible shape, my knave.   (4.14.2–14)

There is something deliquescent in the reality behind the play. It is a deliquescence to the full display of which each judgment, each aspect pointed to, and each character, is necessary, always provided that no single one of these is taken as final. The proportion of comment and judgment on the central characters is higher in *Antony and Cleopatra* than anywhere else in Shakespeare. This further underlines its uniqueness and the difficulties of coming by an adequate final assessment. Antony and Cleopatra are presented in three ways. There is what is said about them; there is what they say themselves; there is what they do. Each of these might correspond to a different "level" of response. Each is in tension against the others. Each makes its continuous and insistent claim on the spectator for judgment in his own right. The pigments vividly opposed to each other on the canvas have to mix in the spectator's eye.

Underlying, however, the bewildering oscillations of scene, the overlapping and pleating of different times and places, the co-presence of opposed judgments, the innumerable opportunities for radical choice to intervene, there is, I think, a deliberate logic. It is this which gives the play its compact unity of effect and makes its movement a sign of angelic strength rather than a symptom of febrility. It is the logic of a peculiarly Shakespearian dialectic. Opposites are juxtaposed, mingled, married; then from the very union which seems to promise strength dissolution flows. It is the process of this dialectic—the central process of the play—which we must trace if we wish to arrive anywhere near Shakespeare's meaning.

II

The first scene opens with Philo's comment on the "dotage" of his general:

> Those his goodly eyes
> That o'er the files and musters of the war
> Have glowed like plated Mars: now bend, now turn
> The office and devotion of their view
> Upon a tawny front. His captain's heart,
> Which in the scuffles of great fights hath burst
> The buckles on his breast, reneges all temper,

> And is become the bellows and the fan
> To cool a gypsy's lust.   (1.1.2–10)

Nothing more has time to be said. Antony and Cleopatra themselves appear. Their first words express the essence of romantic love, a tacit contradiction of all that Philo seems to have just suggested:

Cleopatra. If it be love indeed, tell me how much.

Antony. There's beggary in the love that can be reckoned.

Cleopatra. I'll set a bourn how far to be beloved.

Antony. Then must thou needs find out new heaven, new
     earth.   (14–17)

Again immediately, an attendant announces the arrival of news from Rome. The atmosphere of the Egyptian court changes. We see the opposite effects of the intrusion on the two it most concerns. Antony will not hear the messengers. Cleopatra insists that he shall. Antony is taunted with a wicked caricature of what the news might be, and of the relation in which he stands to Rome. Yet the version is sufficiently like to make Antony blush—from anger, or shame, or both:

>   Your dismission
> Is come from Caesar; therefore hear it, Antony,
> Where's Fulvia's process? Caesar's would I say? Both?
> Call in the messengers. As I am Egypt's queen,
> Thou blushest, Antony, and that blood of thine
> Is Caesar's homager: else so thy cheek pays shame
> When shrill-tongued Fulvia scolds.   (26–32)

Antony's reaction is to pitch his romantic vows higher still, asserting his independence of Rome in terms that should leave no doubt as to where he stands:

> Let Rome in Tiber melt, and the wide arch
> Of the ranged empire fall! Here is my space.

> Kingdoms are clay: our dungy earth alike
> Feeds beast as man. The nobleness of life
> Is to do thus; when such a mutual pair
> And such a twain can do't, in which I bind
> On pain of punishment, the world to weet
> We stand up peerless.   (33–40)

This again has all the ring of absolute and heroic self-committal. Cleopatra's reply, however, is typical both of herself and of the ambivalence that runs through everything in the play:

> Excellent falsehood!
> Why did he marry Fulvia and not love her?
> I'll seem the fool I am not; Antony
> Will be—himself.   (40–43)

Her first words might be oxymoron or plain disbelief. The next call up the vista of Antony's past, with its broken pledges and unconscious insincerities—if they were no more. Her last words are highly ambiguous and turn the whole situation upside-down: She is the helpless creature willfully blinding and deceiving herself, Antony is the self-contained and calculating manipulator of her weaknesses. In replying, Antony is like the man innocent of jujutsu who thinks he is pushing when really he is being pulled:

> But stirred by Cleopatra.
> Now, for the love of Love and her soft hours,
> Let's not confound the time with conference harsh. . . .
> . . . What sport tonight?   (43–47)

Shakespeare gives the operative lines a subtle falsity of note that could equally indicate hearty play acting, slightly awkward self-consciousness, or willful evasion. Cleopatra's answer is realist and comes with a new urgency:

> Hear the ambassadors.   (48)

It drives Antony also to something we can recognize as more fully himself—something that is perceptive and tinged with the masterful as well as the reckless:

> Fie, wrangling queen!
> Whom everything becomes—to chide, to laugh,
> To weep; whose every passion fully strives
> To make itself in thee fair and admired.
> No messenger, but thine; and all alone,
> Tonight we'll wander through the streets and note
> The qualities of people. Come, my queen;
> Last night you did desire it. Speak not to us.   (48–55)

This is not only Antony's view of Cleopatra's character, and a reliable account of what she is really like. It is also an expression of the deliquescent reality at the heart of the play which incarnates itself most completely in the persons of the hero and heroine. After Antony's speech, with this twofold authority it bears, the comment of the soldiers seems peculiarly limited and out of place:

Demetrius. Is Caesar with Antonius prized so slight?

Philo. Sir, sometimes when he is not Antony,
He comes too short of that great property
Which still should go with Antony.

Demetrius.   I am full sorry
That he approves the common liar, who
Thus speaks of him at Rome; but I will hope
Of better deeds tomorrow.   (56–62)

It serves to remind us, however, of the world that stands around the lovers, the world of the faithful soldier who can only understand the soldierly, the world of "the common liar" that enjoys the unpleasant "truth," the world, too, of Rome and Caesar that is radically opposed to the world of Egypt and Cleopatra.

The first scene is only slightly more than sixty lines long. Yet it is sufficient to illustrate all the main features of the play we have pointed to, and extensive enough to set up the swinging ambivalence—the alternatives and ambiguities constantly proposed to choice—which will govern and control our whole reaction to the play. There is the speed and oscillation, the interpenetration of Rome and Egypt and of present and past. Above all there is the dialectic marriage of the contraries and their dissolution through union. The jealousy of Cleopatra towards Fulvia, the outrage of Caesar to Antony's *amour propre*—these negative repulsions can serve to hold the mutual pair together as firmly as positive attractions. Antony and Cleopatra are opposed to the world that surrounds and isolates them. In this isolation their union seems absolute, infinite, and self-sufficient. Yet the war of the contraries pervades the love, too. In coming together they lapse, slide, and fall apart unceasingly.

The outstanding achievement of the first scene is the way in which it begins with the soldiers' condemnation and returns us at the end to the same thing—allowing for this side eighteen lines out of the sixty-two. Yet at the end we are no longer satisfied as to the adequacy of what Demetrius and Philo say. Not that what they say has been disproved by what we have seen of Antony and Cleopatra. They are and they remain a strumpet and her fool. To have any judgment at all is to choose, apparently, either the judgment of the soldiers at the beginning of the scene or the lovers' own self-assessment that immediately follows it. (Coleridge chose the former; Dr. Sitwell and Mr. Wilson Knight take the latter.) To entertain either judgment, however, is not enough. The deliquescent truth is neither in them nor between them, but contains both. *Antony and Cleopatra* is Shakespeare's critique of judgment.

Scene 1 played out romantic love and lovers' quarrels on a lofty stage. It also gave the sharp local comment of the soldiery. Scene 2 takes the theme of love belowstairs and changes key. It also gives the universal comment of the Soothsayer, with its suggestion that everything is already decided, the tragedy is in the nature of things, now is already over, the future past, the present always:

> In Nature's infinite book of secrecy
> A little I can read. . . .
> I make not, but foresee. . . .
> You have seen and proved a fairer former fortune
> Than that which is to approach.   (1.2.9–35)

In place of the "romance" of love, Charmian, Iras, and Alexas give the "reality." The reality in this case is a strong succession of rich, powerful, and adequate males:

> Let me be married to three kings in a forenoon, and widow them all; let me have a child at fifty to whom Herod of Jewry may do homage; find me to marry with Octavius Caesar, and companion me with my mistress.   (25–30)

It reads like a parody of Cleopatra's aspirations, just as the women's bickering and teasing of Alexas mimics Cleopatra's handling of Antony:

> Alexas—come, his fortune, his fortune! O, let him marry a woman that cannot go, sweet Isis, I beseech thee, and let her die too, and give him a worse, and let worse follow worse, till the worst of all follow him laughing to his grave, fiftyfold a cuckold!   (63–68)

This seems a nightmare version of Antony's fate—the reflection in a distorting mirror of the thoughts and feelings that course through Antony after Cleopatra's desertion in the disastrous sea fight.

The group is interrupted in its fortune-telling by the entry of Cleopatra. She is looking for Antony. Her remarks prepare us for the different mood about to establish itself:

> Saw you my lord? . . .
> He was disposed to mirth; but on the sudden
> A Roman thought hath struck him.   (81–84)

Antony is heard approaching. Cleopatra immediately goes off. Now that he is coming she will refuse to see him.

When Antony appears he is surrounded by the messengers

from Rome and immersed in Roman affairs. He veers sav-
agely to the point of view both of the soldiers in the first
scene and "the common liar" in Rome. Throughout the play
this is what marks him off from Cleopatra and makes him a
more complex meeting ground for the opposites than even
she is herself. He can understand and respond to the appeal
of Rome as much as he can understand and respond to
Egypt:

> Speak to me home, mince not the general tongue;
> Name Cleopatra as she's called in Rome;
> Rail thou in Fulvia's phrase, and taunt my faults
> With such full license as both truth and malice
> Have power to utter. O, then we bring forth weeds
> When our quick winds lie still, and our ills told us
> Is as our earing. Fare thee well awhile . . .
> These strong Egyptian fetters I must break,
> Or lose myself in dotage.   (106–18)

The second messenger brings news of Fulvia's death. It is
characteristic of the play that what is hated during life
should find favor once it is dead. Later in this scene that is
reported to be the case with Pompey in the popular reaction
to him:

> Our slippery people,
> Whose love is never linked to the deserver
> Till his deserts are past, begin to throw
> Pompey the Great and all his dignities
> Upon his son.   (187–91)

This is what happens, too, in Antony's case when, once he
is dead, Octavius sings his praises. It also happens when
Cleopatra is thought to have committed suicide and Antony
flings from vituperation to acclamation almost without
pausing. It happens now with Fulvia. Antony says:

> There's a great spirit gone! Thus did I desire it:
> What our contempts do often hurl from us,
> We wish it ours again. The present pleasure,

By revolution low'ring, does become
The opposite of itself: she's good being gone;
the hand could pluck her back that shoved her on.
I must from this enchanting queen break off.

(123–29)

Typically, when he joins the general, Enobarbus summons all the counterarguments. To leave Egypt would be to kill Cleopatra. "She is cunning," Antony says, "past man's thought." "Alack, sir, no," Enobarbus rejoins,

her passions are made of nothing but the finest part of pure love. We cannot call her winds and waters sighs and tears; they are greater storms and tempests than almanacs can report. This cannot be cunning in her; if it be, she makes a show'r of rain as well as Jove. (148–53)

Even if we read Enobarbus's words as irony, the double irony that works by virtue of the constant ambivalence in the play still turns them back to something approaching the truth: and Cleopatra's real distress and anxiety over Antony's departure have already cut through the scene like a knife. The dingdong continues:

Antony. Would I had never seen her!

Enobarbus. O, sir! you had then left unseen a wonderful piece of work. . . .

Antony. Fulvia is dead.

Enobarbus. Sir?

Antony. Fulvia is dead.

Enobarbus. Fulvia?

Antony. Dead.

Enobarbus. Why, sir, give the gods a thankful sacrifice. . . . This grief is crown'd with consolation: your old smock brings forth a new petticoat. (154–71)

Antony, however, has made up his mind to go back to Rome.

Antony does go back to Rome—but not in the mood and not with the motives of thoroughgoing reformation in which he remains at the end of Scene 2. In Scene 3 the alchemy of the Shakespearian process is further at work. It works to make Antony do the thing resolved upon but for reasons the very opposite of those which led him to the resolve. The scene of his departure is chosen for Cleopatra's most sincere avowal. Having tormented Antony beyond all bearing she suddenly breaks off with:

> Courteous lord, one word.
> Sir, you and I must part, but that's not it:
> Sir, you and I have loved, but there's not it:
> That you know well. Something it is I would—
> O, my oblivion is a very Antony,
> And I am all forgotten.   (1.3.86–91)

Antony's final words in the scene almost catch the very idiom of *The Phoenix and the Turtle*:

> Let us go. Come:
> Our separation so abides and flies,
> That thou residing here goes yet with me,
> And I hence fleeting here remain with thee.
> Away!   (101–5)

It is, so to speak, the honeymoon of the contraries—only possible while the lovers are apart.

III

The first three scenes show how pervasive is that quality in technique and vision which we have called the Shakespearian "dialectic." It comes out in single images, it can permeate whole speeches, it governs the buildup inside each scene, it explains the way one scene is related to another. The word "dialectic," of course, is unfortunately post-Hegelian. The thing we wish to point to, however, in

using the word, is Shakespearian. In *Antony and Cleopatra*
Shakespeare needs the opposites that merge, unite, and fall
apart. They enable him to handle the reality he is writing
about—the vast containing opposites of Rome and Egypt,
the World and the Flesh.

Rome is the sphere of the political. Shakespeare uses the
contraries (long before Blake) to give some sort of rational
account of the irrationals there involved. The common
people, for example, is "the common liar." Antony has
already noted that its love is "never linked to the deserver
till his deserts are past." Caesar, too, has his own cold
knowledge of the same fact:

> It hath been taught us from the primal state
> That he which is was wished until he were;
> And the ebb'd man, ne'er loved till ne'er worth love,
> Comes deared by being lacked. This common body,
> Like to the vagabond flag upon the stream,
> Goes to and back, lackeying the varying tide,
> To rot itself with motion.   (1.4.41–47)

The great men, however, behave exactly as they say the
commons do, too. With Antony, Fulvia becomes deared by
being lacked. In Caesar's case it is the same. The threat of
Pompey makes him suddenly appreciate the grandeur of
Antony's leadership, courage, and endurance. The mag-
nanimous praise of Antony in Act 5 is only possible
because Antony by then is dead. The law is general: judgment is a kind of accommodation to the irrational on
reason's part:

>   men's judgments are
> A parcel of their fortunes, and things outward
> Do draw the inward quality after them,
> To suffer all alike.   (3.13.31–34)

Even soldierly "honor" is rooted in the ambiguous. When
Pompey's man mentions his treacherous scheme for dis-
posing of all Pompey's rivals at one blow (the rivals are
also Pompey's guests on board ship), Pompey exclaims:

> Ah, this thou shouldst have done,
> And not have spoken on't. In me 'tis villainy,
> In thee 't had been good service. Thou must know
> 'Tis not my profit that does lead mine honor;
> Mine honor, it. Repent that e'er thy tongue
> Hath so betrayed thine act. Being done unknown,
> I should have found it afterwards well done,
> But must condemn it now.   (2.7.75–82)

The law is general because it reflects the nature of the ter-rene world—the tidal swing of the opposites on which all things balance in a motion that rots them away.

The self-destruction of things that rot with the motion which their own nature and situation dictate is almost obsessive with Shakespeare throughout the play. The political world is the manipulation of the common body they despise by the great men whom the commons can never love until they are safely rid of them. The pattern which remains constant in all the possible groupings is that of open conflict alternating with diseased truce, neither of them satisfactory:

> Equality of two domestic powers
> Breeds scrupulous faction; the hated, grown to strength,
> Are newly grown to love. . . .
> And quietness, grown sick of rest, would purge
> By any desperate change.   (1.3.47–54)

Compacts between the great men merely represent the tem-porary sinking of lesser enmities in front of greater:

> lesser enmities may give way to greater.
> Were't not that we stand up against them all,
> 'Twere pregnant they should square amongst themselves.
>   (2.1.43–45)

Pompey's is a correct appreciation. It is because of him that Octavius and Antony are reconciled. They will rivet the alliance by means of Antony's marriage to Caesar's sister. Enobarbus knows automatically that this union is a certain way of making conflict ultimately inevitable:

you shall find the bond that seems to tie their friendship
together will be the very strangler of their amity.

(2.6.120–22)

Octavia is one of Shakespeare's minor triumphs in the
play, beautifully placed in relation to the main figures and
the tenor of their meaning. Her importance is apt to be over-
looked unless her careful positioning is noted. Her presence
gives a symmetrical form to the main relations of the play.
Octavia is the opposite of Cleopatra as Antony is the opposite of Caesar. She is woman made the submissive tool of
Roman policy where Cleopatra always strives to make the
political subservient to her. (It is the thought of being led in
triumph by Caesar as much as the thought of Antony's
death which finally decides Cleopatra for suicide.) Where
Caesar and Cleopatra are simple and opposite, Octavia—
like Antony—is a focal point for the contraries. There is
nothing in her as a "character study" to account for the
effect her presence has. It is rather that she is transparent to
the reality behind the play and one of its least mistakable
mediators. On the occasions when she appears herself, or
when mention is made of her, it is the interfluent life of this
reality rather than the personality of its vehicle which fills
the scene.

Her first entry is significant. It comes immediately after
the triumvirate and Pompey have made their pact. We have
just heard the following satiric account of Lepidus's
behavior—and Lepidus, like Octavia, has to stand between
the two demi-Atlases:

Agrippa. 'Tis a noble Lepidus.

Eno. A very fine one. O, how he loves Caesar!

Agrippa. Nay, but how dearly he adores Mark Antony!

Eno. Caesar? Why, he's the Jupiter of men.

Agrippa. What's Antony? The god of Jupiter.

Eno. Spake you of Caesar? How! The nonpareil!

Agrippa. O Antony! O thou Arabian bird!   (3.2.6–12)

Then the triumvirate and Octavia come on. Octavia stirs Antony deeply. But the imagery in which his vision of her is clothed carries us past the person described to the "varying tide" by which everything in the play is moved:

> Her tongue will not obey her heart, nor can
> Her heart obey her tongue; the swan's-down feather
> That stands upon the swell of the full tide
> And neither way inclines.   (47–50)

Octavia never escapes from her position midway between the contraries that maintain and split the world. With Antony away in Athens, her brother first falls on Pompey, then finds a pretext to destroy Lepidus. He is now ready to mount his attack on the last remaining rival, his "competitor in top of all design." Hearing of it, Octavia cries:

> A more unhappy lady,
> If this division chance, ne'er stood between,
> Praying for both parts. . . .
>   . . . Husband win, win brother,
> Prays, and destroys the prayer; no midway
> 'Twixt these extremes at all.   (3.4.12–20)

Octavia's is the alternative plight to Cleopatra's for womanhood in the play. The choice is merely between alternative methods of destruction—either at one's own hands or through the agency of the process. The "swan's-down feather," like the "vagabond flag," can only swing on the tide until it rots with motion.

Rome is the world of politics and policy. Its supreme term is Octavius Caesar himself. He, like Octavia, must be brought into relation with the pattern which he helps in part to define. Half his significance is lost if he is seen only as a "character." In Octavius's case we have aids external to the play which help towards a clear focus on what Shakespeare intends by him. He falls recognizably into Shakespeare's studies of the "politician"—the series that begins with Richard III and continues down through Edmund.

Octavius is a notable development in the figure which

started as a machiavel pure and simple. Shakespeare now betrays no sign of alarm, no hint of revulsion or rejection, almost no trace of emotion in putting him into a story. He is taken completely for granted. He has arrived and he will stay. He is part of the structure of things. He is "Rome." In matters of politics and policy it is obvious that only the politicians count: And politics is one half of life. The politician is a perfectly normal person. Given all his own way he would doubtless bring—as Octavius is certain his triumphs eventually will bring—a "universal peace." To be normal like him, of course, and to enjoy the peace he offers, two conditions are necessary. First, one must sacrifice the other half of life; then, one must be prepared to make complete submission. By the time Shakespeare comes to depict Octavius he has refined away all the accidentals from the portrait—the diabolism, the rhetoric, the elaborate hypocrisy, the perverse glamor: everything but the essential deadliness and inescapability. Octavius marks an advance on Goneril and Regan. He shares their impatience with tavern and brothel. He has no share in the lust which entraps even them. We might almost doubt whether Octavius has any personal appetite at all, even the lust for power. His plan to lead Cleopatra in triumph has the appearance of a desire for personal satisfaction, but it is more likely that it fits into an impersonal wish on Caesar's part to subdue all things to Rome. Caesar, of course, is Rome—but a kind of impersonal embodiment. He is more like a cold and universal force than a warm-blooded man. He is the perfect commissar, invulnerable as no human being should be. Egypt has no part in his composition.

Caesar has the deceitfulness of the machiavel, but he plays his cards without any flourish. He can rely on his opponents to undo themselves: they are more complicated than he. He puts the deserters from Antony in the van of his own battle:

> Plant those that are revolted in the vant,
> That Antony may seem to spend his fury
> Upon himself. (4.6.9–11)

The strength and weakness of those ranged against him constitute Caesar's fifth column. The opposition will rot away or eat the sword it fights with.

It is in the last act that Egypt and Rome confront each other singly, the duplicity of Caesar pitted against the duplicity of Cleopatra. There is no doubt as to who shall survive the contest. The tension is maintained throughout the fifth act only by the doubt left in the spectator's mind right up to the end as to which way Cleopatra will jump: Will she accept submission or will she take her own life? The whole play has prepared us for just this doubt. In a sense, whichever way the decision goes it is immaterial. The point of the play is not the decisions taken but the dubieties and ambivalences from which choice springs—the barren choice that only hastens its own negation. Rome, from the nature of things, can admit no compromise. Egypt, equally, can never submit to its contrary. So Cleopatra kills herself.

Cleopatra has been loved by recent commentators not wisely but too well. As Caesar impersonates the World, she, of course, incarnates the Flesh. Part of Shakespeare's sleight of hand in the play—his trickery with our normal standards and powers of judgment—is to construct an account of the human universe consisting of only these two terms. There is no suggestion that the dichotomy is resolvable: Unless we are willing to take the delusions of either party as a resolution, the "universal peace" of Caesar, the Egypt-beyond-the-grave of Antony and Cleopatra in their autotoxic exaltations before they kill themselves.

Cleopatra is the Flesh, deciduous, opulent, and endlessly renewable:

> she did make defect perfection . . .
> Age cannot wither her, nor custom stale
> Her infinite variety: other women cloy
> The appetites they feed, but she makes hungry
> Where most she satisfies; for vilest things
> Become themselves in her, that the holy priests
> Bless her when she is riggish.   (2.2.237–46)

The Flesh is also the female principle. Cleopatra is Eve, and Woman:

> No more but e'en a woman, and commanded
> By such poor passion as the maid that milks
> And does the meanest chares. (4.15.72–74)

She is also Circe:

> Let witchcraft join with beauty, lust with both!
> (2.1.22)

Shakespeare gives Cleopatra everything of which he is capable except his final and absolute approval. Cleopatra is not an Octavia, much less a Cordelia. The profusion of rich and hectic color that surrounds her is the color of the endless cycle of growth and decay, new greenery on old rottenness, the color of the passions, the wild flaring of life as it burns itself richly away to death so that love of life and greed for death become indistinguishable:

> there is mettle in death which commits some loving act upon
> her, she had such a celerity in dying. (1.2.144–46)

The strength of the case Shakespeare put against her is undeniable. The soldiers, and Caesar, and Antony when the consciousness of Rome speaks through him, are right, as far as they go. The strength of the case for her is that it is only Rome that condemns her. And Egypt is a force as universal as Rome—as hot as the other is cold, as inevitably self-renewing as the other is inescapably deadly. And the only appeal that can be made in the play is from Egypt to Rome, from Rome to Egypt. And neither of these is final, because between them they have brought down Antony, the "man of men."

For the tragedy of *Antony and Cleopatra* is, above all, the tragedy of Antony. His human stature is greater than either Cleopatra's or Caesar's. Yet there is no sphere in which he can express himself except either Rome or Egypt, and to bestride both like a Colossus and keep his balance is impossible. The opposites play through Antony and play with him, and finally destroy him. To Caesar (while Antony is in Egypt, and alive) he is:

> A man who is th' abstract of all faults
> That all men follow.   (1.4.9–10)

To Cleopatra he appears instead a "heavenly mingle":

> Be'st thou sad or merry,
> The violence of either thee becomes,
> So does it no man else.   (1.5.59–61)

When she sees him returning safe from the battlefield she cries:

> O infinite virtue, com'st thou smiling from
> The world's great snare uncaught?   (4.8.17–18)

After he is dead she remembers him as a kind of Mars:

> His face was as the heav'ns and therein stuck
> A sun and moon, which kept their course, and lighted
> This little *O*, th' earth. . . .
> His legs bestrid the ocean: his reared arm
> Crested the world: his voice was propertied
> As all the tunèd spheres, and that to friends;
> But when he meant to quail and shake the orb,
> He was as rattling thunder. For his bounty,
> There was no winter in't: an autumn 'twas
> That grew the more by reaping. His delights
> Were dolphinlike, they showed his back above
> The element they lived in. In his livery
> Walked crowns and crownets: realms and islands were
> As plates dropped from his pocket. . . .
> . . . Nature wants stuff
> To vie strange forms with fancy, yet t'imagine
> An Antony were nature's piece 'gainst fancy,
> Condemning shadows quite.   (5.2.79–100)

This, of course, is again the past catching fire from the urgent needs of the present, flaring in memory and imagination as it never did in actuality. Antony is nothing so unambiguous as this. The most judicious account of him is that of Lepidus when he is replying to Caesar's strictures:

> I must not think there are
> Evils enow to darken all his goodness;
> His faults in him seem as the spots of heaven,
> More fiery by night's blackness, hereditary
> Rather than purchased, what he cannot change
> Than what he chooses.   (1.4.10–15)

Here the ambiguities of the play's moral universe get their completest expression: Faults shine like stars, the heaven is black, the stars are spots. Ambivalence need go no further.

IV

The earlier criticism of *Antony and Cleopatra* tended to stress the downfall of the soldier in the middle-aged infatuate. More recent criticism has seen the play as the epiphany of the soldier in the lover, and the reassurance of all concerned that death is not the end. In the view that has been put forward here neither of these is right. The meaning of *Antony and Cleopatra* is in the Shakespearian "dialectic"— in the deliquescent reality that expresses itself through the contraries.

Antony and Cleopatra swims with glamor. Once we lose sight of the controlling structure of the opposites which holds the play together we are at the mercy of any random selection from its occasions. And occasions abound—moments, opinions, moods, speeches, characters, fragments of situation, forked mountains and blue promontories, imposed upon us with all the force of a "giant power." It is, then, eminently understandable that critics should succumb like Antony or hold aloof like Demetrius and Philo.

The Roman condemnation of the lovers is obviously

inadequate. The sentimental reaction in their favor is equally mistaken. There is no so-called "love-romanticism" in the play. The flesh has its glory and passion, its witchery. Love in *Antony and Cleopatra* is both these. The love of Antony and Cleopatra, however, is not asserted as a "final value." The whole tenor of the play, in fact, moves in an opposite direction. Egypt is the Egypt of the biblical glosses: exile from the spirit, thralldom to the fleshpots, diminution of human kindness. To go further still in sentimentality and claim that there is a "redemption" motif in Antony and Cleopatra's love is an even more violent error. To the Shakespeare who wrote *King Lear* it would surely smack of blasphemy. The fourth and fifth acts of *Antony and Cleopatra* are not epiphanies. They are the ends moved to by that process whereby things rot themselves with motion—unhappy and bedizened and sordid, streaked with the mean, the ignoble, the contemptible. Shakespeare may have his plays in which "redemption" is a theme (and I think he has), but *Antony and Cleopatra* is not one of them.

Antony and Cleopatra is an account of things in terms of the World and the Flesh, Rome and Egypt, the two great contraries that maintain and destroy each other, considered apart from any third sphere which might stand over against them. How is it related to the plays of the "great period," the period which comes to an end with *King Lear*?

The clue is given, I think, in the missing third term. *Antony and Cleopatra* is the deliberate construction of a world without a Cordelia, Shakespeare's symbol for a reality that transcends the political and the personal and

> redeems nature from the general curse
> Which twain have brought her to.
>
> (*King Lear*, 4.6.209–10)

One must call the construction deliberate, because after *King Lear* there can be no doubt that Shakespeare knew exactly where he was in these matters. Both *Antony and Cleopatra* and *Coriolanus* follow North's Plutarch without benefit of clergy. Both Antony and Coriolanus were cited by the sixteenth-century moralists as notable examples of heathen men who lacked patience—the one committing suicide, the other rebelling against his country. In *Antony and Cleopatra* suicide is the general fate of those who wish to die. Cleopatra gives the audience a conscious reminder of the un-Christian ethos involved:

> All's but naught.
> Patience is sottish, and impatience does
> Become a dog that's mad: then is it sin
> To rush into the secret house of death
> Ere death dare come to us?   (4.15.77–81)

The Christian world view in Shakespeare's time turned round a number of conceptions which were covered by the Elizabethans in their examination of the meanings of "Nature." The theme of "Nature" runs through the whole of *Macbeth, King Lear,* and *Timon*. Its absence from *Antony and Cleopatra* suggests Shakespeare's satisfaction that for him the theme is exhausted. He is inwardly free now to look at a classical story, deliberately excise the Christian core of his thought, and make up his account of what then remains over.

This explains the effect, I think, of *Antony and Cleopatra*. Freedom from the compulsive theme of the Natures, the conscious security gained from having given it final expression, enabled Shakespeare to handle something new and something which was bound to be intrinsically simpler. Part of the energy absorbed in grappling with theme now bestows itself on technique. *Antony and Cleopatra* gives the impression of being a technical tour de force which Shakespeare enjoyed for its own sake.

The excision also explains, I think, the tone of the play—the sense of ripe-rottenness and hopelessness, the vision of self-destruction, the feeling of strenuous frustration and fevered futility, that which finds its greatest expression in Antony's speech before he gives himself his deathblow:

> . . . now
> All length is torture: since the torch is out,

Lie down and stray no farther. Now all labor
Mars what it does; yea, very force entangles
Itself with strength. Seal then, and all is done.

(4.14.45–49)

The excision, finally, explains what might be regarded as
a diminution of scope in *Antony and Cleopatra*. (We are, of
course, only comparing Shakespeare with himself.) The
theme of Rome and Egypt, however, is simpler than the
theme of "Nature," the trick of using the contraries (again,
for Shakespeare) relatively an easy way of organizing the
universe. It is unusual, at any rate, for Shakespeare to rely
on one trick so completely as he seems to do in *Antony and
Cleopatra*. At times we are almost tempted to believe he
has fallen a victim of habitual mannerism.

One last comment might be made. We referred at the
beginning of this chapter to Shakespeare's surprising
capacity for self-renewal. *Antony and Cleopatra* is not the
aftermath of Lear in any pejorative sense. There is something in it that is new and exciting and profound. Shakespeare remained still the youngest as the greatest of his
contemporaries. In *Antony and Cleopatra* he is making
his own adjustments to the new Jacobean tastes. The play is
Shakespeare's study of Mars and Venus—the presiding
deities of Baroque society, painted for us again and again
on the canvases of his time. It shows us Virtue, the root of
the heroic in man, turned merely into *virtu*, the warrior's
art, and both of them ensnared in the world, every force
entangling itself with strength. It depicts the "man of men"
soldiering for a cynical Rome or whoring on furlough in a
reckless Egypt. It is the tragedy of the destruction of man,
the creative spirit, in perverse war and insensate love—the
two complementary and opposed halves of a discreating
society.

For more obvious, if less great manifestations of the
same discreating society, interested almost exclusively in
love and war (and these both more narrowly conceived and
more overvalued emotionally than they ever are by Shakespeare) we must turn to Beaumont.

JANET ADELMAN

From The Common Liar:
An Essay on *Antony and Cleopatra*

. . . darkling stand
The varying shore o' th' world.

(4.15.10–11)

Tragedies do not normally ask us to identify ourselves
with the minor characters. But in *Antony and Cleopatra* we
participate in the experience of the commentators more
often than in the experience of the lovers: we are forced to
notice the world's view of them more often than their view
of the world. There are, of course, moments of framing
commentary in the other tragedies, moments when we are
more engaged with the commentator and his perceptions
than with the protagonist. Horatio in *Hamlet* and the fool in
Lear are temporarily allowed to assert their points of view.
But such moments are indeed rare; we more readily accept
the protagonist's definition of himself and the world than
the world's definition of him. Even in *Macbeth*, Macbeth's
own sense of himself as loathsome moves us far more than
the world's condemnation of him. But in *Antony and
Cleopatra* the device of framing forcibly dissociates us
from the lovers; their vision of themselves becomes merely

From Janet Adelman, *The Common Liar: An Essay on "Antony and
Cleopatra"* (New York and London: Yale University Press, 1973), pp.
41–49. The footnotes have been omitted.

one in a series of competing visions. For much of the play, we live outside their immediate universe and see them with distressing clarity from perspectives which are alien to them.

This emphasis on alien perspectives accounts, I think, for one of the structural peculiarities of the play. In most of the tragedies, virtually every event in the play is related either directly or by analogy to the tragic plot. The most common charge against the structure of *Antony and Cleopatra* is that it violates this very simple structural principle: there are several distracting scenes that have nothing in particular to do with the tragic plot, that is, with the downfall of the lovers. Even the play's staunchest supporters often find themselves embarrassed by such apparent excrescences as the Ventidius scene (3.1). We cannot blame this apparent structural laxity on the unwieldy nature of the source material; for in fact Shakespeare quite ruthlessly omits everything in Plutarch's account that does not serve his purpose. We must assume, then, that Shakespeare did not give his play that concentration of structure typical of most of the tragedies for reasons of his own.

The world of *Antony and Cleopatra* is defined by violent juxtapositions and contrasts. The most powerful of these contrasts are unavailable to the reader in his study; they are made in purely theatrical terms, through what Charney calls "presentational imagery." In Act 1, Scene 5, we see Cleopatra lounging among her attendants, imagining Antony's soldiership and recalling Caesar and great Pompey, who "would stand and make his eyes grow in my brow" (line 32). There is an absolute indolence about the scene, as though we have all drunk mandragora to sleep out the great gap of time. The next scene must follow immediately upon this one (it is only through the accidents of editorial scene division that it does not); it presents the sharpest possible dramatic contrast. "*Enter* Pompey, Menecrates, *and* Menas, *in warlike manner*" (2.1). Everything about this scene is as upright and energetic as the previous scene was indolent; here we see warfare in good earnest, not the version which Cleopatra chooses to imagine or recall. This scene is by no means necessary to the plot; we do not need to see Pompey in his camp. He serves merely to necessitate the temporary union of Antony and Octavius; a report of his sea power would accomplish the same end. In fact he is so superfluous a character that Shakespeare kills him off in a subordinate clause: Antony "threats the throat of that his officer / That murder'd Pompey" (3.5.19–20). Even the fate of poor Lepidus receives more extended treatment. But we do see Pompey in his own camp; we do see from his perspective, however momentarily. Precisely the same sort of theatrical contrast is made when Ventidius enters in triumph; again the scene has been separated from its complement by editorial whim. In Act 2, Scene 7, we see the world leaders drunk, reclining or dancing; they leave the stage and suddenly "*Enter* Ventidius *as it were in triumph . . . the dead body of* Pacorus *borne before him*" (3.1). As in the Pompey scene, the contrast is made explicit in the stage direction. Moreover, we have just heard the treacherous Menas address Enobarbus as "noble captain" in the last line of Act 2, Scene 7; five lines later, Ventidius is addressed as "noble": the echo should emphasize the theatrical point. Again the scene is unnecessary for the plot; again it provides us with a radically disjunctive perspective.

In the earlier tragedies, we are not given perspectives which are totally unrelated to those of the protagonists; in *Antony and Cleopatra*, we are. We expect to see Caesar at Actium as we expect Malcolm at Dunsinane, but we do not expect to see Pompey at the Mount; it is rather as though we were to pay a momentary visit to Fortinbras before he left Norway or to the captain of the Turkish fleet in *Othello*. To clarify this distinction, let us look for a moment at two scenes: the appearance of Fortinbras in *Hamlet* (4.4) and the appearance of Ventidius here. These scenes are superficially similar: both function fundamentally to contrast a strong and decisive man of action, an efficient soldier, with the protagonist; both are interpolated into the main action and apparently unrelated to it. But it is precisely the similarity in the two scenes of martial activity that allows us to see their fundamental difference. However surprised we are by Fortinbras's appearance in *Hamlet*, he does reappear at the end of the play as a figure of some consequence.

Moreover, Hamlet himself speaks with one of Fortinbras's captains; we are essentially aware of Hamlet's responses in this scene. Fortinbras's appearance is the occasion for a soliloquy; the hero not only watches the action but explicitly comments on the contrast between Fortinbras and himself. But what of Ventidius? He appears on the outer edges of the empire; none of the protagonists witnesses his appearance. They never discuss him in the course of the play, though he discusses them. And while his bearing serves as a contrast to the bearing of the drunken world leaders on Pompey's galley and his fear of carrying the battle further serves to indicate the effects of triumviral degeneracy on subordinate officers, he is related to the protagonists only in the most tenuous way; he cannot in any sense be said to explicate Antony's condition as Fortinbras explicates Hamlet's. Both the Pompey and the Ventidius scenes present a radical contrast to the perspective of the protagonists; and it is precisely in forcing us to move from one perspective to the next abruptly and without mediation that *Antony and Cleopatra* achieves its most characteristic effects. Such unanticipated shifts in perspective force upon us an awareness of *scope*, of how various a place the world is.

In the other tragedies, even the most minor of the characters tend to take part in the one great tragic event. The musicians in *Othello* give us an image, however imperfect, of that harmony which Iago will successfully untune. Macbeth's devilporter identifies his castle as a kind of hell, in case we were in danger of forgetting; and Macbeth is of course his masterdevil. The gravedigger in *Hamlet* represents a point of view strikingly different from that of the over-curious prince; but he introduces us to Ophelia's maimed rites and moreover serves as a significant teacher in Hamlet's education to accept mortality. But what of similar scenes in *Antony and Cleopatra*? The serving men on Pompey's galley do not reflect Antony's condition, nor are they involved in any way in his action. When Lepidus, Maecenas, and Agrippa arrange to meet at Mount Mesena (2.4), they scarcely mention the protagonists; nor is the farewell of these subordinates in any way significant to the protagonists. The varied personages in *Antony and Cleopatra* come forth, posit their own diverse points of view, and then disappear; they remain autonomous and insist that we notice the multiplicity of this world.

This insistence on the varying shores of the world is not common in Shakespearean tragedy. In the major tragedies, the presentation of character and the structure generally function to focus our attention on the protagonists, to force us to participate in their experience and to live for a time within the moral contours of their universe. To participate fully in the tragic experience, we must be willing, for the moment, to see the universe through the eyes of the protagonist and entirely in relation to him: we must experience Lear's storm as he himself experiences it. This concentration of vision allows us to perceive the sufferings of Edgar and the fool on the heath as fragmentary versions of Lear's suffering; it allows us to feel that Gloucester's blinding is part of Lear's experience even before Lear is aware of it. In order to achieve this concentration of vision, we must be given some knowledge of the inner state of the protagonist; we must be allowed to see how he perceives the world before we can participate in his perceptions. Lear on the heath conducts a virtually continuous soliloquy, whether other characters overhear him or not; Hamlet, Othello, and Macbeth constantly tell us how the world seems to them. But this kind of knowledge is usually denied us in *Antony and Cleopatra*; and the dramatic structure functions to diffuse and dissipate our attention throughout a wider universe than that which the protagonists know. We expect to see the universe only insofar as it reflects the experience of the protagonists; but we see the universe as prior to and independent of them.

It is of course true of all the tragedies that the audience sees a more varied world than the protagonists; we never share their vision entirely. But in the other tragedies, the exclusiveness of the protagonist's vision and our partial absorption into it are essential to the tragic effect. Their vision becomes progressively narrowed until fewer and fewer possibilities are left open to them: Lear's world contracts until it does not include the possibility of kindly

daughters, Othello's the possibility of Desdemona's inno-
cence; Macbeth gradually loses sight of any world outside
his own diseased fantasy. In these plays, the audience par-
ticipates both in the narrowing of vision and in an awareness of what is excluded; we share in the constriction
although we see the protagonist trapped by it. *Othello* is
horrifying partly because we are made to experience Othello's abused perception even while we know it is wrong;
for most of *Macbeth*, our experience is as claustrophobic as
Macbeth's. When we are finally given sight of King
Edward's or Cordelia's healing nature, our relief is enormous precisely because we too have been trapped by the
protagonist's vision. Part of the effect of these plays
depends on our ability to see through the protagonist's
eyes, even when we see possibilities unacknowledged by
him. But this progressive narrowing and widening of our
vision is foreign to *Antony and Cleopatra*: there the exclu-
sivity of the protagonists' vision never becomes part of our
experience; we are given competing visions throughout.

Multiplicity of all kinds is essential to the structure of
Antony and Cleopatra: throughout most of the play the
world is an enormously crowded place. This multiplicity is
achieved not only through the introduction of apparently
unrelated characters and scenes but also through a structural principle of varied repetition, rather like a musical
theme and variations. The audience continually sees the
same actions, hears the same metaphors, but always with a
slight variation; and this structural repetition suggests
widely varying versions of experience just as the framing
commentary suggests varieties of judgment. We are given,
for instance, a series of servants who desert their masters
and masters who desert their servants, each of whom comments by implication on the rest. Shortly after Enobarbus
has announced that he will "seek / Some way to leave"
Antony (3.13.200–1), Antony himself addresses his servants "as one that takes his leave" (4.2.29): Enobarbus
weeps over Antony's leave-taking even as he plans his
own. In the next scene, we hear that "the god Hercules,
whom Antony loved, / Now leaves him" (4.3.15–16). This

action reiterates the central action of Actium, in which Antony quite literally leaves his servants; and it complements the action of all those servants who leave their masters throughout the play. Menas deserts Pompey because Pompey is not sufficiently ruthless to deserve service; Alexas and Canidius and the rest desert Antony because Antony has deserted his followers and in some sense himself at Actium; Enobarbus deserts Antony because it appears to him that Cleopatra and his own discretion have deserted Antony. Seleucus deserts Cleopatra for reasons that remain obscure: If his betrayal is not staged (and there is no real reason to assume that it is), then his behavior is, at the least, ungenerous. Dolabella temporarily deserts Octavius for love of Cleopatra; his betrayal of his master's plans is one of the few moments of compassion at the end of the play. Decretas deserts Antony, presumably because dead masters are not profitable to work for; but his eulogy of Antony reminds us that he knows his master's worth and is willing to assert it even to Caesar. If Decretas complicates the pattern of betrayal, Scarus reverses it altogether. He too seems inclined to desert Antony after Actium (3.10.31–32), but in the proof, he is magnificently loyal. Enobarbus dies of a broken heart because he has deserted Antony. Eros kills himself to avoid obeying his master's command; his magnificent disobedience may be seen as a commentary on the disobedience of all the unreliable servants in the play. Antony has previously deserted Fulvia, Octavia, and Cleopatra; Cleopatra seems momentarily to regard his death as a desertion ("Noblest of men, woo't die? / Hast thou no care of me?" 4.15.59–60). Servants and masters desert, in short, with every reason and under every circumstance; the pattern is repeated with endless variation. Our impression is simultaneously that nothing changes and that nothing is the same.

The same sense of endless likeness and endless difference is achieved by this kind of repetition throughout the play: in the reception of bad news, for instance, or in the repeated episodes of handshaking or hand kissing. After Actium, Scarus tells us that Antony has "kissed away / Kingdoms, and provinces" (3.10.7–8); Antony himself kisses Cleopatra and says, "Even this repays me" (3.11.71). Cleopatra wishes that her kiss could quicken the dying Antony (4.15.39), but her kiss kills Iras (5.2.292). Has she the aspic in her lips? We are given both Charmian's figs (1.2.34) and the figs that bring death to Cleopatra and her maidens; the reverberations set up between the first fig and the last suggest a whole complex of attitudes toward life and its pleasures. Decretas's theft of Antony's sword would not be so shocking if we had not seen Eros practice a different swordplay only a few moments before. Eros draws his own sword to kill himself for love of Antony; Decretas steals Antony's sword to make matters right with Caesar. The contrast could scarcely be more sharply drawn than by the repeated use of the sword. The three images of entrapment in the play suggest the variety of perspectives with extraordinary economy. Cleopatra decides to go fishing and imagines each fish an Antony (2.5.11–14); she obviously thinks of herself as an amiable trap. But there is nothing amiable about the image of the trap when she greets Antony after his victory: "com'st thou smiling from / The world's great snare uncaught?" (4.8.17–18). Cleopatra as snare or the world as snare? Which finally captures Antony? Caesar complicates the image further: Cleopatra looks "As she would catch another Antony / In her strong toil of grace" (5.2.346–47). For him, Cleopatra is clearly the snare; nonetheless, there are presumably worse fates than being caught in a toil of *grace*.

The achievement of simultaneous perspectives through varied repetition works throughout the play. When we hear the music of Hercules departing, we are reminded of a thematic pattern of enormous complexity. The music of the departing god is the first we know of his presence; we recognize the supernatural only as it withdraws. This pattern of the presence known too late is a variation of the "She's good, being gone" (1.2.127) theme initiated by Antony's reaction to Fulvia's death and repeated whenever we see someone weep what willingly he did confound; it anticipates such critical moments as Enobarbus's discovery of Antony's full generosity only after he has deserted him, Antony's reaction to the report of Cleopatra's death, and

Cleopatra's deification of Antony after his death. Cleopatra's dream of her emperor and the political tears which Octavius sheds for Antony are variations on the same theme. The function of varied repetition is most striking in the association of love, war, and death, an association posited by widely differing characters with widely differing perspectives. For Philo and Pompey, the association represents the misapplication of a soldier's talents (1.1.6–10; 2.1.12–13). Agrippa is more amused than appalled by the association: "She made great Caesar lay his sword to bed" (2.2.233). The death of the character named Eros, with his sword drawn, is the objectification of the association on stage; in his death, the comic perspective is transformed utterly. Enobarbus's comment on Cleopatra's "celerity in dying" (1.2.145–46) will be similarly transformed when Caesar tells us of Cleopatra's pursuit of easy ways to die. At their suicides, each of the lovers reiterates the association of love and death (4.14.99–101; 5.2.294–95) as part of their transformation of death into reunion. But the sexual suggestiveness of the asp and the Clown's banter insure that we will not forget the other perspectives possible.

The insistence upon scope, upon the infinite variety of the world, militates against the tragic experience. We simply are not permitted the luxury of the tragic vision: our attempt to see the universe solely in terms of the protagonists is continually thwarted. For in *Antony and Cleopatra* the vision of tragedy is only part of the story. The protagonists find themselves to be of primal significance in the universe; but we must see them from other, less comfortable perspectives. We have heard of Antony's almost magical soldiership from Pompey and Caesar. In the Ventidius scene, we see it for a moment with the satiric impulse of a subordinate who works while his master plays: "I'll humbly signify what in his name, / That magical word of war, we have effected" (3.1.30–31). In Decretas, we see briefly from the point of view of a man who seems even more perfectly political than Caesar when he greets Antony's suicide with "This sword but shown to Caesar, with this tidings, / Shall enter me with him" (4.14. 112–13);

but we also see him deliver a potentially dangerous eulogy of Antony to Caesar. The dramatic contrasts and the varied repetitions insist that we move among several versions of experience, among the comic and satiric as well as the tragic.

MARIANNE NOVY

Gender and Acting in *Antony and Cleopatra*

Antony and Cleopatra is the only Shakespearean tragedy that focuses on and indeed glorifies the woman as actor in both senses, doer and pretender, and, not coincidentally, as sexually active. Whether she is asking for a declaration of love from Antony or asking him to return to Rome, Cleopatra is likely to be role-playing. Antony does at times angrily accuse her of deception, but she, unlike the other heroines so accused, makes similar accusations to him:

> Good now, play one scene
> Of excellent dissembling, and let it look
> Like perfect honor.   (1.3.78–80)

Much more than the other tragic heroes, each of them can be mollified; their ability to forgive and start over is closely related to their ability to play many different roles. Furthermore, each of them can also be appreciative audience to the other:

>   Fie, wrangling queen!
> Whom everything becomes—to chide, to laugh,
> To weep; whose every passion fully strives
> To make itself, in thee, fair and admired.   (1.1.48–51)

From *Love's Argument: Gender Relations in Shakespeare* by Marianne L. Novy. Copyright © 1984 by the University of North Carolina Press. Used by permission of the publisher.

243

His legs bestrid the ocean: his reared arm
Crested the world: his voice was propertied
As all the tunèd spheres, and that to friends. (5.2.82–84)

In describing each other, each creates and shares the
audience's admiration for the other; Cleopatra, especially,
becomes artist as well as audience and actor. In the last of
her visions, before her death modeled on Antony's ideals,
the barriers between roles dissolve and each can be both
actor and audience at once:

Methinks I hear
Antony call: I see him rouse himself
To praise my noble act. I hear him mock
The luck of Caesar.   (283–86)

A skeptic may always refuse to believe in the love
between Antony and Cleopatra. Love can never be proved
with mathematical certainty; attempts to show it can always
be taken as pretense or self-deception. As Janet Adelman
has suggested, the trust required of an audience to believe
in love onstage is analogous to the trust required of lovers
to believe in each other.[1] In *Hamlet*, *Othello*, *Macbeth*, and
Lear, the heroes tragically fail to achieve or maintain their
trust in the women who love them, and regain it, if at all,
when it is too late. In *Antony and Cleopatra*, by contrast,
the lovers, for all their jealousy and wrangling, are always
willing to forgive each other and start over after their fights;
thus they accept the ambiguities in each other and in their
relationship and paradoxically achieve something more
like trust than any of the other couples. The role that each
plays allows for and indeed demands the partnership of a
free and independent person.

Why this sharp contrast between Shakespeare's comic
and tragic men (with Antony in between) in their attitude
toward women as actors—in most of the tragic heroes a
suspicion that works to confine women to being audience,
in most of the comic heroes acceptance and participation?
The difference is clearly related not only to genre but also
to gender; women in the tragedies have no obsessive suspi-

cion about men as actors. According to Michael Goldman, all major dramatic characters are actors in the extended sense that they 'go beyond ordinary bounds in ways that remind us of acting. They are capable of some kind of seductive, hypnotic, or commanding expression."[2] Thus audiences onstage and off see in them the *otherness* of the professional actor. The character as actor is strange, exotic, and therefore an object of both repulsion and attraction. I would suggest that within Shakespeare's tragedies, the women's reaction to the men as actors shows much more the positive side of that ambivalence—the sympathy and admiration. The tragic heroes' attitude to the women as actors shows mostly the negative side. There the suspicion of the actor as other coalesces with the general cultural suspicion of the woman as other discussed by Simone de Beauvoir.[3] Much that Goldman says about one group could apply to both:

> The community focuses on them, makes them a cynosure, enjoys seeing them dressed up in their proper costumes at the proper times. But always the attraction springs from and exists in tension with an implied hostility. . . . They are elevated above the community by the role they take on, but their elevation exposes them [cf. woman on pedestal]; they serve at their audience's pleasure. (pp.12–13)

NOTES

1. Janet Adelman, *The Common Liar: An Essay on "Antony and Cleopatra"* (New Haven: Yale University Press, 1973), pp. 105–13.
2. Michael Goldman, The Actor's Freedom: Toward a Theory of Drama (New York: Viking, 1975), p. 17.
3. Simone de Beauvoir, *The Second Sex,* trans. H. M. Parshley (New York: Bantam, 1961), p. xvi. Leslie Fiedler, *The Stranger in Shakespeare* (New York: Stein and Day, 1972), discusses woman as other, but he often identifies Shakespeare's attitude too closely with that of his male characters. Some affinities between women and the theater are noted in Juliet Dusinberre's *Shakespeare and the Nature of Women* (New York: Barnes and Noble, 1975), pp. 11, 247.

S. SCHOENBAUM

Antony and Cleopatra on Stage and Screen

Tastes change, and despite the commonplace (*plus ça change . . .*), the more things change—at least as regards Shakespeare—the more different they are likely to become. *Antony and Cleopatra* is an instance. Despite the fact that its theatrical fortunes include some showy productions, the play has never been a favorite with directors or audiences; that is, not until recently. Its present comparative popularity coincides with the interpretive ferment regarding *Antony and Cleopatra* since midpoint in the present century, and to which the Suggested References of this revised Signet Classic Edition testify.

No record has come down of a particular performance of *Antony and Cleopatra* before the closing of the theaters in 1642. When, after the Restoration, the Lord Chamberlain in 1660 granted the King's Company under Thomas Killigrew a monopoly on the revival of twenty-one plays of Shakespeare, *Antony and Cleopatra* was listed as "formerly acted at the Blackfriars"—clearly implying production by Shakespeare's troupe at the house they took over in 1608. With respect to this piece, Killigrew appears not to have exercised his privilege.

A deterrent to revival must have been the availability, from 1677, of *All for Love*, John Dryden's blank-verse tragedy written (so the title page proclaims) "*in Imitation of Shakespeare's Style.*" In accordance with prevalent neo-classical imperatives, Dryden observes the unities of time, place, and action; the play begins after the battle of Actium and concerns only the lovers' last day. Although echoes and deliberate imitations of *Antony and Cleopatra* color Dryden's texture, *All for Love* is a Shakespearean offshoot rather than adaptation proper. The rival claims of love and honor collide; pathos has its innings. Characters dwindle, in number and complexity. Alexas, the Queen's eunuch, plays his part, but neither Caesar nor Enobarbus makes an entrance, and no clown—deemed unworthy in heroical tragedy—brings Cleopatra's asp. The play ends with the dead lovers seated together in state. Serapion, priest of Isis—not present in Shakespeare—has the last, eloquent word.

> The impression of a smile left in her face,
> Shows she died pleased with him for whom she lived,
> And went to charm him in another world.

Dryden's tragedy did not immediately captivate the town, but eventually it caught on, and for almost a century displaced *Antony and Cleopatra*, which has the doubtful distinction of being the only tragedy of Shakespeare's to go unrevived, even in adaptation, during this period.

We first hear of it on the stage in 1759, when David Garrick, at the height of his frame, mounted *Antony and Cleopatra* at Drury Lane in a lavish production with new costumes, decoration, and scenery. For the script Garrick enlisted the aid of the future Shakespearean editor Edward Capell, who cut ruthlessly—reckoning as expendable the political maneuverings—and combined scenes and characters. Capell transposed speeches: most notably the celebrated description of the lovers' first meeting (2.2.197–224), now spoken by a characterless military flunky, Thyreus (Shakespeare's Thidias) and strategically placed as a set speech on the heels of Antony and Cleopatra's first exit with their train. Of unprepossessing stature, Garrick was deemed an insufficiently commanding Antony. His Cleopatra, however, gave special scope for the talents of Mary Ann Yates, who at thirty would go on to be celebrated for two decades "for everything that was ner-

vous, various, elegant and true in attitudes and action"—
not inappropriate gifts for an actress playing Cleopatra.
Garrick's revival eked out six performances.

By the time *Antony and Cleopatra* in 1813 returned in
pomp to the stage at the new Covent Garden under John
Philip Kemble's management, pictorialism was already
ascendant. No matter that the script was a patchwork con-
flation of Shakespeare and Dryden; this production had for
high points the sea fight at Actium and, for finale, a grand
funeral procession and ode, accompanied by instrumental
music and choral singing ("The Roman glory sets on
Egypt's shore, / And great Mark Antony will rise no
more."). Kemble sought to enlist his sister, the great Sarah
Siddons (most celebrated for her Lady Macbeth), as
Cleopatra, but she refused, declaring "she should hate herself, if she should play the part as it ought to be played."
Lacking such compunctions, Mrs. Faucit took the role,
giving a genteel reading made easier by the conscientious
omission of bawdy references. This version lasted for nine
nights.

In 1833 William Charles Macready—with his thrilling
voice a preeminent romantic actor, but then in poor
health—played Antony and gave what he himself reckoned
a "hasty, unprepared, unfinished performance" that gave up
the ghost after only three nights, during which the Cleopatra of Louisa Ann Phillips was reduced (such was the
company's financial straits) to wearing "a tarnished gar-
ment which your true stage Cleopatra would have trodden
underfoot." Shakespeare's play had its first recorded stage
triumph when Samuel Phelps brought it to Sadler's Wells
in 1849. Phelps cut, transposed, and combined scenes, but
the words were always Shakespeare's, and the playlist tes-
tifies to the elimination of only three small parts, among
them the Queen's treasurer Seleucus. As Antony, Phelps
struck bacchanalian attitudes; his Cleopatra (Isabella Glyn)
posed statuesquely, making her first entrance surrounded
by dancing satyrs and nymphs and Greek boys with cym-
bals. The revelings at Pompey's banquet made a great
impression, and in meeting death Glyn was "sublime." She
became synonymous with "the serpent of old Nile," and as

late as 1867, in her Victorian crinoline costume, was enticing her Antony (Henry Loraine) at the Princess's Theatre in a mangled version that omitted sixteen scenes yet lasted over four hours because of the accretions of spectacle—including, for Pompey, a moonlit galley set on rippling waters.

Reckoning that "surely it is better to have a little of Shakespeare than none at all," Andrew Halliday, at Drury Lane in 1873, left out half the text of *Antony and Cleopatra*—including Pompey's banquet—to concentrate on pageantry and the "Passions of the Single Pair." When Enobarbus (whose death was omitted) described Cleopatra's barge—at the end of Act 1—it appeared with silver pavilion, fluttering cupids, and purple sails, as the passionate pair's first meeting was represented in pantomime. At Actium contending galleys fought a naval battle, and the stage filled with torchbearers for Cleopatra's death. A production first was scored when the audience, ignoring the principals, twice summoned the scene designer for a bow.

Even more sumptuously elaborate was Lillie Langtry's four-and-one-half-hour revival, with purple galleys, Roman chariots, and milk-white steeds, as the century entered its last decade. A mummy sat at the Egyptian feasts, swarthy slaves danced a ballet, and Langtry, beautiful but icy, had a two-story set for Cleopatra's suicide. Janet Achurch brought physical passion to her Cleopatra in 1897, although the "lacerated discourse of her wailings" unnerved George Bernard Shaw; but he liked the moment when the "inexcusably fat" Antony (Louis Calvert), dying of his self-inflicted wound, gave a short burst of laughter upon hearing that Cleopatra had not really killed herself.

In Beerbohm Tree's 1906 production the new century continued old ways. Caesar's reference to Cleopatra appearing in "th' habiliments of the goddess Isis" (3.6.17) inspired a *tableau vivant*—literally, a "living picture"—a silent group of individuals arranged to represent a scene—in which, preluded by voluptuous music, the queen (Constance Collier) in silver crown and robes walked through the streets of Alexandria while the populace screamed. At midpoint the dissolving sphinx which opened the play loomed out of the darkness to "a thrumming, vibrating, aromatic kind of music" suggesting "the maddened luxury of the East, and the exasperating, enigmatic attraction of the queen."

Antony and Cleopatra first came to Stratford-upon-Avon with Frank Benson's touring company in 1898. Benson's uncharacteristically spectacular mounting included Cleopatra's palace with a golden throne. In 1912 at Stratford, Benson, again playing Antony, had for his Cleopatra the young Dorothy Green, later to become a West End favorite in the part.

Not until after the First World War did *Antony and Cleopatra* have a distinctively twentieth-century staging, in the rapid, so-called "non-stop" production by Robert Atkins in 1922 at London's Old Vic. A disciple of the pioneering William Poel, Atkins dispensed with realistic settings and drew the curtain down only once during his thirty-one scenes. Antony (Wilfrid Walter) made his first entrance carrying Cleopatra (Esther Whitehouse) in his arms; in a final tableau she became a "frozen monument of death." Subsequent producers would follow Atkins in relying on symbolic scenery and few intervals. In her first season with the Old Vic, three years later, Edith Evans performed Cleopatra, with Baliol Holloway—he had played Lepidus and the Clown in 1912—for her Antony. For his kaleidoscopic revival at the Old Vic in 1930, with John Gielgud and Dorothy Green and the rest—including Ralph Richardson as Enobarbus—in Renaissance costumes, with Egyptian and Roman touches, Harcourt Williams garnered record receipts, the run being extended.

At the New Theatre (also in London) in 1936, Theodore Komisarjevsky's innovative staging deployed alterations of lighting to signal changes in locale. Even more novel was his choice, for Cleopatra, of the Russian comedienne Eugenie Leontovich, whose accent proved impenetrable: "When you sued staying, / Then was the time for words" (1.3.33–34) became, in one reviewer's malicious phonetic rendering, "Wen you sut staying, / Den was de time for Wurst." Artfully uniting majesty and allure, Edith Evans was again Cleopatra in Glen Byam Shaw's revival at the

Piccadilly Theatre in 1946. Five years later, Laurence Olivier and Vivien Leigh alternated Shakespeare's play with Bernard Shaw's *Caesar and Cleopatra* at the St. James's Theatre. As Antony in the former, Olivier gave an uncharacteristically muted portrayal of a rare spirit gone to seed; Leigh's beauty attracted as much notice as her acting.

At the Shakespeare Memorial Theatre (since renamed the Royal Shakespeare Theatre) in 1953, Peggy (not yet Dame Peggy) Ashcroft was Cleopatra in Glen Byam Shaw's second revival of the tragedy. Red-haired and pale-faced, Greek rather than dusky Egyptian, Ashcroft seduced Antony and audience alike. As Antony, Michael (not yet knighted) Redgrave conveyed the heroism of a character who had held the world in thrall, and also his dissolution and inner turmoil. With an extraordinary display of varie-gated temperament—royal yet not affectedly regal, sincere yet also devious, at once noble and ignoble—Janet Suzman dazzled audiences and critics alike with a triumphant Cleopatra in the Trevor Nunn revival at the same house in 1972. Richard Johnson, his black beard grizzled, was a fit-tingly munificent Antony, while Patrick Stewart, as always magnificent of voice, disapproved of his general's life-style, but managed reluctantly to smile. Presented at the Edinburgh Festival by the Prospect Theatre Company, Toby Robertson's staging in 1977 featured Dorothy Tutin as Cleopatra and Alec McCowen as Antony, with Timothy West as Enobarbus. Derek Jacobi was an imperial Octavius in an all-star cast dressed in high-Renaissance fashion.

In his Royal Shakespeare Company production with Alan Howard and Glenda Jackson, staged at the Royal Shakespeare Theatre in Stratford and the Aldwych in London—two anything but intimate houses—in 1978, Peter Brook disdained spectacle, opting instead for inti-macy. Brook confined the action to a semicircle of glass panels. In an interview in the London *Times* (October 18) after the play opened, he explained his rationale: "What Shakespeare wrote consists of 45 or so short scenes of inti-mate behaviour. There is no pageantry. Everything con-cerns personal relationship. . . . The Empire may be tottering but he keeps it out of sight." Well out of sight: In the later battle scenes, soldiers threw clots of blood onto the panel—blood that remained there until the performance ended. Throughout Jackson artfully conveyed Cleopatra's mercurial shifts of mood; the production achieved a special exaltation in the final death scenes. At its truly intimate alternative house in Stratford, The Other Place, in 1982, Adrian Noble's low-keyed, mostly conversational revival featured Michael Gambon as an ever-generous, aging voluptuary; his Cleopatra (Helen Mirren) cleansed her begrimed face and changed from mourning shift to gold robe for her final, serenely rapturous leavetaking.

Robin Phillips' production at the Chichester Festival in 1984 featured Diana Rigg as Cleopatra and Denis Quilley as a noble Antony led astray by the serpent of old Nile. Cuts were abundant: gone were the drunken high jinks aboard Pompey's galley, nor was the audience informed that the forthcoming report of Cleopatra's death was a ruse (4.13.5–8). Peter Hall's National Theatre production in 1987 made use of a lofty rear masonry wall which could be wheeled apart to serve as a monument, rampart, or military headquarters, and which dominated the bare reddish stage. Messengers or soldiers ran up and down the aisles, smoke curled in from the wings, trumpets and drums sounded. A tall rope rigging sufficed to denote a state banquet aboard ship. The lovers were unmistakeably middle-aged, sustained by passion recollected in a world where great events afforded no tranquility. In gold–embroidered velvet open at the throat, festooned with scarves and baubles, Anthony Hopkins was sturdy, gray-haired and gray-bearded as Antony. Honor waged its unequal battle with love; after the mortal disgrace of Actium, a single kiss from Cleopatra was sufficient to show that for Antony the world was well lost. As he lay dying, he was lifted to Cleopatra in a huge fish net. Judi Dench was a Cleopatra who gave free rein to her emotions: She skipped, giggled, sobbed, schemed ruthlessly, displayed irresistible allure, and died magnificently. She succeeded triumphantly in cutting her capacious surroundings down to size. At the end Cleopatra was, like Hamlet, borne shoulder high by soldiers from the stage in a funeral

cortège. Tim Piggott-Smith made a surprisingly sympathetic Octavius—lanky, youthful, yet (in the end) Machia-
vellian; with him the Empire would carry on.

The first recorded American presentation of *Antony and
Cleopatra* took place at Manhattan's Park Theatre in 1846
in a sumptuous production mounted by George Vander-
hoff, the production's Antony. The Nile flowed by; a
panoramic view depicted the naval engagement at Actium.
But the Nile flowed for only six nights. Succeeding decades
saw occasional revivals. Most lavish was Rose Eyeting's at
the Broadway Theatre in 1877, featuring a specially com-
missioned ballet, and Eyeting as a capriciously tempera-
mental Cleopatra. By contrast, Cora Urquhart Potter made
the Egyptian temptress into (in the critic William Winter's
words) "the belle of the modern ballroom" in Dyrle
Bellow's 1889 production, arranged in six acts and sixteen
scenes. This revival held audiences for fifty-seven performances. In the present century, John Mason Brown began
his famous review of an ill-fated 1937 production by
remarking, "Tallulah Bankhead barged down the Nile last
night as Cleopatra—and sank." For Bankhead, Cleopatra
was a designing courtesan. Ten years later the revered
queen of the American stage, Katharine Cornell, opted for
dignity in her regal portrayal opposite Godfrey Tearle
(looking uncannily like the recently deceased FDR), a
world-weary—literally so—Antony, with Kent Smith a
memorably astringent Enobarbus. The production had
a record 126 performances before heading west to bring
ancient Alexandria and Rome to the environs of Chicago's
stockyards.

The American Shakespeare Festival revival in 1960 at
Stratford, Connecticut, starred two performers best known
for their film work: Katharine Hepburn as a regal, albeit
unseductive yet amusing Cleopatra, and—as Antony—
Robert Ryan, who would go on to impress cinema audiences with his gun-toting roles in *The Wild Bunch* and *The
Dirty Dozen*; in youth a prize fighter, Ryan was outboxed
by Shakespeare's language. At the same house, this time in
1975, in a production conceived by Michael Kahn, a large
Roman banner descended before Cleopatra's monument in

the last act to conceal Antony's body; the Empire had prevailed. Apparently made up to resemble Elizabeth Taylor's film Cleopatra, Salome Jens (as a review noted) gave up the ghost sitting bolt upright in her chair with scarcely a flicker to denote her passing.

Antony and Cleopatra has in recent years had its share of revival during regional Shakespeare seasons in the United States. As presented at Boulder, Colorado, in 1972, the left side of the theater became Egypt—blue colors and warm brown earth tones predominating—while the right side was Rome: all aquamarine, blue, white, and silver. (Another revival at Boulder in 1985, under the summer sky at the Mary Rippon Outdoor Theatre, featured what one reviewer somewhat uncharitably described as a "male menopausal" Antony.) In Tony Richardson's Los Angeles production in 1987, the time frame was updated to the Fascist 'thirties, with Octavius a bare-skulled Mussolini caricature with a personal guard of Blackshirts; Cleopatra was a royal black African (shades of the Duce's conquest of Ethiopia!) with hip-length tresses, just going gray in cornrows, and black attendants, while Antony wore khaki and jodhpurs: Imperialism called the shots. Antony and Cleopatra has also played to throngs in Ashland, Atlanta, and elsewhere.

European productions, while relatively sparse, have sometimes created a stir. At the Comédie Française in 1918, Firmin Gémier (using the sensuous Pierre Loti translation) deployed three orchestras around the auditorium, and concluded the second act with a "carpet of women on the steps, palpitating and motionless, like beautiful reptiles." So wrote the novelist Colette. At the State Theater in Leningrad in 1923, Schillingowsky set his unrevolutionary revival against austerely modern steps and pillars; no naked thighs, as in Paris. In the same year in Vienna, at the Burg Theater, Lotte Mendelsohn ravished audiences as she exercised her wiles on an oddly neurotic Antony. Just after World War II ended Jean-Louis Barrault chose Antony and Cleopatra, as translated by André Gide, for his first Shakespeare production at the Comédie Française.

In recent years Antony and Cleopatra has more than once been revived in the other hemisphere. The play had its first production in China in 1984, when it was presented in repertory by the Shanghai Youth Theater before full houses in a style that apparently owed much to classic Chinese opera. In Tokyo in 1980, as directed and adapted by Koreya Senda, the Haiyuza company offered *Antony and Cleopatra* in a Japanese translation, with brief additional scenes with the queen being lavishly attired by her waiting women for an audience with Herod, or practicing sword play and archery with her women. The banquet scene aboard Pompey's galley, far from being omitted, was a high point of Rex Crampton's production mounted by the Melbourne Theatre Company in Australia in 1983: With perfectly—and painfully—articulated speech, the drunken Lepidus made a valiant and inadvertently hilarious attempt to put to Antony his question about the legendary Egyptian crocodile.

Antony and Cleopatra has twice been produced for television screening. A Royal Shakespeare Company version, mounted on British commercial television in 1978, featured Janet Suzman as the serpent of old Nile. In Jonathan Miller's 1981 BBC Shakespeare Plays television version, Colin Blakely and Jane Lapotaire were plausible middle-aged lovers in a production which, appropriately for the small screen, made much of the nonheroic foibles and failings of the legendary protagonists. The great centerpiece of Shakespeare's tragedy, the scene in which the three world sharers meet aboard Pompey's galley (2.7), was present in curtailed form as we join participants in mid-conversation (called 2.10 in this version). Like all directors of this play, Miller had to decide what sort of setting was best for an Elizabethan play about ancient Rome. His solution was to adopt a baroque setting, derived especially from the paintings of Veronese (1528–1588), in particular *Mars and Venus Bound by Cupid* and *The Family of Darius at the Feet of Alexander*. Venetian pictures such as these inspired Miller to use long tunics of yellow, orange, red, and silver, with lace and rich jewelry, though Octavius's court wore dark blue and green. Discussions of *Antony and Cleopatra* commonly emphasize its panoramic vistas, but Miller (partly because of the conditions of filming) chose to give us great richness enclosed in small interiors, thereby creating a sense of oppressiveness. This concept often worked surprisingly well, but in certain scenes one felt it was inadequate, for instance in the first, where we ought simultaneously to see Antony and Cleopatra and their critics, and the last scene, where we ought simultaneously to see the dead Cleopatra (looking "as she would catch another Antony") and the wry Octavius who offers the comment. But a television screen probably cannot effectively give expansive views. The nature of the medium cannot, however, excuse some of the cuts in Miller's production, notably the omission of the scene in which Antony's soldiers hear "music under the stage" (4.3), denoting the departure of his guardian spirit, and the scene with Seleucus (5.2).

An afterthought: It is perhaps surprising that the part of Cleopatra has only very rarely been performed by a black actress. In the play Cleopatra is said to be "tawny" (1.1.16) and "black" (1.5.28), and although Shakespeare sometimes uses "black" in the sense of brunette, it is clear that he thought of Cleopatra as non-Caucasian. She is also said to be a "gypsy" (4.12.28). In talking about Shakespeare's play it is irrelevant to point out that Cleopatra was in fact not of African descent. Descended from the Ptolemies (Macedonian Greeks who ruled Egypt after the death of Alexander the Great), she was not an Egyptian, though she did dress herself in Egyptian apparel and she spoke Egyptian. Her images on coins show a Mediterranean face. Shakespeare probably had no very clear idea of her lineage, and little or no idea of what an Egyptian might look like, but by calling her "tawny," "black," and a "gipsy" he indicates that he thinks of her as other than European.

Bibliographic Note: The play's fortunes in the British theater from Jacobean times to the 1970s are ably chronicled by Margaret Lamb in *"Antony and Cleopatra" on the English Stage* (1980). Michael Scott, *Antony and Cleopatra* (1983), in the Text and Performance series, concentrates on four productions: Benthall / Olivier (1951), Trevor Nunn

(1972), Peter Brook (1978), and Jonathan Miller's BBC television production (1980). David E. Male's *Antony and Cleopatra* (1984), a booklet of thirty-six pages, concentrates on the productions by Nunn (1972), Brook (1978), and Noble (1982). Jonathan Miller discusses his BBC-TV version in the BBC printed text, *"Antony and Cleopatra": The Production* (1981). There is also a BBC documentary, *Jonathan Miller Directs "Antony and Cleopatra"* (1981).

Suggested References

The number of possible references is vast and grows alarmingly. (The *Shakespeare Quarterly* devotes one issue each year to a list of the previous year's work, and *Shakespeare Survey*—an annual publication—includes a substantial review of biographical, critical, and textual studies, as well as a survey of performances.) The vast bibliography is best approached through James Harner, *The World Shakespeare Bibliography on CD-Rom: 1900–Present*. The first release, in 1996, included more than 12,000 annotated items from 1990–93, plus references to several thousand book reviews, productions, films, and audio recordings. The plan is to update the publication annually, moving forward one year and backward three years. Thus, the second issue (1997), with 24,700 entries, and another 35,000 or so references to reviews, newspaper pieces, and so on, covered 1987–94.

Though no works are indispensable, those listed below have been found especially helpful. The arrangement is as follows:

1. Shakespeare's Times
2. Shakespeare's Life
3. Shakespeare's Theater
4. Shakespeare on Stage and Screen
5. Miscellaneous Reference Works
6. Shakespeare's Plays: General Studies
7. The Comedies
8. The Romances
9. The Tragedies
10. The Histories
11. *Antony and Cleopatra*

The titles in the first five sections are accompanied by brief explanatory annotations.

1. Shakespeare's Times

Andrews, John F., ed. *William Shakespeare: His World, His Work, His Influence,* 3 vols. (1985). Sixty articles, dealing not only with such subjects as "The State," "The Church," "Law," "Science, Magic, and Folklore," but also with the plays and poems themselves and Shakespeare's influence (e.g., translations, films, reputation)

Byrne, Muriel St. Clare. *Elizabethan Life in Town and Country* (8th ed., 1970). Chapters on manners, beliefs, education, etc., with illustrations.

Dollimore, John, and Alan Sinfield, eds. *Political Shakespeare: New Essays in Cultural Materialism* (1985). Essays on such topics as the subordination of women and colonialism, presented in connection with some of Shakespeare's plays.

Greenblatt, Stephen. *Representing the English Renaissance* (1988). New Historicist essays, especially on connections between political and aesthetic matters, statecraft and stagecraft.

Joseph, B. L. *Shakespeare's Eden: the Commonwealth of England 1558–1629* (1971). An account of the social, political, economic, and cultural life of England.

Kernan, Alvin. *Shakespeare, the King's Playwright: Theater in the Stuart Court 1603–1613* (1995). The social setting and the politics of the court of James I, in relation to *Hamlet, Measure for Measure, Macbeth, King Lear, Antony and Cleopatra, Coriolanus,* and *The Tempest.*

Montrose, Louis. *The Purpose of Playing: Shakespeare and the Cultural Politics of the Elizabethan Theatre* (1996). A poststructuralist view, discussing the professional theater "within the ideological and material frameworks of Elizabethan culture and society," with an extended analysis of *A Midsummer Night's Dream.*

Mullaney, Steven. *The Place of the Stage: License, Play, and Power in Renaissance England* (1988). New Historicist analysis, arguing that popular drama became a cultural institution "only by . . . taking up a place on the margins of society."

Schoenbaum, S. *Shakespeare: The Globe and the World*

(1979). A readable, abundantly illustrated introductory book on the world of the Elizabethans.

Shakespeare's England, 2 vols. (1916). A large collection of scholarly essays on a wide variety of topics, e.g., astrology, costume, gardening, horsemanship, with special attention to Shakespeare's references to these topics.

2. Shakespeare's Life

Andrews, John F., ed. *William Shakespeare: His World, His Work, His Influence,* 3 vols. (1985). See the description above.

Bentley, Gerald E. *Shakespeare: A Biographical Handbook* (1961). The facts about Shakespeare, with virtually no conjecture intermingled.

Chambers, E. K. *William Shakespeare: A Study of Facts and Problems,* 2 vols. (1930). The fullest collection of data.

Fraser, Russell. *Young Shakespeare* (1988). A highly readable account that simultaneously considers Shakespeare's life and Shakespeare's art.

———. *Shakespeare: The Later Years* (1992).

Schoenbaum, S. *Shakespeare's Lives* (1970). A review of the evidence and an examination of many biographies, including those of Baconians and other heretics.

———. *William Shakespeare: A Compact Documentary Life* (1977). An abbreviated version, in a smaller format, of the next title. The compact version reproduces some fifty documents in reduced form. A readable presentation of all that the documents tell us about Shakespeare.

———. *William Shakespeare: A Documentary Life* (1975). A large-format book setting forth the biography with facsimiles of more than two hundred documents, and with transcriptions and commentaries.

3. Shakespeare's Theater

Astington, John H., ed. *The Development of Shakespeare's Theater* (1992). Eight specialized essays on theatrical companies, playing spaces, and performance.

Beckerman, Bernard. *Shakespeare at the Globe, 1599–1609* (1962). On the playhouse and on Elizabethan dramaturgy, acting, and staging.

Bentley, Gerald E. *The Profession of Dramatist in Shakespeare's Time* (1971). An account of the dramatist's status in the Elizabethan period.

———. *The Profession of Player in Shakespeare's Time, 1590–1642* (1984). An account of the status of members of London companies (sharers, hired men, apprentices, managers) and a discussion of conditions when they toured.

Berry, Herbert. *Shakespeare's Playhouses* (1987). Usefully emphasizes how little we know about the construction of Elizabethan theaters.

Brown, John Russell. *Shakespeare's Plays in Performance* (1966). A speculative and practical analysis relevant to all of the plays, but with emphasis on *The Merchant of Venice, Richard II, Hamlet, Romeo and Juliet,* and *Twelfth Night.*

———. *William Shakespeare: Writing for Performance* (1996). A discussion aimed at helping readers to develop theatrically conscious habits of reading.

Chambers, E. K. *The Elizabethan Stage,* 4 vols. (1945). A major reference work on theaters, theatrical companies, and staging at court.

Cook, Ann Jennalie. *The Privileged Playgoers of Shakespeare's London, 1576–1642* (1981). Sees Shakespeare's audience as wealthier, more middle-class, and more intellectual than Harbage (below) does.

Dessen, Alan C. *Elizabethan Drama and the Viewer's Eye* (1977). On how certain scenes may have looked to spectators in an Elizabethan theater.

Gurr, Andrew. *Playgoing in Shakespeare's London* (1987). Something of a middle ground between Cook (above) and Harbage (below).

———. *The Shakespearean Stage, 1579–1642* (2nd ed., 1980). On the acting companies, the actors, the playhouses, the stages, and the audiences.

Harbage, Alfred. *Shakespeare's Audience* (1941). A study of the size and nature of the theatrical public, emphasizing the representativeness of its working class and middle-class audience.

Hodges, C. Walter. *The Globe Restored* (1968). A conjectural restoration, with lucid drawings.

Hosley, Richard. "The Playhouses," in *The Revels History of Drama in English*, vol. 3, general editors Clifford Leech and T. W. Craik (1975). An essay of a hundred pages on the physical aspects of the playhouses.

Howard, Jane E. "Crossdressing, the Theatre, and Gender Struggle in Early Modern England," *Shakespeare Quarterly* 39 (1988): 418–40. Judicious comments on the effects of boys playing female roles.

Orrell, John. *The Human Stage: English Theatre Design, 1567–1640* (1988). Argues that the public, private, and court playhouses are less indebted to popular structures (e.g., innyards and bear-baiting pits) than to banqueting halls and to Renaissance conceptions of Roman amphitheaters.

Slater, Ann Pasternak. *Shakespeare the Director* (1982). An analysis of theatrical effects (e.g., kissing, kneeling) in stage directions and dialogue.

Styan, J. L. *Shakespeare's Stagecraft* (1967). An introduction to Shakespeare's visual and aural stagecraft, with chapters on such topics as acting conventions, stage groupings, and speech.

Thompson, Peter. *Shakespeare's Professional Career* (1992). An examination of patronage and related theatrical conditions.

———. *Shakespeare's Theatre* (1983). A discussion of how plays were staged in Shakespeare's time.

4. Shakespeare on Stage and Screen

Bate, Jonathan, and Russell Jackson, eds. *Shakespeare: An Illustrated Stage History* (1996). Highly readable essays on stage productions from the Renaissance to the present.

Berry, Ralph. *Changing Styles in Shakespeare* (1981). Discusses productions of six plays (*Coriolanus*, *Hamlet*, *Henry V*, *Measure for Measure*, *The Tempest*, and *Twelfth Night*) on the English stage, chiefly 1950–1980.

————. *On Directing Shakespeare: Interviews with Contemporary Directors* (1989). An enlarged edition of a book first published in 1977, this version includes the seven interviews from the early 1970s and adds five interviews conducted in 1988.

Brockbank, Philip, ed. *Players of Shakespeare: Essays in Shakespearean Performance* (1985). Comments by twelve actors, reporting their experiences with roles. See also the entry for Russell Jackson (below).

Bulman, J. C., and H. R. Coursen, eds. *Shakespeare on Television* (1988). An anthology of general and theoretical essays, essays on individual productions, and shorter reviews, with a bibliography and a videography listing cassettes that may be rented.

Coursen, H. P. *Watching Shakespeare on Television* (1993). Analyses not only of TV versions but also of films and videotapes of stage presentations that are shown on television.

Davies, Anthony, and Stanley Wells, eds. *Shakespeare and the Moving Image: The Plays on Film and Television* (1994). General essays (e.g., on the comedies) as well as essays devoted entirely to *Hamlet*, *King Lear*, and *Macbeth*.

Dawson, Anthony B. *Watching Shakespeare: A Playgoer's Guide* (1988). About half of the plays are discussed, chiefly in terms of decisions that actors and directors make in putting the works onto the stage.

Dessen, Alan. *Elizabethan Stage Conventions and Modern Interpretations* (1984). On interpreting conventions such as the representation of light and darkness and stage violence (duels, battles).

Donaldson, Peter. *Shakespearean Films/Shakespearean Directors* (1990). Postmodernist analyses, drawing on Freudianism, Feminism, Deconstruction, and Queer Theory.

Jackson, Russell, and Robert Smallwood, eds. *Players of Shakespeare 2: Further Essays in Shakespearean Performance by Players with the Royal Shakespeare Company* (1988). Fourteen actors discuss their roles in productions between 1982 and 1987.

————. *Players of Shakespeare 3: Further Essays in Shake-spearean Performance by Players with the Royal Shakespeare Company* (1993). Comments by thirteen performers.

Jorgens, Jack. *Shakespeare on Film* (1977). Fairly detailed studies of eighteen films, preceded by an introductory chapter addressing such issues as music, and whether to "open" the play by including scenes of landscape.

Kennedy, Dennis. *Looking at Shakespeare: A Visual History of Twentieth-Century Performance* (1993). Lucid descriptions (with 170 photographs) of European, British, and American performances.

Leiter, Samuel L. *Shakespeare Around the Globe: A Guide to Notable Postwar Revivals* (1986). For each play there are about two pages of introductory comments, then discussions (about five hundred words per production) of ten or so productions, and finally bibliographic references.

McMurty, Jo. *Shakespeare Films in the Classroom* (1994). Useful evaluations of the chief films most likely to be shown in undergraduate courses.

Rothwell, Kenneth, and Annabelle Henkin Melzer. *Shakespeare on Screen: An International Filmography and Videography* (1990). A reference guide to several hundred films and videos produced between 1899 and 1989, including spinoffs such as musicals and dance versions.

Sprague, Arthur Colby. *Shakespeare and the Actors* (1944). Detailed discussions of stage business (gestures, etc.) over the years.

Willis, Susan. *The BBC Shakespeare Plays: Making the Televised Canon* (1991). A history of the series, with interviews and production diaries for some plays.

5. Miscellaneous Reference Works

Abbott, E. A. *A Shakespearean Grammar* (new edition, 1877). An examination of differences between Elizabethan and modern grammar.

Allen, Michael J. B., and Kenneth Muir, eds. *Shakespeare's Plays in Quarto* (1981). One volume containing facsimiles of the plays issued in small format before they were collected in the First Folio of 1623.

Bevington, David. *Shakespeare* (1978). A short guide to hundreds of important writings on the subject.

Blake, Norman. *Shakespeare's Language: An Introduction* (1983). On vocabulary, parts of speech, and word order.

Bullough, Geoffrey. *Narrative and Dramatic Sources of Shakespeare*, 8 vols. (1957–75). A collection of many of the books Shakespeare drew on, with judicious comments.

Campbell, Oscar James, and Edward G. Quinn, eds. *The Reader's Encyclopedia of Shakespeare* (1966). Old, but still the most useful single reference work on Shakespeare.

Cercignani, Fausto. *Shakespeare's Works and Elizabethan Pronunciation* (1981). Considered the best work on the topic, but remains controversial.

Dent, R. W. *Shakespeare's Proverbial Language: An Index* (1981). An index of proverbs, with an introduction concerning a form Shakespeare frequently drew on.

Greg, W. W. *The Shakespeare First Folio* (1955). A detailed yet readable history of the first collection (1623) of Shakespeare's plays.

Harner, James. *The World Shakespeare Bibliography*. See headnote to Suggested References.

Hosley, Richard. *Shakespeare's Holinshed* (1968). Valuable presentation of one of Shakespeare's major sources.

Kökeritz, Helge. *Shakespeare's Names* (1959). A guide to pronouncing some 1,800 names appearing in Shakespeare.

———. *Shakespeare's Pronunciation* (1953). Contains much information about puns and rhymes, but see Cercignani (above).

Muir, Kenneth. *The Sources of Shakespeare's Plays* (1978). An account of Shakespeare's use of his reading. It covers all the plays, in chronological order.

Miriam Joseph, Sister. *Shakespeare's Use of the Arts of Language* (1947). A study of Shakespeare's use of rhetorical devices, reprinted in part as *Rhetoric in Shakespeare's Time* (1962).

The Norton Facsimile: The First Folio of Shakespeare's Plays (1968). A handsome and accurate facsimile of the first collection (1623) of Shakespeare's plays, with a valuable introduction by Charlton Hinman.

Onions, C. T. *A Shakespeare Glossary*, rev. and enlarged by R. D. Eagleson (1986). Definitions of words (or senses of words) now obsolete.

Partridge, Eric. *Shakespeare's Bawdy*, rev. ed. (1955). Relatively brief dictionary of bawdy words; useful, but see Williams, below.

Shakespeare Quarterly. See headnote to Suggested References.

Shakespeare Survey. See headnote to Suggested References.

Spevack, Marvin. *The Harvard Concordance to Shakespeare* (1973). An index to Shakespeare's words.

Vickers, Brian. *Appropriating Shakespeare: Contemporary Critical Quarrels* (1993). A survey—chiefly hostile—of recent schools of criticism.

Wells, Stanley, ed. *Shakespeare: A Bibliographical Guide* (new edition, 1990). Nineteen chapters (some devoted to single plays, others devoted to groups of related plays) on recent scholarship on the life and all of the works.

Williams, Gordon. *A Dictionary of Sexual Language and Imagery in Shakespearean and Stuart Literature*, 3 vols. (1994). Extended discussions of words and passages; much fuller than Partridge, cited above.

6. Shakespeare's Plays: General Studies

Bamber, Linda. *Comic Women, Tragic Men: A Study of Gender and Genre in Shakespeare* (1982).

Barnet, Sylvan. *A Short Guide to Shakespeare* (1974).

Callaghan, Dympna, Lorraine Helms, and Jyotsna Singh. *The Weyward Sisters: Shakespeare and Feminist Politics* (1994).

Clemen, Wolfgang H. *The Development of Shakespeare's Imagery* (1951).

Cook, Ann Jennalie. *Making a Match: Courtship in Shakespeare and His Society* (1991).

Dollimore, Jonathan, and Alan Sinfield. *Political Shakespeare: New Essays in Cultural Materialism* (1985).

Dusinberre, Juliet. *Shakespeare and the Nature of Women* (1975).

Granville-Barker, Harley. *Prefaces to Shakespeare*, 2 vols. (1946–47; volume 1 contains essays on *Hamlet, King Lear, Merchant of Venice, Antony and Cleopatra,* and *Cymbeline*; volume 2 contains essays on *Othello, Coriolanus, Julius Caesar, Romeo and Juliet, Love's Labor's Lost*).

———. *More Prefaces to Shakespeare* (1974; essays on *Twelfth Night, A Midsummer Night's Dream, The Winter's Tale, Macbeth*).

Harbage, Alfred. *William Shakespeare: A Reader's Guide* (1963).

Howard, Jean E. *Shakespeare's Art of Orchestration: Stage Technique and Audience Response* (1984).

Jones, Emrys. *Scenic Form in Shakespeare* (1971).

Lenz, Carolyn Ruth Swift, Gayle Greene, and Carol Thomas Neely, eds. *The Woman's Part: Feminist Criticism of Shakespeare* (1980).

Novy, Marianne. *Love's Argument: Gender Relations in Shakespeare* (1984).

Rose, Mark. *Shakespearean Design* (1972).

Scragg, Leah. *Discovering Shakespeare's Meaning* (1994).

———. *Shakespeare's "Mouldy Tales": Recurrent Plot Motifs in Shakespearean Drama* (1992).

Traub, Valerie. *Desire and Anxiety: Circulations of Sexuality in Shakespearean Drama* (1992).

Traversi, D. A. *An Approach to Shakespeare,* 2 vols. (3rd rev. ed, 1968–69).

Vickers, Brian. *The Artistry of Shakespeare's Prose* (1968).

Wells, Stanley. *Shakespeare: A Dramatic Life* (1994).

Wright, George T. *Shakespeare's Metrical Art* (1988).

7. The Comedies

Barber, C. L. *Shakespeare's Festive Comedy* (1959; discusses *Love's Labor's Lost, A Midsummer Night's Dream, The Merchant of Venice, As You Like It, Twelfth Night*).

Barton, Anne. *The Names of Comedy* (1990).

Berry, Ralph. *Shakespeare's Comedy: Explorations in Form* (1972).

Bradbury, Malcolm, and David Palmer, eds. *Shakespearean Comedy* (1972).

Bryant, J. A., Jr. *Shakespeare and the Uses of Comedy* (1986).

Carroll, William. *The Metamorphoses of Shakespearean Comedy* (1985).

Champion, Larry S. *The Evolution of Shakespeare's Comedy* (1970).

Evans, Bertrand. *Shakespeare's Comedies* (1960).

Frye, Northrop. *Shakespearean Comedy and Romance* (1965).

Leggatt, Alexander. *Shakespeare's Comedy of Love* (1974).

Miola, Robert S. *Shakespeare and Classical Comedy: The Influence of Plautus and Terence* (1994).

Nevo, Ruth. *Comic Transformations in Shakespeare* (1980).

Ornstein, Robert. *Shakespeare's Comedies: From Roman Farce to Romantic Mystery* (1986).

Richman, David. *Laughter, Pain, and Wonder: Shakespeare's Comedies and the Audience in the Theater* (1990).

Salingar, Leo. *Shakespeare and the Traditions of Comedy* (1974).

Slights, Camille Wells. *Shakespeare's Comic Commonwealths* (1993).

Waller, Gary, ed. *Shakespeare's Comedies* (1991).

Westlund, Joseph. *Shakespeare's Reparative Comedies: A Psychoanalytic View of the Middle Plays* (1984).

Williamson, Marilyn. *The Patriarchy of Shakespeare's Comedies* (1986).

8. The Romances (*Pericles, Cymbeline, The Winter's Tale, The Tempest, The Two Noble Kinsmen*)

Adams, Robert M. *Shakespeare: The Four Romances* (1989).

Felperin, Howard. *Shakespearean Romance* (1972).

Frye, Northrop. *A Natural Perspective: The Development of Shakespearean Comedy and Romance* (1965).

Mowat, Barbara. *The Dramaturgy of Shakespeare's Romances* (1976).
Warren, Roger. *Staging Shakespeare's Late Plays* (1990).
Young, David. *The Heart's Forest: A Study of Shakespeare's Pastoral Plays* (1972).

9. The Tragedies

Bradley, A. C. *Shakespearean Tragedy* (1904).
Brooke, Nicholas. *Shakespeare's Early Tragedies* (1968).
Champion, Larry. *Shakespeare's Tragic Perspective* (1976).
Drakakis, John, ed. *Shakespearean Tragedy* (1992).
Evans, Bertrand. *Shakespeare's Tragic Practice* (1979).
Everett, Barbara. *Young Hamlet: Essays on Shakespeare's Tragedies* (1989).
Foakes, R. A. *Hamlet versus Lear: Cultural Politics and Shakespeare's Art* (1993).
Frye, Northrop. *Fools of Time: Studies in Shakespearean Tragedy* (1967).
Harbage, Alfred, ed. *Shakespeare: The Tragedies* (1964).
Mack, Maynard. *Everybody's Shakespeare: Reflections Chiefly on the Tragedies* (1993).
McAlindon, T. *Shakespeare's Tragic Cosmos* (1991).
Miola, Robert S. *Shakespeare and Classical Tragedy: The Influence of Seneca* (1992).
———. *Shakespeare's Rome* (1983).
Nevo, Ruth. *Tragic Form in Shakespeare* (1972).
Rackin, Phyllis. *Shakespeare's Tragedies* (1978).
Rose, Mark, ed. *Shakespeare's Early Tragedies: A Collection of Critical Essays* (1995).
Rosen, William. *Shakespeare and the Craft of Tragedy* (1960).
Snyder, Susan. *The Comic Matrix of Shakespeare's Tragedies* (1979).
Wofford, Susanne. *Shakespeare's Late Tragedies: A Collection of Critical Essays* (1996).
Young, David. *The Action to the Word: Structure and Style in Shakespearean Tragedy* (1990).

————. *Shakespeare's Middle Tragedies: A Collection of Critical Essays* (1993).

10. The Histories

Blanpied, John W. *Time and the Artist in Shakespeare's English Histories* (1983).

Campbell, Lily B. *Shakespeare's "Histories": Mirrors of Elizabethan Policy* (1947).

Champion, Larry S. *Perspective in Shakespeare's English Histories* (1980).

Hodgdon, Barbara. *The End Crowns All: Closure and Contradiction in Shakespeare's History* (1991).

Holderness, Graham. *Shakespeare Recycled: The Making of Historical Drama* (1992).

————, ed. *Shakespeare's History Plays: "Richard II" to "Henry V"* (1992).

Leggatt, Alexander. *Shakespeare's Political Drama: The History Plays and the Roman Plays* (1988).

Ornstein, Robert. *A Kingdom for a Stage: The Achievement of Shakespeare's History Plays* (1972).

Rackin, Phyllis. *Stages of History: Shakespeare's English Chronicles* (1990).

Saccio, Peter. *Shakespeare's English Kings: History, Chronicle, and Drama* (1977).

Tillyard, E. M. W. *Shakespeare's History Plays* (1944).

Velz, John W., ed. *Shakespeare's English Histories: A Quest for Form and Genre* (1996).

11. *Antony and Cleopatra*

In addition to the titles concerned with stage history on pages 256–57, and those recommended in Section 9, The Tragedies, of this list of Suggested References, the following are recommended:

Adelman, Janet. *The Common Liar: An Essay on "Antony and Cleopatra"* (1973). Part of this book is reprinted above.

Barnet, Sylvan. "Recognition and Reversal in *Antony and Cleopatra*." *Shakespeare Quarterly* 8 (1957): 331–34.

Bloom, Harold, ed. *Modern Critical Interpretations: William Shakespeare's "Antony and Cleopatra"* (1988).

Brower, Reuben A. *Hero and Saint: Shakespeare and the Greco-Roman Tradition* (1971).

Charney, Maurice. *Shakespeare's Roman Plays: The Function of Imagery in the Drama* (1961).

Coates, John. " 'The Choice of Hercules' in *Antony and Cleopatra*." *Shakespeare Survey* 31 (1978): 45–52.

Dollimore, Jonathan. *Political Tragedy* (1984).

Drakakis, John, ed. *Antony and Cleopatra [New Casebooks]* (1994).

Erickson, Peter. *Patriarchal Structures in Shakespeare's Drama* (1985).

Goldman, Michael. *Acting and Action in Shakespearean Tragedy* (1985).

Granville-Barker, Harley. *Preface to Shakespeare,* I (1946).

Kahn, Coppélia. *Roman Shakespeare: Warriors, Wounds and Women* (1997).

Kernan, Alvin. *Shakespeare, The King's Playwright: Theater in the Stuart Court 1603–1613* (1995).

Knight, G. Wilson. *The Imperial Theme* (1951).

Knights, L. C. *Some Shakespearean Themes* (1959).

MacCallum, M. W. *Shakespeare's Roman Plays and Their Background* (1910).

Mack, Maynard. "The Jacobean Shakespeare: Some Observations on the Construction of the Tragedies." *Stratford-upon-Avon Studies 1: Jacobean Theatre* (1960), pp. 11–41. Reprinted in the Signet Classic edition of *Othello*.

Miola, Robert. *Shakespeare and Classical Tragedy* (1992).

———. *Shakespeare's Rome* (1983).

Riemer, A. P. *A Reading of Shakespeare's "Antony and Cleopatra"* (1968).

Spencer, T. J. B. "Shakespeare and the Elizabethan Romans." *Shakespeare Survey* 10 (1957): 27–38.

Sprengnether, Madelon. "The Boy Actor and Femininity in *Antony and Cleopatra*." In *Shakespeare's Personality*, ed. Norman N. Holland, Sidney Homan, and Bernard J. Paris (1989), pp. 191–205.

Traversi, Derek. *Shakespeare: The Roman Plays* (1963).